CENTRE FOR EDUCATIONAL RESEARCH AND INNOVATION

GW00641018

Successful Services
for our Children
and Families at Risk

ORGANISATION FOR ECONOMIC CO-OPERATION AND DEVELOPMENT

ORGANISATION FOR ECONOMIC CO-OPERATION AND DEVELOPMENT

Pursuant to Article 1 of the Convention signed in Paris on 14th December 1960, and which came into force on 30th September 1961, the Organisation for Economic Co-operation and Development (OECD) shall promote policies designed:

- to achieve the highest sustainable economic growth and employment and a rising standard of living in Member countries, while maintaining financial stability, and thus to contribute to the development of the world economy;
- to contribute to sound economic expansion in Member as well as non-member countries in the process of economic development; and
- to contribute to the expansion of world trade on a multilateral, non-discriminatory basis in accordance with international obligations.

The original Member countries of the OECD are Austria, Belgium, Canada, Denmark, France, Germany, Greece, Iceland, Ireland, Italy, Luxembourg, the Netherlands, Norway, Portugal, Spain, Sweden, Switzerland, Turkey, the United Kingdom and the United States. The following countries became Members subsequently through accession at the dates indicated hereafter: Japan (28th April 1964), Finland (28th January 1969), Australia (7th June 1971), New Zealand (29th May 1973), Mexico (18th May 1994), the Czech Republic (21st December 1995) and Hungary (7th May 1996). The Commission of the European Communities takes part in the work of the OECD (Article 13 of the OECD Convention).

The Centre for Educational Research and Innovation was created in June 1968 by the Council of the Organisation for Economic Co-operation and Development and all Member countries of the OECD are participants.

The main objectives of the Centre are as follows:

- *to promote and support the development of research activities in education and undertake such research activities where appropriate;*
- *to promote and support pilot experiments with a view to introducing and testing innovations in the educational system;*
- *to promote the development of co-operation between Member countries in the field of educational research and innovation.*

The Centre functions within the Organisation for Economic Co-operation and Development in accordance with the decisions of the Council of the Organisation, under the authority of the Secretary-General. It is supervised by a Governing Board composed of one national expert in its field of competence from each of the countries participating in its programme of work.

Publié en français sous le titre :

DES SERVICES EFFICACES POUR LES ENFANTS ET FAMILLES À RISQUE

FOREWORD

The research reported in this book develops a theme identified from previous work described in *Our Children at Risk* (OECD, 1995a), which noted the integration of services as a way to provide more effective, holistic, client-oriented and preventive support to families and to children who are at risk of failing in school and the transition to work.

In order to achieve as comprehensive an understanding as possible of the concept of services integration, a broad approach has been taken. It considers not only statutory provision such as education, health and social services but also private support, emanating from business and charities.

The complexities of working systems such as these are addressed by considering their operation at four levels: mandating is concerned with laws and policies; strategic with the ways those policies are interpreted by senior management, in the context of guiding system development; operational with the ways in which the delivery of services are managed on the ground; and the field level with the ways in which services are working for professionals and clients.

The book is organised into three main parts. Part One gives the broad picture. The first two chapters provide an historical introduction to the concept of services integration from an international perspective and an account of the study's methodology. Chapter 3 synthesises changes in laws and policies towards the goal of services integration in 13 countries, based on national reports. The remaining chapters of Part One provide a summary of the main research findings, draw conclusions and discuss some policy implications and challenges. Part Two provides brief vignettes of the case studies in Australia, Canada, Europe, and the United States that were completed during the course of the study. Part Three supplies more specific information of laws and policies for participating countries.

The work took place between 1993 and 1995 and would not have been possible without generous support by the countries involved and in particular through grants from the United States Department of Education, the United States Department of Health and Human Services, the Dutch SVO and the Charles Stewart Mott foundation of the United States of America.

The main part of the report was prepared by Dr. Peter Evans and Dr. Philippa Hurrell of the OECD Centre for Educational Research and Innovation (CERI) supported by a large number of experts who helped to conceptualise, execute, report and evaluate the work.

This book is published on the responsibility of the Secretary-General of the OECD.

TABLE OF CONTENTS

Part I

Introducing the problem and the study:
An historical overview, the main findings, conclusions and policy challenges

Part II

Case study abstracts

Section 1 – Case study abstracts carried out by OECD experts

Section 2 – Case study abstracts carried out by countries

Part III

Legislation and policy: country details

Annexes:

ACKNOWLEDGEMENTS

The work described in this book was made possible by the full co-operation of a very large number of individuals and institutions.

The following experts, Mrs. Josette Combes of ACEPP (Association Collectifs Enfants, Parents, Professionnels), Paris, France; Mrs. Jennifer Evans of the Institute of Education, University of London, United Kingdom; Professor Mary Lewis of the University of Houston, Texas, United States; Mrs. Lucienne Roussel, Inspector General of the Ministry of National Education, Paris, France; and Professor Richard Volpe of the University of Toronto, Canada, helped to conceive and execute the work with great enthusiasm and commitment.

The following institutions gave their total support during the completion of the case studies.

AUSTRALIA

- **Canberra:** The Department of the Prime Minister and Cabinet; The Department of Employment, Education, Training and Youth Affairs; The Department of Human Services and Health; The Department of Social Security; The Attorney General's Office.

- **New South Wales:** In *Sydney:* Arthur Phillip High School; Burnside (Uniting Church in Australia); South Sydney Youth Services; City Central Youth Access Centre; Inner West Youth Access Centre; Cleveland Street High School, Cranebrook High School; Jamison High School; Nepean High School; Barnado's Penrith Centre; Penrith Police Citizens' Youth Club; The Wirraway Community Centre. In *Newcastle:* Newcastle Youth Access Centre; Jasper-Gateshead High School; Lake Macquarie Police Citizens' Youth Club; The Eastlakes Community Network Committee; Jesmond High School – Hunter Adolescent Support Unit; The Annexe – Worimi School.

- **South Australia:** In *Adelaide:* The Commonwealth Employment Service; Department for Education and Children's Services, Family and Children's Services, Child and Adolescent Mental Health Services; The Beafield Education Centre; Paralowie R-12 School; Fremont High School; Seaton High

School; Port Adelaide Youth Access Centre; Salisbury Youth Access Centre; Possibility 14. In *Ceduna*: Murat Bay District Council; The Aboriginal Pre-Kindergarten, Murat Bay Children's Centre; Crossways Lutheran School; Ceduna Area School; Spencer Institute of Technology and Further Education; South Australia Independent Schools Board Inc., Malvern.

– **State of Victoria:** In *Melbourne*: the Directorate of School Education; the Catholic Education Office; Melbourne Deaneries STAR Project; Preston Koori Youth Access Centre, Brunswick youth Access Centre; Footscray Youth Access Centre; Melbourne Youth Access Centre; Crossroads Housing and Support Network Collingwood College; Kensington Community High School. In *Bendigo*: Bendigo Senior Secondary College.

CANADA

– **Toronto:** The Council of Ministers of Education.
– **Alberta:** In *Edmonton*: The Ministry of Education; Ministry of Health; Ministry of Family and Social Services; Ministry of Justice; Commissioner of Services for Children; Community Services Consultancy Ltd; Wellington Junior High School; St. Nicolas Catholic Junior High Programme: "Partners for Youth". In *Lethbridge*: Lethbridge City Council; Lethbridge Co-ordination of Services for Children Initiative; Pre-school Assessment Treatment Centre; Lethbridge Regional Hospital; Parents Place; Family and Community Development Program; School Districts 9 and 51; Canada Employment; Youth Employment Centre; Paediatric Neuromuscular Unit; Programme "Outreach". In *Calgary*: The City of Calgary; Calgary Board of Education; Calgary Catholic School Board; Alcohol and Drug Abuse Commission (AADAC); Calgary Health Services; Alberta Mental Health; Alberta Children's Hospital; Federation of Calgary Communities; Opening doors Steering Committee; Adolescent Treatment Centre; Thornhill Community services; McDougall Centre; Huntington hills University of Calgary.

– **New Brunswick:** Department of Education; Department of Health and Community Services; In *Woodstock*: The Office of the Mayor; School District 12; Atlantic Provinces Special Education Authority; Family and Community Social Services; Centennial Elementary School; Woodstock Junior High School; Woodstock High School; Carelton Victoria Child Development Services Inc.; The Woodstock Access Centre; The Probation service.

– **Ontario:** The Ministry of Education and Training; Ministry of Health; Ministry of Community and Social Services; Ministry of Inter-Governmental Affairs; Ontario Association of Children's Aid Societies. In *Timmins*: The Office of the Mayor; Ministry of Education and Training; Ministry of Health; Ministry of Community and Social Services; Ministry of Northern Development and

Mines; MPP; The Area Inter-Ministerial Management Committee; Laurentian University; Integrated Services for Northern Children; South Cochrane Child and Youth Service (Children's Mental Health Centre); Jeanne Sauve Youth Services; Children's Treatment Centre. In *Kitchener:* The City of Kitchener; Eastwood Collegiate Institute; The Waterloo County Board of Education; The Mutual Insurance Group; The Rotary Club; The Volunteer Action Centre of Kitchener. In *Sudbury:* The Ministry of Education and Training; Ministry of Health; Ministry of Community and Social Services; Federal Department of Indian and Northern Affairs; Better Beginnings, Better Futures Association.

– *Saskatchewan:* Saskatchewan Education; Saskatchewan Social Services; Saskatchewan Health Services; The League of Educational Administrators; Saskatchewan School Trustees Association; Saskatchewan Federation of Home-School Associations; Princess Alexandra Community School; Princess Alexandra Community Association; Riversdale Community and School Association; Riversdale Business Improvement District. In *Saskatoon*; Saskatoon Police Service; Planning and Development, Saskatoon. In *Prince Albert* : Prince Albert Regional Education Services; Prince Albert Regional Social Services; Prince Albert Police Department; St. Mary's School; Prince Albert Regional Health Services; West Flat Citizens' Group.

FINLAND

– *Hameenlinna:* Hämeen lääninhallitus; Hämeen lääninhallitus kouluosasto; Hämeen lääninhallitus sosiaali- ja terveysosasto; Hämeenlinnan kaupungin erityispalvelut; A-Klinikka; Ammatillinen opettajakorkeakoulu (Hämeen-linna); Hämeenlinnan kaupungin nuorisotoimisto; Hämeenlinnan seudun kansanterveystyön kuntayhtymä; Hämeenlinnan perusturvavirasto; Vanajan koulukoti; Harvialan koulukoti; Hämeenlinnan perhetukikeskus; Hämeenlin-nan ammattioppilaitos; Hämeenlinnan poliisilaitos; Kiipulasäätiö.

– *Helsinki:* Opetushallitus; Sosiaali- ja terveysalan tutkimus- ja kehittämiskes-kus, STAKES; Äitiys- ja lastenneuvola, Myllypuron terveyskeskus; Oulunkylän erityisensikoti; Käpylän pikkulastenkoti; Koulupsyko-logipalvelut (Helsingin kaupunki); Kotipalvelu (Helsingin kaupunki); Päiväkoti (Helsingin kaupunki); Helsingin yliopistollinen keskussairaala; Auroran lastensairaala; Helsingin kaupungin sosiaalivirasto; Ensikotien liitto.

– *Jyvaskyla:* Keski-Suomen lääninhallituksen kouluosasto; Keski-Suomen lääninhallituksen sosiaali- ja terveysosasto; Keski-Suomen perheneuvola; Mannerheimin Lastensuojeluliiton Keski-Suomen piiri; Suomen mustalais-lähetys; Jyväskylän kaupungin hallinto; Jyväskylän yliopisto; Nenäinniemen ala-asteen koulu ja päiväkoti; Huhtaharjun koulu; Huhtasuon sosiaali- ja terveyskeskus; Hovilan nuorisokoti ja työpaja.

GERMANY

Deutsches Jugendinstitut (DJI).

– **Bremen:** Senator für Gesundheit, Jugend und Soziales; Stadtteilkonferenz, Huchting; Stadtteilfarm Huchting; Kindertagesheim (KTH) Dietrich Bonhoeffer; Kindertagesheim (KTH) Höpost; Mütterzentrum; Haus der Familie.

– **Duisburg:** Industrie- und Handelskammer Duisburg; Dezernat für Schule und Jugend der Stadt Duisburg; Jugendamt Duisburg; Arbeitsamt Duisburg; Stadtrat; Regionale Arbeitsstelle für Ausländerfragen (RAA) Duisburg; auerbetriebliche Berufsbildungseinrichtung; Bertolt Brecht Berufsschule.

– **Leipzig:** Sächsisches Staatsministerium für Kultus; Sächsisches Staatsministerium für Soziales, Gesundheit und Familie; Regionale Arbeitsstellen für Ausländerfragen (RAA); Dezernat für Schule, Jugend und Sport der Stadt Leipzig; Jugendamt Leipzig; Christlicher Verein junger Männer (CVJM), Leipzig; 21. und 51. Mittelschule; Schülerclub Grunau.

NETHERLANDS

– **Zoetermeer:** The Ministry of Education, Culture and Science.

– **Emmen:** Bureau of the Drenthe Educational Priority Area; New Dordrecht preschool playgroup.

– **Rotterdam:** City Fund for Reduction of Educational Disadvantages Rotterdam (FAO); Foundation "De Meeuw"; Protestant Educational Services Foundation Rotterdam (DCO); "De Beukelburg" school; Foundation for Welfare in Afrikaanderwijk. Erasmus University.

– **Rijswijk:** Ministry of Health, Welfare and Sports.

PORTUGAL

– **Lisbon:** Ministério da Educação; Ministério do Emprego e da Segurança Social; Ministério da Justiça; Casa Pia de Lisboa; Colégio Pina Manique; Colégio de N. St. da Conceição; Direcção de Serviços de Saúde Mental; Instituto de Apoio à Criança; SOS Criança (linha telefónica); Santa Casa de Misericórdia de Lisboa; Jardim Zoológico de Lisboa; Aldeia de Santa Isabel; Câmara Municipal de Lisboa; Junta de Greguesia; Escola do 1° Ciclo n°5 da Amora – Quinta da Princesa; CEBI – Centro Comunitário de Alverca; Núcleo de Intervenção Comunitária para a Prevenção da Toxicodependência; Chapitô; Centro de Observação e Acção Social; Centro de Estudos para a

Intervenção Social; Escola Preparatória de Vila Franca de Xira; Escola Secundaria de Linda-a-Velha; Secretariado Eutre Culturas; Centro Social do Bairro 6 de Maio.

- **Porto:** Centro Regional de Segurança Social do Norte; A Casa do Caminho; Projecto de Luta contra a Pobreza de Ringe; Fundação para o Desenvolvimento da Zona Histórica do Porto

UNITED STATES OF AMERICA

- **Washington DC:** The Department of Education; The Department of Health and Human Services; The Department of Housing and Urban Development; The White House Domestic Policy Council; Council of Chief State School Officers; National Governors Association; The Institute of Educational Leadership.

- **California:** In *Sacramento:* The Department of Social Services; The Department of Health Services; The Department of Education; California Child Development Programs Advisory Committee; California Assembly Office of Research; California Legislature Assembly Committee on Human Services; California Research Bureau; The Foundation Consortium for School Linked Services; California Legislative Budget Committee. In *San Diego:* The Office of the Superintendent, San Diego City School District; Department of Health Services; Department of Social Services; Department of Health Services; The Private Industry Council; The Children's Hospital and Health Centre; Alexander Hamilton Elementary School; Hoover Health and Social Services Centre; New Beginnings Council; The Healthy Start Program.

- **Missouri:** Missouri Department of Social Services; Department of Elementary and Secondary Education; Department of Health; Department of Mental Health; The Family Investment Trust.

- **Kansas City:** LINC (Local Investment Commission); Futures Advisory Committee; 21st Century Communities; Heart of America Family Services united Way; Women's Employment Network; KCMC Child Development Corporation; Goppert Child Development Centre; Southeast High School; Swope Parkway Neighbourhood Clinic; Family Focus Centre; Partnership for Kids; Full Employment Council; Adult Basic Education; Employment Security; Penn Valley College.

- **St. Louis:** Grace Hill Neighbourhood Services; Family Preservation Services; LINC, Parents as Teachers (PAT); 21st Century communities; Crisis Nursery; Penrose Family Support Centre; St. Charles Employment Training Office; Caring Communities.

- **New York:** The National Center for Social Work and Education Collaboration; The Edwin Gould Foundation; The Fund for New York City Public Education; The Aaron Diamond Foundation; The Youth Development Institute; The Children's Aid Society; The Door; Community School, IS 218/PS5; Project HighRoad, IS 183; The Clearpool School and Camp Clearpool.

SUMMARY

This report explores the ways in which many countries are moving towards the co-ordination and integration of their human services to meet the needs of children and families said to be at risk. The drive is for services which are preventive and remedial, effective, efficient and economical. The study, as a whole, analyses change at four levels. First, laws and policies; second, strategic level decision-makers; third, service co-ordinators; and fourth, the professionals who supply the services on the ground and their clients. The work covers the pre-school, school age and transition to work periods. The report is divided into three parts. In the first, a synthesis of information from country reports, case studies and literature reviews, from Europe, North America and Australia is given. In the second part, case studies of good practice in Australia, Canada, Finland, Germany, Netherlands, Portugal and the United States of America are summarised and in the third developments in countries' laws and policies are described. Further technical information, relating to the methodology of the study, is provided, in the annexes.

In the first part of the report, after headline statements, illustrating the nature of the problems presented by children and youth at risk and their families to education systems, the first chapter continues with an historical description, in a small number of countries, of the way that the policy goal of services integration has waxed and waned over the course of this century. It notes that, for many countries, the involvement of the education authorities is giving a new impetus to the process of services integration. Chapter 2 provides a brief account of the methodology used in the study. In Chapter 3, some legal and policy developments are noted. Chapter 4 provides a classification of integrated services on the basis of the actors involved, the structures in which they work, the mechanisms which operate to help in integrated service delivery, and the physical location of the service. These are identified as useful dimensions, generalisable across communities and countries. Chapter 5 summarises the main empirical outcomes of the study covering the evaluations that have taken place, perceived advantages and disadvantages and factors which facilitate or inhibit the co-ordination of services. The results indicate that, in general terms, an integrated service approach is preferred by all actors involved. In brief, administrators value the economies and professionals value an improved service and heightened job satisfaction with less stress.

Chapter 6 draws the main conclusions and identifies policy challenges. It notes that the need for a new approach to service delivery for those at risk stems from changes in the economies of many countries, changes in family structures and changes in the way in which the healthy development of the child and young person is understood. Narrowly defined categorical services can no longer meet these needs. They must be holistic and preventive. Integrated services seem to flourish under policies which encourage decentralisation and include as wide a range of statutory services as is necessary, functioning collaboratively with the community and the private sector. This new balance provides policy challenges in the areas of ownership, in the relationships between government departments/ministries and professional interests, on resourcing and on the relationship between government departments/ministries and local administrations and arrangements. To understand these changes fully and to help in implementation, new evaluation instruments must be developed.

Part I

INTRODUCING THE PROBLEM
AND THE STUDY

**An historical overview, the main findings, conclusions
and policy challenges**

INTRODUCTION

by

Peter Evans and Philippa Hurrell

ILLUSTRATING THE PROBLEM

The following headline statements highlight the nature of the problems that schools are perceived to be facing in coping with children and youth at risk:

- The OECD report *Our Children at Risk* (OECD, 1995a) identified 15 to 30 per cent of children of school age as being "at risk" of failing in school.

- In Australia, it has been concluded that family conflict, family fragmentation and family dislocation are major causes of youth homelessness, which in turn is associated with educational under-achievement and early school leaving (The Burdekin Report, 1989).

- In Ontario, Canada, one third of all adolescents drop out of high school, and "runaways swell the numbers of the homeless in our urban centres, in disconcertingly large and increasing numbers" (Children First, 1990).

- A report from Saskatchewan, Canada, states that "children and young people are coming to school hungry, emotionally and physically abused and neglected, destructive and violent in their behaviour, with physical and learning disabilities, with language and cultural needs, with health or medical needs and suffering from the stress of family breakdown" (Saskatchewan Ministry of Education, 1992).

- In Germany, 25 per cent of children in the kindergarten are described as having "oddities" (Haberkorn *et al.*, 1988).

- In Portugal, an unknown number of children who are not supported by their families live on the streets.

- In the United States, 20.4 per cent of children live in poverty (National Center for Children in Poverty, 1993).

These observations state powerfully the kinds of problems that are faced by countries' education systems. According to Mawhinney (1994):

"On their own schools cannot effectively address the entangled problems of youth such as drug abuse, homelessness, and violence. The programmatic approach to the development of policy for children's services has failed."

For some, a new approach is required, since social services are:

"too fragmented, overspecialised and overburdened, and they have limited outreach capacity and are working in isolation from one another" (Children First, 1990).

The co-ordination of agencies and services, that try to meet the range of problems outlined above in supporting the social and educational needs of children and youth at risk and their families, forms the focus of this report.

HISTORICAL ORIENTATION

Wanting to integrate services is not a new idea, but an enduring one, subject to a cyclical trend of policy making, in which enthusiasm for co-ordination has waxed and waned (Challis et al., 1988; Kagan, 1993). The following sections briefly and selectively provide an historical orientation to the issues, and then consider some of the main reasons why, as part of the educational reform agenda, services co-ordination is currently in the ascendant.

Providing co-ordinated, comprehensive services for those in need has been accepted as a socially desirable goal in many countries throughout this century. It has been approached usually through developments in both public and private sectors and in their collaboration. Six examples of different patterns are described below, from Finland, Germany, the Netherlands, Portugal, the United Kingdom and the United States. These countries were selected because of the ready availability of information.

Finland

In Finland, Jauhiainen (1993) discusses the development of the student welfare system in compulsory education over the past 130 years. School welfare can be divided into three fields: health, psycho-social welfare, and counselling and guidance. Child welfare was initiated in the 1920s by a voluntary organisation, "The Mannerheim League". This spread throughout Finland, with its clinics working in close co-operation with schools. School social work also started at about this time – as did counselling arrangements. Nowadays, local authorities employ specialist educational psychologists, school doctors, public health nurses and student counsellors in schools to deal with the students' well-being. Between the 1960s and 1980s, Finland attained the level of a modern Nordic welfare state by which time the school health care system based in secondary schools had reached its zenith. Later, it was extended to post-compulsory institutions, including universities, and additional emphasis was put on mental health provision.

For children under school age, maternity and child clinics run by the health authorities guide parents on the care of children up to seven years old. They are concerned with physical and psycho-social health and there is a growing trend to enhance their role in the support of children. However, most of the work in this area is carried out in child welfare and family counselling centres run by local authorities.

The child guidance clinics have changed their role over the past 15 years, focusing rather less on school issues and becoming more family-centred. This development has been enabled by the increase in the employment of school-based personnel specialising in the psycho-social well-being of students.

However, economic recession in the last few years has led to major reforms in government administration, including decentralisation. This is seen by some as potentially threatening to these services.

Germany

In Germany, the current philosophy of social care is based on earlier determined principles of an obligation to work and of subsidiarity. Public social welfare was planned to contribute to public security and order. Developments undertaken during the 1920s were taken up again after 1945. *Länder* youth offices (of the old West Germany) were given the task of co-ordinating and promoting the work of local youth welfare offices as part of local self-government. The principle of subsidiarity – whereby help and care are first seen as the responsibility of the family, relatives and the neighbourhood, then of voluntary and statutory agencies and, finally, of national organisations – was also strengthened (Schafers, 1981). The 1960s witnessed the start of more recent discussions concerning the co-operation and co-ordination of services. The idea developed through the 1970s and was consolidated by the recent Children and Youth Services Act (1990) which gave new impetus to service co-operation. This act (derived from the idea of the "world of life" based on Habermas's concept of Lebenswelt) supports standards of modern youth protection which include: primary and secondary prevention; a client needs orientation (implying decentralisation); integration of service provision; an orientation towards enabling clients to find work and deal with life; client involvement in decision-making; and a systems orientation (Habermas, 1981). It also encourages co-operation with other agencies, such as non-statutory bodies, in developing action plans and identifying the best solutions for clients.

The description given above refers to the *Länder* of western Germany. Since unification, this model has been applied in the new *Länder*, where youth policy had developed from an entirely different basis. For example, the principle of subsidiarity did not apply in eastern Germany since the responsibility for youth care rested entirely with the public authorities. Professional training and the nature of the relevant professions was also very different. Now, collaborative projects are beginning to emerge.

The Netherlands

In the Netherlands, "youth policy may be characterised as facet policy" (Geelen *et al.*, 1994; Veenman *et al.*, 1995). This means that developing and implementing youth policy is not the single responsibility of one department or of a separate set of actions. Instead, each government department is obliged to take youth into account in its policy making, while the Youth Policy Section of the Ministry of Health, Welfare and Sport serves to co-ordinate the whole process.

In general terms youth policy is seen as an investment in youth contributing to the growth of social capital. Specific youth policy, for those at risk, is inter-sectoral in nature and aimed at supporting youth where the usual structures have been weakened. Its objectives are to promote opportunities for young people, to prevent drop-out and to assist those who have already discontinued their education (Ministry of Welfare, Health and Cultural Affairs, 1993). Two important responsibilities include monitoring, analysing and publicising societal developments which are of significance for youth and promoting cohesion between the salient parties.

To achieve these goals, the Ministry of Welfare, Health and Cultural Affairs (1994) has reported recently that the improvement of integration in youth policy has involved stronger co-operation between, for example, education, primary health care, youth welfare work, manpower services, justice, police and the social services. In developing these co-ordination strategies both provinces and municipalities have been given a key role in their implementation. Central government remains in charge of directing the:

> "macro-framework for youth care and preventive policy. The responsibility of the provinces is to direct the remedial youth care, which is organised at regional level. The task of the municipalities, in co-operation with the provinces, is to direct local preventive policy. One of the central themes within remedial youth care is the pursuit of a clearly recognisable entry to the compartmentalised system of youth welfare work" (Veenman *et al.*, 1995).

Although, for many years, Dutch education has had the preparation of students for the labour market as one of its goals, more recently, following the report of the Rauwenhoff Committee (1990), the alignment of education and labour market policies have been given especial priority, the goal being to give all pupils a qualification that will give them entry to work. A number of reforms to the education system have been put into practice to achieve this goal. A central theme has been to smooth the transition from school to work. This has been achieved by creating more flexible opportunities for those students who find the academic side of schooling too hard, by giving more hands on experience and developing the co-operation between education and employers concerned with the apprenticeship system.

Portugal

In Portugal, public child support services have existed since the Middle Ages as "misericordias", with the first nursery schools emerging towards the end of the 19th century. However, it was not until the 1960s that public institutions began to develop social policy frameworks and to provide support in the co-ordination of private institutions. In 1984 legislation allowed for the State, in co-operation with other agencies and organisations, to implement a network of child and family social protection services. The present support services for children are now divided between the Ministries of Education, and Employment and Social Security. More recently policy has favoured the role of private initiatives, and has developed the responsibilities of Private Institutions of Social Solidarity (IPSS). Ramirez (1992) points to the need to increase awareness that local services need to form partnerships with the regional offices of different ministries, businesses, private organisations, the general population, and municipalities – who all share responsibility for the well-being of Portuguese citizens.

In Portugal, the concepts of "partnership" and "multi-dimensionality" are emerging slowly with the recognition that the problems of children at risk are linked to low levels of education in their families, deficiencies in food, health and housing, lack of pre-school care, and the devaluation of school by parents who give a preference to work (Cardoso, 1994).

The United Kingdom

In the United Kingdom, the Webbs (1909) (see Webb and Webb, 1963) argued for their "principle of prevention" through which the community, via a variety of agencies, would address the main causes of destitution:

> "at the incipient stages, when they are just beginning to affect one or other members of a family, long before a family as a whole has sunk into the morass of destitution".

Volunteer workers would have a key role:

> "the modern relation between the public authority and the voluntary worker is one of systematically organised partnership under expert direction".

The theme of their work – that what was needed was a co-ordinated, comprehensive attack on social problems which would bring together the different strands of public policy and the actions of different social agencies to bear on one particular population group – was taken up again in the United Kingdom in the 1960s and 1970s. The Seebohm Report (1968), for instance, initiated a re-organisation of local authority social services departments and brought together previously separate agencies. The intent was to increase flexibility and create more generic social workers, since overspecialisation was seen as being dissonant with the complex multiple needs of families and communities.

At the government level there were attempts to develop a joint framework for social policy – an initiative that was abandoned in the early 1980s as support for co-ordination waned (Challis et al., 1988). Nevertheless, by 1989, integration was back in the ascendant. The Children Act was passed which promoted partnership between local authorities and parents, and between the various local authority departments, over care for children in need. More recently the Single Regeneration Act (1994) has combined the funds of 20 separate programmes in five government departments to create greater flexibility in meeting local needs.

The United States of America

In the United States, a similar pattern can be identified. From the 1920s to the 1940s, co-ordinated efforts on social policy – referred to as "services integration" – were made initially by "united charities", area projects and neighbourhood councils. In the 1950s, concern about multi-problem families resulted in the development of integrated services programmes in a number of cities. Additional programmes were stimulated by the growth of the civil rights movement, the war on poverty, and the development of the notion of "the Great Society" (Kahn and Kamerman, 1992).

A major services integration initiative was launched in 1971 by the Department of Health, Education and Welfare in Washington which led to the reorganisation and consolidation of human service agencies at the state level in some States. It, too, ran out of steam, and was followed in the 1980s – in the context of budget cutting and decentralisation initiatives – by an increase in new and narrow categorical programmes. As in the United Kingdom, by the late 1980s new services integration initiatives had emerged involving the federal government and foundations, with both administrative and local level aspects. They tended to emphasise community-based solutions, including education, which focussed on holistic strategies for family units, inter-agency agreements, instruments for developing case plans, case management, pooled and decategorised funding, and the co-location of services (Kahn and Kamerman, 1992).

Some of the failings of current service delivery systems have been identified by Kusserow (1991) and appear in Table 1. Although based on the experience in the United States, the analysis could equally well apply elsewhere.

Thus the interest in providing, and the need to offer co-ordinated services to meet the needs of children and families has not abated. During the 1990s, new efforts have been made in many countries which, unlike earlier initiatives that emphasised top-down approaches, have been bottom-up, community-based and have involved a range of services especially education.

Table 1. **The main failings of current service delivery systems**

Problem	Examples
Needed services are difficult to access	• Clients must travel to multiple locations • Clients must complete many applications, undergo multiple assessments
Needed services are unavailable	• Specialised service is not available in every geographic area • Available services are insufficient to meet demand
Services delivered lack continuity	• Service providers fail to co-ordinate the planning of their services • Comprehensive service plans not developed for clients
Services are crisis-oriented	• Preventive services are inadequate; clients must wait for problems to reach crisis levels before receiving services
Service programmes lack accountability	• Programmes receive funding based on number of clients served rather than on outcome of service provided Few providers collect data to evaluate the success of their programmes

Source: Kusserow, 1991.

OTHER FACTORS PRESSING FOR CHANGE
TOWARDS GREATER SERVICES CO-ORDINATION

The developments, briefly identified above, evidence renewed interest in the co-ordination of both policy making and the delivery of services. A number of themes, which together emphasise a preventive approach, can be identified and these have stimulated further interest in integrated service reforms. These are discussed briefly below under the headings of: the socio-economic context; decentralisation; theoretical developments; and the effects of changing family roles on schooling.

The socio-economic context

Fluctuations in the economies of OECD countries; the growth of unemployment and poverty; transformations in demographies (in particularly, increases in the proportion of elderly citizens and decreases in birth rate); rises in the numbers of immigrants; alterations in family structures; and the growing need for literate and skilled workers have all created pressures for reform. Recent reforms cover the whole range of human services, including education, and for students are broadly aimed at improving skills, attitudes and competencies for entry into the labour market. The purpose of these reforms is to reduce human and financial waste, and thus improve efficiency and effectiveness. They are aimed at all students, but inevitably they impact strongly on children and youth at risk (for a fuller account see OECD, 1995a).

Decentralisation

Government policies, to decentralise decision-making and to pass budgets to local institutions, have enabled communities to link their support work more closely to need. These policies have stimulated the growth of partnerships between public and private sectors. For instance, they have provided additional opportunities for local funding (from businesses, foundations, and so on) to be used in concert with public funding for "bottom-up" reform and system development.

Theoretical developments

Ecological theories of child development stress its biological, psychological and social aspects. Patterns of behaviour are believed to develop in synchrony with other evolving relationships. This approach stresses the holistic development of children within particular cultural contexts and emphasises the need to support not only the individual but also social structures such as the family and community. Many writers (e.g. Wilson, 1990) have pointed to the interdependence of the different domains mentioned earlier. For instance, poverty has implications for access to health care, educational success and subsequent employment prospects. Evidence from longitudinal studies in the United Kingdom, also supports the link between poverty, family structure and educational success (Pilling, 1990).

Effects of the changing role of the family on schooling

The changing role and organisation of the family is too widely accepted to need documenting here. However, the implications of this trend for schools have received less attention. Hagen and Tibbitts (1994), for example, note that changes in family structures in Norway call into question the role that schools traditionally have played. Teachers are responsible for acting as a "human link" between municipal services and children's families. This quite limited role is premised on the assumption that parents should have the main responsibility for the well-being of their children. But what if parents do not take full responsibility for the welfare of their children? Who should intervene? In these circumstances teachers have continued to question the limits of the role they can play in helping to co-ordinate services for children. In Australia, too, schools have found that the current climate of poverty and family dislocation has led to welfare services being so over-stretched and crisis-oriented, that by the time they respond, students have been lost to the school system. This means that schools themselves must then act both to co-ordinate support services and also to modify their own arrangements (Coopers *et al.*, 1992).

Thus the extent to which schools can adapt to these circumstances and still attain their main goals requires further consideration – particularly as social conditions become more difficult, and the performance required of schools becomes more demanding. In the past, education systems have not been closely involved in co-ordination efforts. For example, in the United States, Kagan (1993) has argued that schools have allowed themselves to become over-stretched in attempts to deal single-handedly with social problems at the expense of educational goals. However, she goes on to point out that these new and growing pressures stemming from social change have exposed weaknesses and led to the recognition that education systems need to collaborate more widely with other agencies.

THE ROLE OF EDUCATION SYSTEMS IN INTEGRATED SERVICES

The involvement of education in co-ordination efforts is a recent and welcome development. It has provided new impetus and purpose, as well as financial and other resources. It also offers the potential to improve the comprehensiveness of service delivery.

Including education systems in this wider co-operative venture has not been without its difficulties. A number of issues identified by participating countries, with reference to pre-school, school and transition to work periods, are presented below.

The pre-school period

In Finland, Ojala (1989) reveals a number of historical tensions linked to pre-school provision. He points out that the national responsibility for day care rests with social welfare authorities but that school authorities participate by providing pre-school education for 6-year-olds, and by training pre-school teachers. The lowering of the school entry age from 7 to 6 will require close co-operation between welfare, health and education services (Aalto, 1991).

The various Head Start programmes in the United States (*e.g.* Zigler and Muenchow, 1992) also provide examples of cross-departmental collaboration (including federal and state agencies) in the provision of pre-school education. Recent programmes and grants (The Child Care and Development Block Grant, 1991) to support child care for children at risk are attempts to rationalise national child care and pre-school policy by requiring more co-ordinated planning within the State. At the same time, the responsible state agency must link new services with other federal, state, local child care, and child development programmes. A good example of public-private sector co-operation is provided by the New Start programme in Kansas City, Missouri in the United States. There, federal Head Start money has been combined with other public and private sector funding to provide all day, year round child care (normally Head Start programmes are half day only) along with the services of family advocates who link families with other agencies. This development reflects the significant role attributed to parental involvement in effective integrated networks.

In Germany, co-operation has developed between kindergartens and day care centres. Evaluations have shown that 25 per cent of all children show "oddities" in their behaviour (Haberkorn *et al.*, 1988), and that kindergartens are the focus of preventive efforts involving links with child guidance services.

Despite encouraging developments, areas of weakness needing policy change have been identified. In the Netherlands, for example, the government recognises that children from disadvantaged families are less likely than those from more advantaged families to attend day care facilities thereby increasing their educational disadvantage.

The school period

In Australia, the National Equity Programme for Schools (NEPS) is nested within the government's Social Justice and Access and Equity strategies. NEPS brings together, into a single framework, a range of formerly separate programmes which deal with issues that put children at risk such as homelessness and drug abuse and is aimed at improving educational outcomes for all students. One particular component of NEPS is the STAR (Students at Risk) (Department of Employment, Education and Training, 1992) programme introduced in 1990 as part of the Youth Social Justice Strategy to increase school retention. The initiative is intended for at risk students and although supported projects should be school based, those which involve co-ordination and contact with Youth Access Centres (centres which help youth to access work and training – see later section on transition to work) or health, welfare, housing agencies and business are encouraged. The considerable extent of implementation in the States and Territories can be seen from the 1993 National Report on Schooling in Australia (MCEETYA, 1993).

A new programme to support families to keep their children at school is being introduced, which will provide family counselling, support services and a grant for incidental expenditure until their children are 16 when they can then enter the AUSTUDY programme which provides financial assistance to students to promote equality of educational opportunity, by encouraging them to complete their education.

In addition the Department of Employment, Education, Training and Youth Affairs (DEETYA), within its general co-ordinating responsibilities, has implemented pilot projects to address homelessness, mainly amongst school-age young people. These projects include the co-ordination of services within the protocols. In addition the full integration of all financial inputs is one feature of Aboriginal Education Programmes (AEPs) intended to improve standards of education in that community. A recent report on education for Aboriginal and Torres Strait Islander Peoples also recommended (Commonwealth of Australia, 1994 – recommendation 2) in the context of self-determination and choice that responsibility should be as local as possible and co-ordination "up" the system as high as possible to ensure the efficient delivery of educational programmes or relevant support services. The National Strategy for Equity in Schooling (MCEETYA, 1994) calls, in the case of children and youth at risk, for:

> "the whole school community (...) to have access to information about, and opportunities to work with, non-educational support services (for example, medical/dental/psychological, income support, counselling) for students in each priority group" and that:

> "other appropriate support programmes (for example, health, safety, welfare, translation/interpretation services, income support) are co-ordinated with educational policies and processes to achieve optimal results for students in each priority group".

In Germany, schools increasingly are seen as the central pivot of children's lives, where failure, truancy and drop-out are regularly observed. A change in perspective, supporting "world-of-life" oriented youth services, has led to co-operation between schools and youth welfare services. This is encouraged by the Children and Youth Services Act (1990). All is not plain sailing, however, and problems exist at both the philosophical and practical levels. According to Raab (1994), the concept of school social work is at the heart of a contradiction in which school is seen as providing the same opportunities for all, but also acting to legitimise social inequality. However, recent trends, related to family change and growing violence, have led to the establishment of school social work as a "normal" youth service. At a practical level, teachers and social workers, not surprisingly, have developed different methods of working and ideas about education. Teachers wish to impart knowledge, but social workers view the development of children more holistically. A lack of appreciation of each other's working principles is certainly an obstacle to successful co-operation. However, school social work activities – including counselling, developing the interests of students, stimulating the use of meta-cognitive strategies, and linking the school and the community – seem to be in line with educational goals. The successful interaction of these two groups requires that both parties change their ways of working. Such changes, even if handled diplomatically, are bound to lead to tensions. Nevertheless, a number of programmes have been successful in this area, and evaluations reveal that students feel more at home in school and increase their problem-solving skills, and that relationships between disadvantaged and non-disadvantaged groups improve (Schmidt, 1992).

The United States is expanding the role of schools in meeting students' general needs. The Department of Education noted that "All children in Chapter One programmes (i.e. disadvantaged pupils) must have access to health and social services. [They] might be delivered at the school or linked to off-site but accessible, health clinics and social service agencies (...)". This recommendation was given legal status under the 1988 Hawkins-Stafford Elementary and Secondary School Improvement Amendments (PL 100-297), and is being implemented in some States (for example, Florida and Vermont).

While school-based provision is common in Europe, as well as in some States of the United States, concerns have been raised in that country about its feasibility. Some worry that schools lack the necessary experience; that difficulties will arise in funding arrangements; that schools primarily are oriented towards "normal" pupils; that they lack space; that non-educational personnel will be responsible to educational authorities; and that pressure to raise standards may exhaust energy for other support work.

As a result, Chaskin and Richman (1992) suggested that no single institution should be allowed to dominate children's services, since bureaucratic inertia and a reduction in pluralist, citizen-based planning might result. Furthermore, school catchment areas may not be co-terminous with those of family-oriented services. Nevertheless, examples of carefully supported school-based programmes have proved successful, and school-based provision would seem to be the preferred and obvious choice given that obstacles, such as those noted earlier, can be overcome. Certainly, the trend in the United States appears to be in this direction (Kagan, 1993).

In the school period, the delivery of co-ordinated services in educational institutions is a reality in some countries, but only an aspiration in others. In Finland, the goal has been to develop schools as "miniature welfare states" – functioning as centres for teaching, health care, social work and career guidance. This objective has much in common with Zigler's vision of 21st century American schools (Zigler, 1989).

The transition to work period

All countries recognise the importance of keeping children in school in order to develop competencies which are acceptable to employers. Careers counselling is often provided in schools to facilitate the transition to work, often in co-operation with employment services. In Australia, Youth Access Centres (YACs) function to assist children and youth at risk in their transition from school to work. They do this through information, advice, counselling and referral to other agencies. They focus on education, employment and training information but also on other relevant information for disadvantaged young people under 21 years, including accommodation, health and income support. They thus have the role of co-ordinating services for children and youth at risk, for example by assisting in the development of inter-agency strategies. This has led to the strengthening of links between youth service organisations, increasing knowledge of each other's working practices, the development of closer working relationships and the identification of duplication. This practice has led to increased employment access for young people (an outcome enhanced by YAC's outreach services, which include mobile offices), and an increased recognition of the role of YACs. YACs also operate a schools liaison programme (SLP) which, as the name suggests, links the YAC service to secondary schools and helps them to anticipate future needs. The SLP provides information as part of early and successful intervention in schools in preventing unemployment, homelessness and other problems. Recent evaluations, among clients of YACs, proved very favourable (Department of Employment, Education and Training, 1994).

Nevertheless, despite apparent success, a recent review of the functioning of YACs recommends a better co-ordination of service delivery and an increase in attention to the problems faced by disadvantaged youth. This includes implementing the youth training initiative (YTI). Integrated services are to be supplied through case management procedures for individual clients, which are intended to facilitate access to a wide range of government and non-government services and programmes aimed at assisting young people into work or worthwhile training opportunities. Clients identified as being at risk are eligible immediately for case management in contrast to others who must wait for 13 weeks. Within this scheme there is also a youth training allowance which provides financial support to young unemployed people as well as a clear message of endorsement of the relationship between education and training and satisfying employment criteria. In 1995, the government introduced an element of competition into the case management process by involving the private sector and introducing a regulatory authority.

In Germany, important changes have occurred in the working practices of agencies which support disadvantaged youth in the transition to work which reflect changes in the labour market. Over the past 10-15 years, a system of assistance for young people with vocational problems (*Jugendberufshilfe*) has been established. This provides a variety of programmes for career preparation, as well as supporting and complementing vocational training for youth at risk. The programmes have a social pedagogic quality, and are jointly financed by the Federal Institute of Labour, communities and non-statutory agencies which provide social and youth services. Statutory agencies do not, as yet, play an important role in them. However, the new Children and Youth Services Act obliges these agencies to take positive actions to aid untrained and unemployed youth (Braun et al., 1993).

Recognising that many vocational problems are caused by failure at school, programmes for disadvantaged youth intended to help them in the transition to work should, out of preference, begin in school. In Germany, such initiatives include: schemes to help young people develop career plans early on; information programmes for students and parents about career and educational opportunities (involving co-operation with careers advice, youth and social services); a vocational training preparation year (to allow disadvantaged youth to gain qualifications, develop ideas about their future careers, and to strengthen basic skills); a vocational training preparation year which imparts knowledge necessary for certain fields of work (and also helps career orientation); programmes that offer full vocational training to disadvantaged youth in inter-firm training centres (with the support of socio-pedagogues and special learning aids); and social work services in vocational schools.

Programmes, such as these, usually result from the joint actions of several organisations. For instance, in Munich, the Volkshochschule (VHS) – an adult education centre – developed its programme in co-operation with the Munich employment office, vocational schools and social services. Students in danger of dropping out of school receive counselling and support. The fundamental idea is that young people in need of support in a crisis might prefer help from a "neutral" service provided outside of school by social workers. Counselling and assistance are also offered to vocational school teachers. Help is provided in a neutral surrounding, young people can get information and advice from careers officers. Educational courses are offered to students to compensate for those missed at school. Problems that need to be addressed include the lack of long-term funding for the programme, and some reservations amongst teachers about social work professionals (Ballauf, 1994).

In Bremen, socially disadvantaged women are supported by "Quirl", a scheme partly funded by the Federal Youth Plan. Training programmes were developed in collaboration with the VHS, the Workers Educational Centre, and different non-statutory agencies providing youth services. A day care centre for children and a kindergarten were integrated into the programme because, without them, young women would find it difficult to participate. These facilities were financed by the Labour Office, the Social Services Department, and the Ministry for Women and Youth.

In spite of the school-based services that are already provided in Finland, additional support is given to those who are failing. Indeed, it is recognised that the school system needs to meet new and broader challenges (Takala, 1992). Takala argues that schools need to cross traditional boundaries and collaborate more with families, as well as social, health, employment and leisure services. He advocates a higher level of integration between education and work, and reports the positive effects of student "work projects" in which those labelled as "school allergics" develop relevant skills and attitudes, and achieve subsequent reintegration into society. Similar findings have been reported by Valde (1993).

Likewise, in the Netherlands additional measures have recently been developed to smooth the transition from school to work for children and youth at risk since a disproportionately large number of at risk youth are also unemployed. As noted above, a particular objective of Dutch education policy is to "contribute to the preparation for joining the labour force and participating on the labour market" (Ministry of Education and Science, 1989) – an objective which has received especial attention in recent years (Rauwenhoff Committee, 1990).

During junior secondary education individualised pre-vocational education has been developed for those students who wish to go on to further vocational training (IVBO). These courses will provide a general preparation for work and adult life. For those who do not make the necessary standards for either the higher levels of vocational education or the apprenticeship system there are short vocational courses to train youth without qualifications to be novice employees. Recently this scheme has been modularised to help students gain the necessary breadth of training to eventually obtain a vocational qualification.

The Netherlands has also introduced an apprenticeship system, not dissimilar in structure to the German dual system where responsibility is shared between educational bodies, the government and employers' and employees' organisations. The system operates at three levels. The first aims to develop professional operational skills, the second stresses independent working in middle management and the third on management and independent entrepreneurship. Students without vocational certificates can enter the system but in this case the course is longer.

Part-time non-formal education has developed as a special service which offers non-qualifying education for those young people who either cannot or will not participate in compulsory mainstream education under the part-time ruling. Usually these students lack the training for entry onto the labour market and the course develops personal and social talents for present and future living. This system focuses on combating early school-leaving in co-operation with vocational education. It will also be absorbed into the Regional Training Centres and as a consequence will be offered to all participants in education and vocational training.

Labour market-oriented training schemes for the unemployed, lasting for one year, are also available to every registered job-seeker in need of training and are also available for youth. As in the dual system this scheme is jointly administered.

Despite the apparent comprehensiveness and individualised nature of many of these courses, this form of vocational training has so far failed to prevent low success rates of approximately 50 per cent. As a consequence, extra measures have been introduced by the government for children and youth at risk. Educational policy measures intended to provide as many young people as possible with qualifi-cations relevant for labour market entry, have been introduced which attempt to keep children in education, either until they have obtained the necessary qualifica-tions, or to reduce early school leaving. In addition, special projects have also been introduced which quite specifically attempt to align education and labour market entry requirements for youth at risk. Essentially these approaches (Veenman *et al.*, 1995) augment the support for students who can no longer cope with the demands of the regular education provision. These supports take the form of individualised planning that take the employment and educational aspirations of the student into account, provide particular training in labour and social skills needed for success in the work place and arrange for particular work placements with employers and continuing support for them. In doing this a wide range of services are involved and co-ordinated by staff. What is required is:

> "intensive co-operation with a variety of institutions such as the employment office, the school, the social services, trade and industry, the social environ-ment of the young person and if need be the probation and after-care service" (Veenman *et al.*, 1995).

Services integration for youth in the transition to work is more complicated than for any other age group. In addition to the myriad education, health and welfare services which provide for younger children, employment services and pri-vate companies must also form part of the collaborative network. Public sector services, and especially schools, are required to form partnerships with private companies that have contrasting philosophical outlooks and functions. A frequent unwillingness (or inability) on either side to approach the other, discovered in national case studies, appears to be a problem. Schools seldom have sufficient resources to provide intensive careers support for children at risk; companies on the other hand, often are unwilling to court "early" school-leavers, preferring instead to focus their interests on young people with further or higher education.

The concept of services integration

Recently there has been considerable discussion about the meaning of the concept of services integration. An early statement from the United States Department of Health, Education and Welfare in the 1970s described services integration as follows:

> "Services integration refers primarily to ways of organising the delivery of services to people at the local level. Services integration is not a new programme to be super-imposed over existing programmes; rather, it is a process aimed at developing an integrated framework within which ongoing programmes can be rationalised and enriched to do a better job of making services available within existing commitments and resources. Its objectives must include such things as: *i)* the co-ordinated delivery of services for the greatest benefit to people; *ii)* a holistic approach to the individual and the family unit; *iii)* the provision of a comprehensive range of services locally; and *iv)* the rational allocation of resources at the local level so as to be responsive to local needs" (Kusserow, 1991, p. 10).

The development of American thinking on defining services integration has been fully described by Kagan (1993) and will not be repeated here. Her final "comprehensive definition" recognises a number of different levels at which services integration can operate. These are the client, programme, policy and organisation levels. A comprehensive evaluation of services integration would need to cover all these levels – a conclusion anticipated in the design of the CERI study.

However, for many, the idea of services integration implies too strong an interaction between agencies. A preferred term is co-ordination. In an international context inevitably various terminological issues arise. In Germany, for example, the term services integration is not used, but those of collaboration or co-ordination are well accepted. In the Netherlands, the term networking appears to be in wide use which seems closer to the idea of co-ordination as described in Table 2 which contrasts co-operation and co-ordination (Mulford and Rogers, 1982).

Co-operation is a word often used to refer to the informal joint activities of organisations, with reciprocal trade-offs in the absence of rules. Co-ordination, on the other hand, refers to the sharing of goals, decision-making, tasks, and the allocation of resources.

More recently the term collaboration has entered into this vocabulary and has been used to describe the different processes involved in bottom-up and top-down initiatives involved in co-operation and co-ordination. In a practical manual on school-linked integrated services, Melaville and Blank (1993) use the term collaboration to describe a bottom-up, multi-year community development process for changing human service systems. It begins with a loosely organised group of people in the community who recognise the need for change. They identify key local people who can inspire commitment to achieving a shared set of goals, and develop a strategic plan for action that targets priority neighbourhoods. Chosen community leaders work together to study the needs of residents and how services are being

Table 2. **A comparison of co-operation and co-ordination processes**

Criteria	Co-operation	Co-ordination
1. Rules and fomality	No formal rules	Formal rules
2. Goals and activities emphasised	Individual organisation goals and activities	Joint goals and activities
3. Implications for vertical and horizontal linkages	None, only domain agreements	Vertical or horizontal linkages can be affected
4. Personnel resources involved	Relatively few – lower-ranking members	More resources involved – higher-ranking members
5. Threat to autonomy	Little threat	More threat to autonomy

Source: Mulford and Rogers, 1982.

provided. Their goal is to develop an inter-agency service delivery prototype for combining resources in ways which improve pro-family services. Formal organisational changes are made in government structures. An on-going process develops in which technical tools such as common intake and assessment forms, common eligibility determination, management information systems, and inter-agency case management, are utilised. Issues relating to the confidentiality of client information are resolved. Collaboration then becomes permanently institutionalised through joint efforts in training, education, supervision, community outreach, and in the enhancement of sensitivity to cultural diversity.

In contrast a top-down account of collaboration has been given by Bruner (1991). For him collaboration begins at the state level and involves dealing with the problems of separate rules, regulations and funding, and negative power struggles between departments. At the second stage, collaboration involves demonstration projects in which the State supports bottom-up initiatives. The third step involves the promotion of successful projects throughout the State. Finally, the fourth step is seen as worker-family collaboration to identify needs and set goals. These goals are more likely to be met in the context of flexible, comprehensive services.

CONCLUDING COMMENT

Efforts to integrate or co-ordinate services have a long tradition in many countries. Involving education systems has been identified as a new thrust which has given momentum to this approach across the pre-school, school and transition periods. It involves a wide range of actors as well as changes in administrative arrangements, attitudes and practices. It is a strategy which has been adopted by many countries with very different welfare traditions. Countries recognise that many of the problems encountered by children as they are growing up cannot be dealt with effectively through "a bureaucratised, categorised, fragmented policy and programme world that lacks capacity for holistic approaches to *whole* individuals and whole families" (Kahn and Kamerman, 1992).

Integrating services is more than a uni-dimensional solution to a complex problem but represents a commitment to a new approach which is preventive and holistic in nature, which stresses early identification, and which has as its main goals the preservation of families, and the solving of their problems. In the same vein, Kahn and Kamerman (1992) have noted that "a major strategy has been to focus on the family unit rather than the child, to intervene from a community base rather than remove the child from the home, and to stress pooled funding in developing a co-ordinated set of outcome-oriented strategies which are derived from a number of agencies and professional perspectives".

2

INTRODUCING THE CERI STUDY

by

Peter Evans and Philippa Hurrell

The principal goal of the CERI study was to bring together and analyse information from a number of Member countries concerning policies and practices related to the ways in which initiatives have been taken to bring together, co-ordinate or integrate a range of statutory and non-statutory services to meet the educational, social, health and employment needs of children and youth at risk and their families.

DEFINITIONS

The definition of children and youth at risk developed in the earlier study (OECD, 1995*a*) is also adopted in this report. They are children, who are "failing in school and unsuccessful in making the transition to work and adult life and as a consequence are unlikely to be able to make a full contribution to active society". Poverty, family and community factors each were identified as predicting at risk status, as were poor knowledge of the majority language, the type of school attended, and its location.

The multiplying effect of risk factors was noted. One risk factor is no more likely than zero risk factor to predict difficulty. However, if two or three risk factors are present, the chances of an unfavourable outcome increase four times. With four risk factors the chances of a negative outcome are increased 10 times. These factors, of themselves, suggest the need for multiple service input if complex problems are to be effectively addressed.

As noted earlier, the purpose of the empirical part of the study was to collect information to describe new and effective approaches to services integration. It was recognised from the outset that this would be a complex task requiring consideration of factors operating across a broad spectrum of types of service delivery. In this context, a broad definition of services integration was agreed upon by participants. Services integration was defined (OECD, 1993), as referring to co-ordination, co-operation or collaboration between two or more services. A broad definition, such as this, was required in order to cover the wide range of examples that were anticipated to be present in Member countries.

METHODOLOGY

The study was carried out between 1993 and 1995. The main part of work involved the collection of detailed information from country reports, case studies and national literature reviews concerning the ways in which, mainly but not exclusively, education, health and social services are being co-ordinated to meet the needs of children and youth at risk and their families during the pre-school, school and transition to work periods. From these three sources, information was sought in four principal areas of implementation which were derived from earlier work by Evans et al. (1989).

- At the mandating level, information was collected on legal frameworks and policies (national and state levels).
- At the strategic level, data was gathered from senior managers and co-ordinators on the functioning of identified services.
- At the operational level, information was sought on issues such as budget and personnel allocation, and their relationship to problem identification and prioritisation.
- At the field level, data was gathered on the way in which services work in practice, including the service delivery process and outcomes for professionals and clients.

The mandating level

As noted above, information was gathered from country reports and case studies. A structure for the country reports was agreed, and reports were submitted by 13 countries [Belgium (the Flemish community), Canada (Alberta, Manitoba, Ontario, Quebec and Saskatchewan), Finland, France, Germany, Italy, the Netherlands, Portugal, Slovenia, Sweden, Turkey, the United Kingdom (England and Wales, Northern Ireland, Scotland), and the United States of America]. These provided information on the mandating level including, in the first part of the reports, data on laws and policies pertaining to services integration, and on social security benefits for various at risk groups. In addition, information was sought on funding, the implications of decentralisation, communication between departments or ministries, and communication within services themselves. Further information was requested on responsibility and implementation of integrated services, as well as on monitoring service quality and the development of preventive strategies. Finally, information was requested on the role of voluntary services, parental participation, client rights and client choice.

The second part of the reports covered the availability of integrated services for children and youth at risk and their families at national and local levels. Information was sought separately on services for pre-school children, school children, youth in the transition to work, and families. The information requested included the size of the population at risk, and the extent of coverage of, and satisfaction with, the services provided. Countries were also asked to give examples of integrated services. A copy of the questionnaire is provided in Annex 1, taken from OECD (1993). The work, organised thematically is reported in Chapter 3 of this book, and Part III supplies country details.

Strategic, operational and field level

In common with the country report structure, considerable planning and consultation went into the preparation of the framework for the case studies (OECD, 1994). Semi-structured interview schedules were written for the strategic, operational and field levels. For the last level, different schedules were designed for professionals and clients. A self-completion questionnaire was also devised which covered factual issues (see Annex 1).

The semi-structured interview schedules were divided into four main parts according to a "CIPP" (Context, Input, Process, Product) structure, adapted from Stufflebeam (1971). These descriptors were also used to structure the initial case study reports to provide consistency. However, mainly to improve readibility this scheme has not been adhered to in the shorter published accounts. A description of the CIPP structure, taken from OECD (1994) is given in Annex 2. Briefly, under the heading of *context*, descriptive information was gathered on the area served, the nature of the clients, the services and the extent of their integration. Under the heading of *input* came the areas of support for integration, initial planning, resources and evaluation. Under the heading of *process*, those involved in decision-making and planning were identified as well as strategies for implementing chosen approaches. Under the heading of *product*, the benefits and problems associated with services integration were covered, as well as certain issues relating to clients.

A team of seven (five OECD experts and two members of the Secretariat) carried out the case studies. Six worked in pairs and focused on the operational and field levels. The seventh gathered information at the strategic level. In the first year (1993), visits were made to Finland, Germany and Portugal. In these countries each pair focused on a particular age period – pre-school, school, or transition to work. Three days were spent in each country. A country briefing was given on the first day and the remainder of the time was spent at various sites.

In the second year (1994), visits were made to Canada and the United States. In each of these countries the data gathering plan was slightly different from that used in the first year. Each pair of experts visited a single province or State and, as far as possible, divided their time up equally between sites concerned with the three age levels. Thus each pair attempted to cover the whole age range. In Canada, case studies were written on Alberta, Ontario, New Brunswick and Saskatchewan. In the United States, the three areas visited were California, Missouri and New York City. A country briefing session was held in Washington on the first day of the study week.

In the final year (1995), the team visited Australia. Here the pattern was as for the United States. The first day comprised a country briefing followed by visits to Youth Access Centres in the Sydney area. After this, the group again split into pairs and carried out studies in New South Wales, South Australia and Victoria. The seventh team member visited the country's capital city, Canberra.

Although the original plan was to carry out the case studies systematically and consistently at all of the sites, this goal was not wholly achieved. As far as possible data was collected in a consistent way, using the interview schedules and the self-completion questionnaire, but there was substantial variation. For instance, at some sites interviews with individuals were not possible and the team was introduced to large groups. Nevertheless, having noted this, the case studies themselves were reported as far as was possible in a consistent manner using the CIPP framework across the strategic, operational and field levels and across the pre-school, school and transition periods.

After the case studies were completed they were sent to the sites for validation. At the same time country nationals were asked to carry out literature reviews on work completed in their country. The information from these was used to enrich the case study reports.

The following chapters of part I provide a synthesis of country reports from 13 Member countries, and case studies from seven countries. Finland and the Netherlands also provided their own case study material. The countries visited were self-selecting with the proviso that examples were taken from each of the major world regions of the OECD. Part II provides "vignettes" of practical developments and Part III, "vignettes" of countries' laws and policy innovations. Further case studies will be available in a future OECD publication dealing with integrated services in Australia, Canada, Finland, Germany, the Netherlands, Portugal and the United States.

3

THE MANDATING LEVEL: LEGISLATION AND POLICY

by

Janet Friedman, Peter Evans and Philippa Hurrell

INTRODUCTION

To gather information at the mandating level, participating countries were asked to submit country reports based on a questionnaire concerning legislation and policies relevant to the integration of services for four target groups at risk: pre-school children, school children, youth in transition to work, and families of children and youth at risk (see Annex 1). The problems faced by children and youth at risk, as well as by their families, are often diverse and multi-causal in nature, presenting major challenges for policy makers and service providers who seek to develop effective approaches to meet the needs of those currently at risk, to identify and implement preventive measures to help reduce the numbers at risk, and to decrease the magnitude of the problems in the future.

This chapter focuses on the mandating level in an effort to examine and understand the legal frameworks and policies adopted by government ministries and departments as they relate to services integration. The report is based on information, gathered mainly in 1994, from the following countries: Belgium (Flemish Community), Canada (with reports received from Alberta, Manitoba, Ontario, Quebec, and Saskatchewan), Finland, France, Germany, Italy, the Netherlands, Portugal, Slovenia, Sweden, Turkey, the United Kingdom (with reports received from England and Wales, Northern Ireland and Scotland), and the United States of America. More detailed information on the participating countries is provided in Part III of this book.

PHILOSOPHY

Most of the countries report a positive philosophy or outlook towards the increased integration of services and speak of the value of co-operation, coherence, co-ordination, and collaboration, sometimes drawing distinctions between the degrees of integration resulting from each of the above. While the modes and degrees of implementation of services integration differ substantially from country to country, the motivations for favouring the concept fall into two broad categories:

– humanitarian interests; and

– economic concerns.

Countries often begin by speaking of children's fundamental rights to an education which meets their individual needs to enable them to develop to their fullest potential, and become active, productive members of society. Incorporated in this idea are the principles of equality of opportunity and access to a range of services in support of their education. In France, for instance, the idea is expressed that even if the school cannot abolish the inequalities that mark the conditions of life of children and youth, it must at least contribute to the equality of opportunity. It should permit all to acquire a level of recognised qualification which will enable them to express their capacities and enter into an active life. In Portugal, the Constitution states that education should contribute to overcoming economic, social, and cultural inequalities as well as towards building understanding and tolerance.

Responses to the questions relating to all of the age groups consider the inter-relatedness of children's social, health, psychological, and nutritional needs (to name but a few), as well as the impact of family circumstances on children's abilities to perform in school and ultimately to reach their potential. In this context, services integration should be seen not as an end in itself, but as a means to providing a more comprehensive, more effective, and more accessible range of services in response to children and families.

From an economic perspective, countries frequently refer to services integration within the context of fiscal constraints for an increasing population perceived to be at risk. Budgetary limitations have become even more severe in times when countries are experiencing periods of slow or negative economic growth. In the face of these constraints, countries are seeking ways to ensure and maximise the effectiveness of programmes and to optimise the use of available resources. The Netherlands report mentions the underlying considerations for initiatives in services integration as "economy, efficiency, and effectiveness" (which have been called the three auditing Es). The government of Alberta, Canada, reports having "established three-year business plans across departments to ensure the province works efficiently and effectively to provide necessary services for all citizens while reducing the provincial deficit". Besides promoting inter-departmental integration in the public sector, governments are seeking ways to stimulate increased collaboration and co-operation between the public and private sectors.

LAWS AND POLICIES PROMOTING SERVICES INTEGRATION

Within the context of a supportive philosophy, as well as economic pressures and other justifications for greater services integration, the reports indicate that governments in virtually all of the countries are legislating and creating national policy frameworks to mandate services integration. Policy approaches vary in the degree to which they are prescriptive regarding how the integration is to be implemented, often delegating to the regional or, in many cases, the local level the autonomy to organise programmes, negotiate working agreements, and establish partnerships based on community needs assessments. A number of models or scenarios for integration emerge from the legislation which countries have reported including:

- *co-ordination of planning* among separate entities for service delivery – including joint needs assessments and collaboration on grant proposals;
- *co-ordination of service delivery* among separate entities – including shared responsibility for implementing programmes, division of labour to avoid duplication of services, shared responsibility for funding, and shared resources among entities including information, staff and materials;
- *merging separate existing services* into one unified entity; and
- *creating new programmes or entities* with an inter-disciplinary focus.

Co-operation may be inter-disciplinary, inter-sectoral, and/or between different levels of government. While several programmes will be discussed which have the potential to influence integration from the bottom up – that is, local efforts or demonstration projects which may influence national policy – in large part, the focus will be on efforts filtering from the top down: the mandating level, the legal frameworks and policies adopted by government ministries and departments which provide the impetus to facilitate services integration. Governments are encouraging and stimulating integration in a number of different ways including:

- creating co-ordinating bodies or appointing co-ordinators for the purpose of enhancing communication and collaboration between separate entities;
- tying funding or targeting increased levels of funding to collaborative planning efforts and/or co-ordinated multi-disciplinary service delivery approaches;
- simplifying and standardising eligibility requirements and application processes across programmes;
- granting waivers to existing regulations for demonstration projects which promote an integrated approach;
- identifying goals which require a multi-disciplinary approach as a means to their attainment;

— merging or replacing previously separate, limited and/or uni-dimensional entities into those which adopt a broader, multi-disciplinary, more holistic approach; and

— supporting research and disseminating information regarding effective practices based on an integrated approach.

Legislation and policies promoting services integration will be discussed within the framework of each of the four target groups, although it should be noted at the outset that some of the programmes have been mandated to integrate and co-ordinate efforts across age groups.

Pre-school children

In many countries, legislation and policies regarding pre-school children include provisions for a multi-disciplinary approach involving a broad range of social welfare, nutritional, health, and educational services, and often promoting co-operation amongst various community services. The need to encourage the early involvement of parents, the necessity for early detection of possible problems, the importance of appropriate intervention to address these problems, and the need to provide family support services are considered important elements in service provision. Countries described provisions from before birth to help provide advantages for healthy growth and development. For example, in Finland, a programme of maternity benefit which encourages mothers to receive regular prenatal health care also provides them with financial benefit or equipment and materials needed for the child's first year of life, including a child's first book.

As regards early childhood care and education programmes, the importance of the link between home and school and the need for parents to take an early and active role in their children's education were stressed. In countries reporting increasing numbers of mothers participating in the work force as well as increasing numbers of single parent families, the need and demand for full-day year-round care is growing. In response to increasing need for day care in Germany, the 1990 Children and Youth Aid Services Act (KHJG) affirmed that all children in need should have day care services. In 1991, the government issued a declaration stating that it would establish a legal right to day care with effort to provide adequate places. In most countries, early childhood care is provided at a cost to parents by a host of service providers, of which the government may be one; however, many children who receive care outside their homes do so within the context of the private sector. In fact, only in the Flemish community in Belgium, was it reported that pre-school education is provided free of charge for all children aged 2.5 to 6. While it is not compulsory, most Flemish children do attend, and it was reported that the programme has not previously targeted specific measures for children at risk. It is significant that despite access to pre-school education, 85 per cent of the repeaters in the first school year come from socially underprivileged families. To address this fact, additional staffing is now being made available, both for the first school year and for 4- and 5-year-old children in early education, with the main objective being "to detect and back up children who are threatened in their development and education as early as possible so as to prevent educational failure".* * In Portugal, a work group comprised of the representatives of the Secretaries of State for Educational Reform and Social Security was established in 1991, for the purpose of assessing the need to create kindergartens and planning for their establishment.

An early government-funded example of services integration for pre-school children, incorporating provisions for a multi-disciplinary approach including a broad range of social, nutritional, health and educational services, is the Head Start Programme in the United States. Head Start has long encouraged early involvement of parents in their children's education and included provision of family support services as a basic component. By channelling funds directly to local programmes and including a provision that communities contribute funds or services, the United States government stimulated early collaboration amongst local community services as well as the development of creative partnerships for the delivery of comprehensive services to pre-school children and their families. Head Start programmes are operated by a range of providers including schools, non-profit organisations, and social service agencies, but again, only a fraction of those in need are enrolled. Recently, the United States government has awarded a number of collaboration grants to States, and using these, communities, based on local needs, have sought to update and enhance the original Head Start model while building stronger ties between Head Start and other major early childhood programmes. For example, Kansas City, Missouri's New Start Programme, by combining funding from Head Start with private, state, and federal sources, has succeeded in offering a full-day year-round programme (whereas most Head Starts are half-day programmes) with the services of a "family advocate" at each site who serves as a case manager, linking each family with needed services such as adult literacy classes, job training, and drug treatment programmes.

Early childhood programmes are sometimes administered by ministries or departments separate from the education ministries or departments providing compulsory school education, a factor which can serve to inhibit integrated planning of curriculum and service co-ordination with schools serving older students. The reports indicate that countries are adopting approaches to linking early childhood education more closely with schools serving older children. For example, in the Flemish community in Belgium, the vision is to integrate early childhood and

---

* In the whole text, quotations with no reference are taken from the country reports (*cf.* list of documents at the end of the bibliography).

primary education, providing continuous care up to the age of 12. In Ontario, Canada, one-third of child care centres are based in schools. School boards are encouraged, in a joint policy of the Ministry of Community and Social Services and the Ministry of Education and Training, to take a more active role in promoting and co-ordinating child care programmes in schools and in the community. The Education Act has been changed to allow schools to hold a child care licence if they wish. Plans are to bridge these two systems and develop common guidelines.

An additional example is provided in the efforts in Saskatchewan, Canada, to develop a co-ordinated, comprehensive plan for meeting children's needs entitled "Action Plan for Children". As part of a similar Community Action Programme for Children in Alberta, Canada, community programmes will receive funding to reduce the risks of social, emotional, health, development and learning problems of children at risk, 0-6 years of age, and their families with the goals of prevention and intervention at the earliest possible point in the origin of risk, using an integrated approach to providing services. Alberta also has in place Programme Enhancement Grants, which provide support for co-ordinated service delivery and additional hours of early childhood instruction as well as compensatory programming to help disadvantaged students increase their readiness for and performance in school. These approaches are structured to look across disciplines and ministries or departments when formulating new plans for providing services for children. In England and Wales, the Children Act of 1989, represents a major step towards promoting partnerships between local social service departments and local education authorities, requiring that they work together in the review and co-ordination of all services for children under the age of 8.

The Better Beginnings, Better Futures Project in Ontario, Canada, exemplifies inter-ministerial co-ordination amongst the Ministries of Health, Education and Training, and Community and Social Services, as well as the federal Department of Indian and Northern Affairs, and involves research into a holistic primary prevention model of social, emotional and behavioural, cognitive and physical health problems in economically disadvantaged communities beginning with prenatal/infant and pre-school programmes. Plans include following the children through to their mid-twenties. Integration was promoted by tying funding from the project to communities being able to document an integrated approach for service planning and delivery. In Germany, inter-service "preventive and supportive" programmes have been developed for pre-school children with behavioural problems, with co-operation being fostered between kindergartens or day care centres and child guidance.

In Slovenia, the education system is currently undergoing reform, and expectations are to give the population at risk more consideration than it has received in the past. A preventive approach is being adopted and efforts are being targeted at "school newcomers", recognising the need to identify problems early and to focus on the transition to school which may be an especially vulnerable and difficult time for children. Services are being integrated with the Advisory Centre for Children, Young People and Parents where professional assistance may be obtained from psychologists, paediatricians, and others.

The Netherlands report draws attention to the fact that the proportion of children from disadvantaged backgrounds participating in various types of child-care is far less than that of children from middle and upper class backgrounds. The report indicates that by the time disadvantaged children attend school, many are "considerably delayed in their language and cognitive development". Furthermore, despite participation in the Educational Priority Policy Programme, a programme which provides additional resources and services for students at risk in high con-centration poverty areas, performance remains below average, particularly for non-Dutch children, and continues to decline the longer the students are in school. In the United States, currently only 36 per cent of eligible children with documented need are served by Head Start. Plans are to increase funding for this programme so that by 1998 all eligible children will receive Head Start services.

The above discussion highlights some of the approaches which countries are taking to providing co-ordinated, comprehensive, integrated services for young children. Encouraging elements are those involving co-operation with community services, co-ordination across disciplines, parent involvement, and efforts to create closer ties with schools providing compulsory education to older children. Concerns remain targeting services specifically at disadvantaged students to achieve real cognitive gains and future success in school, as well as improving service access and availability for children at risk.

School children

The reports indicate that many countries are passing legislation and promoting policies which encourage services integration for school age children. Countries repeatedly acknowledged in the reports the inability of schools alone to solve the problems of at risk children. Co-ordinated approaches, linking community services in an effort to help children at risk to overcome their at risk status and reach their full potential, are increasingly being sought.

Several countries reported employing the strategy of targeting additional resources to schools with high concentrations of poverty, and at the same time, mandating collaborative efforts with other community services such as health and social services. An example of programmes targeting resources is a programme in France, *Zones d'éducation prioritaires* (ZEP), which assumes that the school alone cannot combat the effects of poverty, and that education is enriched by a partner-ship with the various levels of government, as well as the cultural and social services organisations operating in the area. The Netherlands' Educational Priority

Policy Programme, which identifies "educational priority areas" (EPAs), is another example, incorporated into official legislation in 1993 in the Primary Education Act and the Secondary Education Act. In this programme, extra resources are made available to primary schools with at least 75 per cent disadvantaged students on the one hand, on the other hand to networks of schools with high concentrations of children at risk (children of parents of low socio-economic status and from ethnic minorities), including special schools and secondary schools, and areas with high concentrations of Gypsies or travellers. Activities, related to themes in the national policy framework to fight educational disadvantage, have been developed in co-operation with external organisations. In Portugal, schools receive priority intervention if situated in zones or localities where isolation is an obstacle to retaining teachers and where a significant number of children have learning difficulties. In Italy, in the pilot project on the *Dispersion scolaire* phenomenon, zones with high numbers of at risk students have been identified, and the project aims to improve instruction, co-ordinate with community psychological, social and health services, and optimise existing resources. "In Northern Ireland, one of the government's top policy priorities is Targeting Social Need (TSN). TSN aims to meet greatest need, reduce unfair social and economic differentials and promote equality and equity by focusing resources more precisely on Northern Ireland's most disadvantaged areas and people, Protestant and Catholic". In the United States, the Chapter One Programme of the Elementary and Secondary Education Act is the government's largest elementary and secondary education programme, targeting nearly 7 billion dollars each year to schools with large concentrations of poor and educationally deprived children. With the proposed re-authorisation of this programme, the new law will include a provision to require schools to co-ordinate services with those of other community health, educational and social services, thus tying funding to integrative measures. All of these programmes recognise the need for early intervention and detection of problems while bringing additional resources to bear on addressing these problems.

Targeting schools with high concentrations of at risk students and encouraging community participation is also a plan being followed in Manitoba, Canada. There, schools are eligible to receive funds from the Student Support Grants Programme, and proposals must focus on all of the following: curriculum adaptation and development, instructional and assessment practices, positive and supportive learning environments, parental involvement, staff development, and community participation. In a draft policy statement on educational policy for at risk students, "Community participation identifies integration of services as an effective initiative in assisting at risk students to overcome personal, social, and economic barriers to learning and achieve success in school". The inter-relatedness and necessity for all of the elements to be addressed are recognised. Similarly, in Alberta, Canada, funds are being targeted through the Enhanced Opportunity Grant to certain schools enrolling large numbers of students with exceptional educational, social and economic needs.

Legal frameworks in other countries are instituting major reforms to promote partnerships between local authorities. For example, in England and Wales, the Children Act of 1989, is seen as "the most important reform of the law concerning children in this century". The law "promotes partnership between local authorities and parents, and between the various local authority departments, over care for children in need". The Education Reform Act, 1988, and the Education Act 1993 and related enactments encourage quality and diversity as well as parental choice of school, and encourage local education authorities, social service departments, and other local services to collaborate. In Germany, the Children and Youth Services Act (KHJG) focuses on prevention and calls for public services to involve voluntary service providers in planning and co-ordination of all relevant local activities. The law is consistent with local and regional efforts towards "clearer target group orientation", *i.e.* schemes are provided on a clearer analysis and an inventory of young people's characteristics and needs; and local/regional (or even neighbourhood) approach, *i.e.* schemes are based on a local approach and a local needs analysis. In Italy, Law 142/90 calls for public administrations to collaborate to govern activities of common interest. Another important law, 309/90 calls for preventive initiatives in education and for co-ordination with health services. Similarly, in Portugal, the law calls for co-operation with special services from the community health centres to work with the schools to provide for the healthy development of students. The Programme of Promotion of Health Education was recently created to integrate health activities into the curriculum and co-ordinate activities on important issues such as drug addiction and AIDS. In Quebec, Canada, two laws have been passed with statutes which complement each other: *i)* the Law on Public Instruction mandates co-operation between schools and community health and social services, and *ii)* the Law on Health and Social Services calls for services of both a preventive and curative nature, and requires that these be made available in schools. In fact, in 1993, the Minister of Health and Social Services and the Minister of Education issued a joint publication entitled *Health and Social Services in Schools: Guide to Ensure Concerted Action between Local Community Service Centres and School Boards*, outlining the services to be offered to young people in schools.

For the first time, in 1994, the United States has adopted formal social policy goals at the national level through passage of the Goals 2000: Educate America Act. This legislation stated that by the year 2000, "All children in America would be ready to learn". The goals also include a statement that, "Every school will promote partnerships that will increase parental involvement and participation in promoting the social, emotional and academic growth of children". The law provides funds to States that want to create and implement plans for achieving the National Goals.

"The commitment to implement these goals in a collaborative manner is one of the forces moving the United States towards a variety of service delivery reform initiatives (...)." The goals represent an example of a growing emphasis on defining and measuring outcomes of social programmes, as opposed to focusing on inputs such as budgets and manpower. The shift to measuring outcomes leads to a broader vision beyond individual programmes and disciplines and helps to move away from a fragmented approach towards service delivery.

In the Flemish community in Belgium, policy exists for schools to work in close co-operation and collaboration with Psycho-Medical-Social (PMS) centres in diagnosing learning problems, including "problems resulting from the socio-cultural background of pupils". The PMS centres operate with teams consisting of psychologists, education specialists, social workers, physicians and paramedics, who provide assistance and counselling to parents, students, and teachers and monitor students throughout their education. As a result of recent legislation, a special programme of "home-school" liaison which targets Gypsies, travellers, and immigrant disadvantaged students uses contractual collaboration agreements between schools and other community services. In Turkey, where children at risk come under the rubric of special education, a General Directorate of Special Education, Guidance and Counselling Services has recently been established, and co-operation protocols put in place, between ministries, universities and voluntary institutions to carry out activities and studies. Laws in Finland require municipalities to provide support, guidance, and all necessary measures "to remove the social and mental difficulties attached to schooling and the pupil's development, and in order to develop co-operation between school and home".

As seen in the examples cited above, legislation has been passed in several countries to encourage services integration for school children. The fact that this legislation is seen as so innovative by the countries themselves, clearly indicates the confidence that officials feel in pursuing a much more integrative approach.

Youth in transition to work

The slow economies which many countries are experiencing, as well as the potential for societal disruption resulting from such negative behaviours as alcohol abuse, alcohol addiction, and violent crime, are causing countries to seek preventive measures and address problems of truancy, drop-out, and the difficulties in obtaining employment in the interest of avoiding ultimately more costly problems to the individual and society. Services for this age group, frequently have been delegated to several ministries or departments including education, labour, social services, health and justice, thus presenting a challenge for policy makers engaged in the process of reform towards a more integrated approach to service provision.

Efforts to integrate services for youth in transition to work often include "stay-in-school" measures to combat truancy and drop-out. In Canada, the federal Stay-In-School Initiative includes three major goals: to raise public awareness of the issue of school drop-out, to mobilise stakeholders to undertake action, and to provide services to at risk students aged 12-18 to help them to achieve the goal of graduation enlisting the aid of schools and community agencies. In England and Wales, the government has attached particular importance to the issue of truancy and disaffection and has supported expenditure by local education authorities in England and Wales of over 55 million pounds over the four years 1993-97 on projects to tackle these problems. In Belgium, two projects, which started in 1991 in the cities of Antwerp and Ghent to prevent problematic behaviours, began as attempts to work in close collaboration with welfare organisations to identify problems early, to set up plans of action, and to involve outside parties in co-operative efforts with teachers. It is perhaps instructive that these programmes evolved into efforts to improve the entire school climate.

Other measures often employed by countries involve partnerships between the public and private sectors in an effort to supply job training and apprenticeship programmes such as those documented in Belgium for the Flemish community, Canada, Finland, England and Wales, the Netherlands, and the United States. In some countries, the co-operation of employers with schools is enlisted on humanitarian grounds, but in other instances, governments have sought to provide economic incentives to stimulate private sector involvement in providing job training and experience to young people at this crucial transition period. In Germany, for example, a "dual system" of vocational education is provided. This system includes a formal vocational training diploma with apprenticeships involving both schools and companies. Training places are very much dependent on the economy, causing young people to face what "researchers describe as the 'two thresholds' in the process of the transition from school to work: a first in finding a training place as an apprentice; and the second in staying in the company in which he or she has been trained or even to stay in the occupation or occupational field for which he or she has been trained". Responsibility for administering the dual system rests with several bodies. The Vocational Training Act regulates the various aspects related to the in-company provision of "dual system" vocational training; *i.e.* whereas the curriculum and the organisation of courses offered at the part-time vocational schools is the responsibilitly of the educational authorities of the *Länder*, the part of training which is offered on the job is controlled and regulated by the Federal Ministry of Education, Science, Research and Technology and the responsible regional/local bodies designated in this law. At the local or regional level tripartite committees composed of employers, employees and representatives of public authorities seek to co-ordinate efforts. "Despite the tripartite structure of these committees, a lack of co-operation between schools and enterprises as well as lacking co-ordination between school-based and on-the-job training have been frequently criticised by experts and the social partners." Reunification and high unemployment have placed strains on the system including a decrease in the number of available training places, and as a result, state manpower services training schemes have replaced some of the regular "dual system" apprenticeships. The Federal Institute of Labour provides the funding for the schemes, but provision is delegated to commercial or non-profit organisations. In some instances, the Institute does grant financial assistance to apprentices or participants in specific training schemes.

In the Flemish community in Belgium, students from the age of 15 or 16, may attend classes two days a week and for the remainder, gain professional hands-on experience by entering into a part-time labour or apprenticeship contract. As an incentive to employers, a special fund was set up to offer premiums to businesses who take on these students. A similar programme for unemployed 18-25 year olds offers employers a temporary reduction in the employers' contribution to social security for entering into a work-training contract offering these youths a part-time permanent labour contract (at least half-time), thus benefiting both parties. In addition, in the Netherlands, the government offers subsidies to companies for the supervision of trainees. A non-statutory programme, but one which represents a similar model is the Youth Credits programme, originally introduced in England and Wales in April 1991, which offers credits to youths who are thinking about what to do when they reach age 16 or 17. Youth may use the credits, which have a financial value, to present to an employer in exchange for provided approved training leading to a National Vocational Qualification.

Countries are targeting funds and efforts towards ensuring suitable education and training programmes specifically for 16-17 year-olds in the hope of providing appropriate preparation for youth. The programmes aim to reduce the incidence of behaviour problems and juvenile crime while stemming the tide of unemployment and "marginalisation" which can lead to a downward spiral into poverty. In England and Wales, the government guarantees "a suitable training place for all 16-17 year-olds who are not in full-time education, are unemployed, and are seeking training". In 1992, the Swedish government increased the responsibility of the school after compulsory education with the "17th programme", where for everybody who had not applied for or been admitted to any of the 16 available national programmes, the school has the obligation to provide an individually designed programme, adapted to each student's conditions and wishes, with the goal of eventually creating an interest in one of the nationally established programmes. In Portugal, in 1991, the government passed legislation which defines a general course of pre-training created by a common agreement of the Ministry of Employment, Social Security, and Education for young people aged 15 to 21 who have not completed compulsory education. In Northern Ireland, careers education is a mandatory part of the curriculum.

In the Netherlands, the Guaranteed Youth Employment Scheme gives young people the right to a minimum wage, earned either through work experience or participation in vocational training, and includes provisions for co-operation with job centres and among sectors including education, health, justice and social services. In the United States, the 1994 School-to-Work Opportunities Act to be jointly administered by two departments, the Department of Education and the Department of Labour, is intended to enable all States to develop School-to-Work systems involving partnerships of employers, educators, labour organisations, and others to prepare young people for careers in high skill, high wage jobs. The law requires programmes to include core components and goals, but does not specify how requirements are to be met, thereby allowing States and communities the latitude to create new programmes or build upon existing successful projects according to local needs and changes in the local economy (see later for a discussion of funding).

Governments are mandating measures to ensure that career education and guidance services are integrated into the curriculum. In Finland, the Labour Force Services Act of 1993 gives schools more responsibility for vocational guidance including career planning as well as support for placement into training and employment. In 1994, the government went a step further in making additional funding available to schools for the provision of careers education and guidance at an earlier age. The funding is specifically for the provision of career guidance for students in years 9 and 10 (when pupils reach 14 and 15 years old). Rather than regulating the manner in which the integration of these services will occur, schools have been delegated the responsibility to determine how this education and guidance will be organised at the local level. Similarly, in Ontario, Canada, careers education is compulsory in grades 7 through 9. In England and Wales as well as Scotland, the Careers Service provides impartial information services, career guidance, and assistance to enter appropriate education, training, and work, and is expected to operate in conjunction with schools, local businesses, colleges, training providers, and other groups. These government measures have a preventive orientation in helping students to plan for the future and to formulate goals at an early age; at the same time they have the potential to broaden students' horizons and visions as to the possible career paths which are available to them.

Countries documented a large number of programmes targeted at this age group to effect a truly well-integrated approach to helping youth to make a smooth transition to work. The funding and attention that these programmes are receiving suggest that policy makers are attaching great importance to addressing the needs of this group.

Families of children and youth at risk

In this area, several countries reported legislation which combines a broad spectrum of child and family services under one set of legal requirements with efforts to increase flexibility of funding. One such law in Ontario, Canada, the Child and Family Services Act, "has been instrumental in establishing a common set of principles, definitions, expectations, and funding and accountability requirements for a broad range of children's services". The services include child development services, child treatment services, child and family intervention services, child welfare services, young offender services, and community support services.

In Finland, the recently enacted Planning and State Subsidies Act combines legislation for both health and social services and seeks to increase municipalities' ability to plan and implement welfare and health services suitable to their needs. The act contains fewer regulations and universal norms for service delivery than earlier legislation and provides a fixed sum of state subsidies based on factors such as population density and rate of employment. Finland reports a growing tendency on the part of municipalities to unite previously separate social welfare and health agencies.

Services integration is also occurring with regard to youth care, youth welfare, and youth protection in the Netherlands. The Youth Care Act which took effect in 1989 laid down a coherent framework for voluntary youth care, judicial youth protection and juvenile criminal law. Implementation of the act is the joint responsibility of the Minister of Welfare, Health and Cultural Affairs and the Minister of Justice who are jointly responsible for the planning and funding of provisions. The Welfare Act of 1994 defines the scope of welfare services including local youth work, regional and national youth work organisations, organisations for international youth activities, child care, host parents projects, and child care facilities, but does not apply to provisions covered by the Youth Care Act. In common with the Youth Care Act, the Welfare Act in the Netherlands aims at decentralisation and co-operation. A 1993 policy paper, "Cross-sector Youth Policies: Young People Deserve the Future", recommended that government agencies should keep a distance from the functioning of youth welfare schemes, leaving sufficient room for citizens and voluntary organisations to carry out their responsibilities. Key objectives were defined in another Netherlands policy memorandum, "Welfare Policies in the 1990s: Co-operation Along New Lines", including improved co-ordination of youth welfare policies by setting up and maintaining linkages with other levels of government, social organisations, and international organisations. In Germany, the Children and Youth Services Act calls for co-operation of youth welfare agencies with schools, training institutions and public health services, and the government must present an annual Youth Report to Parliament which includes an analysis and inventory of schemes, policy directives, and every third year, an overview of the status of children and youth welfare. The law creates a new concept of youth aid focusing on prevention with youth offices taking responsibility for a variety of tasks including among others, family and parent counselling and support for families in difficulty. Local authorities are required to develop youth aid plans based on a needs analysis and co-ordination of all local services.

Countries reported broad based efforts to promote regeneration and revitalisation of economically distressed areas, measures which overcome the often cited barrier of programmes rooted firmly within individual ministries or departments. This more global approach is reflected in measures such as the Single Regeneration Budget, which took effect in England and Wales in April, 1994, that "will bring into one pot 20 separate programmes (from 5 government departments) to provide flexible support for regeneration and economic development in a way that meets local needs and priorities". A Ministerial Committee on Competitiveness is charged with regeneration policies and their co-ordination. One of the major efforts at regeneration is represented in the 31 City Challenge Partnerships which are currently implementing detailed 5-year action plans in deprived neighbourhoods which seek to improve services and facilities for children and their families.

In the United States, two government departments, the Department of Housing and Urban Development and the Department of Agriculture, will select Empowerment Zones and Enterprise Communities, located in both urban and rural areas. These localities will be eligible for a combination of new funding and tax incentives for a variety of programmes provided by local organisations including non-school services for children and families. "This approach represents a major innovation in co-ordinating and focusing federal resources from many different agencies on high-risk communities, and requires an unprecedented degree of state and local level collaboration as well. The Enterprise Board to oversee implementation of this initiative includes the Secretaries of all domestic Cabinet agencies".

In Scotland, urban regeneration is underway with four Scottish Office-led partnership initiatives and 18 other smaller renewal initiatives. Training, economic development, and environmental renewal programmes are promoted in the partnership areas, with local authorities being encouraged to entrust management of projects to community groups and voluntary organisations. In Northern Ireland, there are a number of urban regeneration programmes to tackle inner city problems. Annual action plans address the needs of children and youth at risk and their families. In Ontario, Canada, the Integrated Services for Northern Children project is an example of inter-agency and inter-ministerial co-ordination designed to improve access for children at risk and their parents who live in remote northern areas of the province to a host of professional services, including those of psychiatrists, psychologists, speech pathologists, teacher diagnosticians, physiotherapists, occupational therapists, psychometrists, and satellite workers.

Another area of concern in several countries is to promote efforts to keep families intact rather than removing children to institutions or foster care. In 1993, the United States adopted the Family Preservation and Family Support Programme towards this goal, and is stimulating and promoting integration by providing additional funding to those States and communities which include maternal and child health, and mental health communities in their planning. In Germany, the Children and Youth Services Act includes provision for support to families including counselling regarding matters related to educating and raising children, counselling for families facing difficulties and socio-therapeutic schemes for children and youth and their families. In Scotland, the recent White Paper on local government reform dealt with issues surrounding the relationship between children's problems and those of their families, and emphasised that social work departments should draw on a wide range of services to help avoid the need for a child to go into care. Through a community care programme, local authorities are required to plan in conjunction with health boards, housing authorities, voluntary agencies, and the private sector, and provide services to vulnerable people such as the elderly, mentally ill, and the physically disabled. In Portugal, the Project of Aid to Family and Children, comprised of representatives of the sectors of justice, social action, and health, was created in 1992 to improve interpersonal relationships within the family, to identify situations involving child abuse or maltreatment, and to develop programmes to aid these children and families.

The above measures indicate that countries are recognising the inter-relatedness of social and educational policies and legislating a wide variety of mandates to integrate services across disciplines and sectors. Communities are given the latitude to plan to adapt to local needs.

LAWS AND POLICIES INHIBITING SERVICES INTEGRATION

Specific laws were rarely cited as inhibiting services integration, but generally, when they were mentioned, the barriers were not created by the terms of the laws so much as by the fact that several laws were duplicative in their goals and target populations, and responsibility for implementing each of the laws was delegated to a different ministry or organisation. For example, the Finnish report described three laws, one for mental health care, another for specialised health care, and another for child welfare which share similar goals but are implemented by three different organisations. Resultant problems include lack of comparability of statistics from different service providers, problems of division of labour and collaboration between service providers, and a lack of appropriate resources. Lack of suitable, established channels for inter-agency collaboration on a regular basis, and lack of a co-ordinator or co-ordinating body were also frequently noted. Separate financial regulations and funding schemes, varying eligibility requirements, and differing management structures under which ministries and departments operate were all cited as barriers to integration. For example, in the United States, where 76 major programmes spend more than $100 million each to provide services and support for children and families, ten Cabinet departments and one independent agency under the jurisdiction of 19 separate Congressional committees manage these programmes and complicate efforts to integrate services. Fragmentation and discontinuity of service provision may result from different organisations being responsible for aspects of a problem or for different stages of a person's life. Long term efforts are needed and specific attention needs to be given to important transition points such as starting schools, beginning secondary education, selecting vocational training, and entering the world of work.

The demand for confidentiality regarding clients' circumstances was frequently listed as a barrier. When the need for confidentiality is interpreted too strictly, professionals are hampered in their ability to share information and to collaborate on appropriate courses of action. Governments may play a constructive role in ensuring clients' rights while eliminating confidentiality as a barrier, as is the case in Finland. The Act on Municipal Educational Administration of 1992 requires the maintenance of confidentiality, outside their duties, on the part of municipal employees and members of municipal authorities, but obliges health services and educational institution staff to share with each other and the municipal authorities all information pertinent to the implementation of their duties.

Fear of loss of autonomy or authority and competition for resources may also serve to hinder integration efforts. A number of reports mention educators' concerns and frustrations regarding schools being side-tracked from their main responsibility to educate and train students, although the reports also reflect that educators are well aware that students at risk come to school with a host of other health, nutritional, social, and psychological needs which can affect their educational performance. Agencies with specific and limited missions may view themselves in competition with one another for funding, resources, and sometimes even clients. Competition between institutions may lead to the provision of counselling and advice based on the narrow focus or interests of the organisation. Their limited vision may lead to professionals reacting to an immediate crisis with a very short-term, limited response as opposed to addressing the causes and the range of problems affecting the family which may require the resources of several different services. Competition may well exist between programmes primarily concerned with prevention of problems and those concerned with the remediation. The fragmentation of services may leave clients in need perplexed and frustrated by the complexity of the process of obtaining services as well as unable to secure the aid they require and are eligible for. Organisations may be wary of integration efforts as simply an excuse for cutting budgets and personnel. Even advocacy groups, if their purposes and goals are too narrowly defined may fear integration and seek to preserve the particular, sometimes narrow orientation of the programme.

Lack of training in co-operation and collaboration is another often noted barrier, particularly for service providers such as teachers who rarely receive specific instruction in fostering co-operation between home and school. Researchers in Finland found that only one quarter of teacher trainees had received qualifications for co-operation between school and home. Of teachers already employed, only 10 per cent thought they had received sufficient qualifications for co-operation as part of their training. Additional specific training for policy makers and managers in framing and implementing co-operative agreements and collaborative programmes, was also mentioned by countries as an important measure to enhance services integration.

Strongly held cultural traditions – typified by the United States – valuing self-help, voluntary assistance, and private rather than government intervention, may hinder government efforts towards integration. The phenomenon of "compartmentalisation", in the Netherlands defined as "the pooling of social forces along political and denominational lines", has led to groups founding their own organisations, perhaps working towards similar goals, but in relative isolation. Frequently the emphasis is on the particular social, political or religious group, and therefore counter to services integration. Competition may exist between various sectors of the society – such as urban and rural communities – leading to lack of cohesive effort towards shared purposes and goals. Sparsely populated areas may also represent a challenge for countries to ensure that services are within access of those separated by distance from large population centres. In addition, jurisdictional problems may arise as to which level of government is responsible for providing a programme to whom and who should be paying for it. The report from Alberta, Canada, for example, refers to communities with a large aboriginal population where federal and provincial jurisdictional issues can arise.

PLANNED CHANGES TO LAWS AND POLICIES CONCERNING SERVICES INTEGRATION

A number of governments have described impending changes aimed at improving co-ordination and integration of services in the near future. For example, affecting pre-school and school age children in the Netherlands, legislation is currently being discussed in Parliament to improve co-operation between schools, local authorities and other institutions. It makes provisions for schools and local authorities to deviate from current legislation if it is obstructing effective policies, thus granting localities the opportunity to re-allocate resources (for example, to provide pre-school services or to lengthen the number of hours of teaching per day). Another provision will allow schools and municipal authorities to pool resources in a fund which may be used, for example, to pay staff to organise local activities aimed at fighting disadvantage. In Northern Ireland, a new early years policy, which will guide development of day care and education services for young children, will be published in 1994 following an inter-departmental review.

In a measure for school age children, with the re-authorisation of the United States government's Chapter One Programme for educationally disadvantaged students, funds will be targeted to schools in communities with very high poverty concentrations who will be mandated to co-ordinate their activities with other educational, health, and social services programmes. In schools where the poverty level is at least 50 per cent, local education agencies would be required to ensure that children are screened for early identification of health or nutritional problems.

For youth in transition to work, beginning in 1994 in England and Wales, the Careers Service will be directly managed by the Department of Employment (now the Department for Education and Employment), ensuring that a certain minimum standard of service is provided across the country to schools that have been charged with including career guidance in their curricula.

As regards children and families at risk, the government of Alberta, Canada, has mandated the Commissioner of Services for Children to "review and reform the services for children and families provided by the departments of Health, Education, Justice and Family and Social Services". His task includes developing a plan for a new approach to service delivery for children and families. In Manitoba, Canada, an educational policy specifically for at risk students is currently being developed. Also, in Saskatchewan, Canada, the government has made the Integrated School-Linked Services initiative under the Saskatchewan Action Plan for Children, a priority project. "Ongoing work by a Minister's Working Committee is focused on encouraging and facilitating the exploration by local communities of new configurations of services delivery and collaborative approaches to better meet the complex needs of children and families. While no new money is available, government is committed to realigning services, creating a policy framework that provides guidelines to schools and communities, and investigating and removing barriers to an integrated service delivery system."

Another example of change in favour of integration in England and Wales is the recently enacted Single Regeneration Budget which brings together 20 previously separate programmes from five government departments for the purpose of revitalising economic development in accordance with local needs and goals.

In the effort to overcome fragmentation and duplication of services, the Flemish community will implement a decree to combine into one multipurpose centre, various services for several problem groups including an obligation "to devote special attention to population groups that bear an increased risk for diminished welfare chances (thus also children and youth at risk and their families)". Functions will include: information and advice, reception, counselling and treatment, prevention, sensitisation, and a structural problem approach to a wide variety of social and psycho-social problems. The decree also calls for compulsory collaboration and consultation among the various Centres for General Welfare Work and the requirement that each centre consults and collaborates with other public and private welfare or social services providers.

THE IMPORTANCE OF LEGISLATION

The role of legislation and national policy initiatives which support services integration described in the country reports is largely one of providing goals, as well as identifying directions and areas deserving attention, and providing financial support. While the interpretation and precise modes of service delivery and imple-mentation are generally left to the localities to match local needs, the governments play a vital role in mandating and ensuring that the broader needs and goals of at risk children and families are addressed in an integrated, comprehensive manner and that services are made available to populations at risk throughout the country. Thus, governments can help to mitigate some of the effects of barriers to integra-tion, such as conflicting interests of rural and urban sectors of the society, and the over-narrow goals of certain interest groups.

The country reports suggest that at the same time, local or community initia-tives, by developing successful approaches to meeting the needs of at risk children and families, may become the basis on which future government legislation and policies will be built. It is at this level that experimentation and the seeds of change are often sown, and therefore, local demonstration and research projects are invalu-able to informing national policy. Frequently, community initiatives seek govern-ment funding to support new programmes and consequently, governments' invest-ment in such initiatives may yield important breakthroughs and innovations or refinements of methods to successfully address problems. The relationship between services integration due to government legislation and policies, and that due to local or community initiatives, is a complementary one, each enhancing and sup-porting the other.

BENEFITS

Views on the extent to which governments should intervene in the lives of individuals or families vary considerably from country to country, as do the range and level of services and benefits funded and provided by the national government. The levels of benefits are difficult to compare between countries since services are often not equivalent. The complexity of benefit programmes also complicates com-parisons and has important implications for efforts to integrate services. Benefits which come under the jurisdiction of different departments or ministries frequently have varying eligibility requirements which complicate integration efforts and may inhibit clients' ability to negotiate the system and receive the services that they need. Comparable measures of programme benefits are generally not available, and only a few countries provided tables detailing social security benefits for children and youth at risk and their families. Differences in governmental philosophies clearly emerged from the responses to the questions.

For example, in Finland, society's role in providing services and benefits is widely accepted with the government providing a broad array of universal services and cash benefits to families and children – for maternity, adoption, care of sick children, income maintenance, and housing. Child allowances are the biggest item for income transfer to families. Similarly, in England and Wales, "social security benefits for children aim to recognise the additional costs incurred by families with children as compared with other groups". These benefits are payable to all families with respect to all children.

In the United States a debate continues on which services and benefits to grant and to what extent the federal government should be involved in regulating or providing services to citizens. Controversy also exists regarding the extent to which States and local communities should be free to decide how to respond to the needs of individuals and families. "Federal programmes have traditionally focused primarily on children and families at risk, rather than providing universal services." Several strategies have been encouraged as preferable to government intervention including self-help, voluntary assistance from family, neighbours and the community, and assistance from private agencies and support organisations. "In many cases federal funds constitute only a small percentage of all spending for a particular service – e.g., for maternal and child health. But by attaching legal 'strings' or requirements for the funds, the federal government influences how the funds are spent [and] who is eligible for the funds".

Another interesting consideration regarding benefits is the issue of work versus entitlement to benefits. In the Netherlands, under the Guaranteed Youth Employment Scheme, the government has taken steps to provide young people with work or training, the philosophy being that young people should not be independently entitled to benefit and "that young people should have work instead of benefit". The policy represents a preventive approach by providing jobs and/or training on which young people may build a future, as opposed to benefit provision which provides financial support, but lacks specific provision of opportunities for skills development and growth towards a career and independent livelihood.

FUNDING

Countries reported reforms in funding schemes and efforts to increase the flexibility granted to municipalities to free them to integrate services and reallocate resources to meet local needs. For example, in Finland, the government has passed health and welfare legislation encouraging municipalities to be more economical at the same time as granting municipalities greater opportunities to use funds to integrate health and welfare services. Whereas previously, state subsidies were paid to municipalities annually according to approved costs of welfare and health services, under the new legislation, the Planning and State Subsidies for Welfare Act of 1992, funding is a fixed sum based on factors such as population density, rate of unemployment, and area, regardless of the total costs of service delivery. Therefore, if the municipality accomplishes its duties economically, it saves money, since it is assured a fixed sum; if it raises the total costs of welfare and health services provision, it must pay the additional costs from its own coffers, thus encouraging economical service delivery.

Through Scotland's urban regeneration programme, the Scottish Office provides 75 per cent of approved expenditure on selected projects and requires local authorities to supply the balance, thus stimulating community group and voluntary organisation action in solving complex urban problems in partnership with the government.

In the United States, the School-to-Work Opportunities Act of 1994, is an example of how the national government can stimulate state and local integration efforts. The law provides multiple sources of support including federal grants to States, waivers, direct grants to local partnerships, and grants to areas with high poverty rates. The law encourages co-ordination of state, local and other federal resources and provides funding for initial demonstration periods only, after which other sources of funding and support must be utilised. In another new piece of legislation promoting services integration, the Goals 2000 programme, the law provides funds for the purpose of replicating and disseminating information about successful co-ordinated programmes.

DECENTRALISATION

Several governments described policies of decentralisation of services for children and families at risk, sometimes involving intermediary level regional boards or departments, but ultimately entailing the delegation of increasing levels of responsibility and autonomy to localities, with the intent of increasing responsiveness, extending choice, expanding access, reducing bureaucracy, elevating empowerment and local planning, and increasing economic efficiency. Governments frequently set the course by identifying goals and responsibilities for service provision, but the details of implementation are only broadly described and left to the discretion of the localities.

Decentralisation may lead to smaller municipalities seeking to merge with larger ones, as was the case in Sweden, where expanded responsibility delegated to municipalities led to consolidation into larger municipalities able to offer a broader range of services and alternative solutions in schools, child care and care of the elderly. Structures need to be of a sufficient, critical size to shoulder effectively the statutory responsibilities delegated to them. The Scottish report speaks of commu-

nities' motivations for consolidation and merging, and the implications of decentralisation: "The larger an authority, the greater its capacity to develop specialist
services and provide the full range of social work facilities. The smaller an authority
the more it will need to look to larger authorities, co-operative arrangements with
other authorities and independent providers for services and expertise". Several of
the reports made note of the constructive, supporting role which networks, particularly at the regional or "inter-municipality" level, play in terms of supplying technical assistance and training, enhancing communication amongst entities, and in
some cases, service delivery. Governments, then, need to consider the implications
of decentralisation for smaller, local entities, particularly in widely dispersed, rural
or sparsely populated areas.

Another important implication of decentralisation is the need to ensure that
jurisdictions are carefully determined and responsibilities clearly defined to avoid
competition and duplication of services as well as to enhance co-operation.

COMMUNICATION AMONG MINISTRIES AND SERVICES

It is perhaps in relation to communication amongst ministries or departments
that the reports indicated the greatest need for improvement in the development of
efficient, open, reliable, frequently and regularly used channels. Countries report
interaction between staff of various ministries or departments, but frequently on an
informal or ad hoc basis, lacking structural supports for regular communication to
occur. Some reports indicated frustrations with ministries or departments working
in isolation from one another, and problems related to legislators who enact laws
which affect the same target group, but are delegated to separate ministries or
departments. Several countries have documented steps to improve inter-departmental and inter-ministerial communication.

The creation of interagency or interdisciplinary task forces or committees to
tackle particular issues, to prepare legislation, to formulate policy statements, and/
or to develop goals which cross sectors or jurisdictions, was reported by many
countries as promoting services integration. For example, in the Netherlands, the
Consultative Committee on Youth Policy is a forum for formal consultation between
the Ministry of Welfare, Health and Cultural Affairs, the Ministry of Education,
Culture and Science, and the Ministry of Justice to co-ordinate youth care and youth
protection issues. Voluntary organisations and employers' groups are also represented on the committee. In Ontario, a Committee of Assistant Deputy Ministers
meets regularly to discuss key issues that cross jurisdictional boundaries. There is
permanent representation from the Ministries of Community and Social Services,
Health, and Education and Training, with other ministries attending as needed. In
England and Wales, a Ministerial Committee for Regeneration will consider regeneration policies and their co-ordination. Also in England and Wales, before their

merger, the Department of Education and the Department of Employment have supported the National Training Targets by jointly producing and distributing a Fact Pack on the targets and their individual departmental plans for achieving them. In the United States, an inter-agency Community Empowerment Board has been established to oversee efforts to develop the Empowerment Zones/Enterprise Communities as part of a major urban regeneration effort. In Belgium's Flemish community, the Interdepartmental Commission on Immigrants, the Flemish Intersectoral Commission for the Fight Against Poverty, and the Interdepartmental Commission on Juvenile Affairs are examples of important means of communication which supplement communication and promote services integration. In Portugal, interdepartmental units including professionals from a variety of disciplines and fostering services integration include the Commissions of Protection of Minors and the Commission for the Integration of Immigrants and Ethnic Minorities. In Scotland, the AIDS Prevention Co-ordinating Group for Scotland has been established, including health boards and local authority representation as well as national representatives from the voluntary sector, the Health Education Board for Scotland and the Police and Prisons' services.

Another means of boosting communication between organisations is creating inter-agency units which share responsibility for monitoring and evaluation, thereby also identifying areas needing improvement or additional services. For example, in Scotland, provision for children and youth placed in secure units is inspected by the Social Work Services Inspectorate and Her Majesty's Inspectorate of Schools.

Some countries reported combining related offices or departments into one unit. For example, in England and Wales in 1994, the government brought together the Regional Offices of the Department of Trade and Industry, the Department of Employment (Training, Enterprise and Education Directorate), the Department of the Environment, and the Department of Transport. It is hoped that the new integrated offices will strengthen links between the programmes and provide more accessible services to local governments, businesses and individuals.

As regards the question of how government legislation and policy are communicated to the relevant services, countries provided scant information on this topic, and spoke to the question on two levels. First, they discussed government efforts to communicate and promote their support for services integration. Largely, responses indicated that the statutes themselves, by including provisions requiring integrative measures such as the formation of inter-departmental committees, or by incorporating measures which tie funding to communities demonstrating implementation of plans to co-ordinate services across disciplines, are effective communicators of the governments' intentions to support services integration.

More often, however, countries responded to the question on the level of how information regarding the specific policies or legislation is disseminated. Several countries indicated government circulars, policy/programme memoranda, and other guidance as the primary means of dissemination of information. In Saskatchewan, Canada, regional offices of the various departments such as Health, Social Services, Education, and Training, act as conduits for information throughout the province regarding policies and initiatives. In Quebec, "A Guide to Health and Social Services", jointly published by the Ministry of Health and Social Services and the Ministry of Education, provides guidance as to the health and social services which should be offered in schools. In Alberta, Canada, which has a committee for the Co-ordination of Services for Children composed of Assistant Deputy Ministers (from the Departments of Family and Social Services, Health, Education and Justice), and a Working Committee of officials from the same departments, a partnership has been established with five communities to identify ways to improve services for children and families. To disseminate information on the pilot sites, a newsletter is published regularly and distributed to the larger service community. An annual forum also serves to enhance communication as elected officials and staff from all levels of government meet with community members to share successes and concerns. In Turkey, to raise public awareness, 1993 was designated as "The Year of Special Education". It highlighted the needs of children receiving special education, many of whom are at risk. A guidebook has been published and TV and radio programmes have been prepared for the purpose of increasing public awareness and support.

AUTHORITY, IMPLEMENTATION AND SERVICE QUALITY

In most of the countries, according to government laws and policies, authority and responsibility for implementation of integrative measures are delegated to one particular ministry or department, or in some cases, to two or more ministries or departments, by way of interdepartmental committees that are charged with collaboration to ensure that integrative measures are implemented. Some duties may be delegated to an intermediate regional level or, in some cases, state or provincial level. These duties may include service delivery to individuals, but more often include administrative and support functions, such as encouraging collaboration and co-operation between institutions. Responsibility for implementing integrative measures is generally delegated to the local level. Local governments, health, welfare and social service authorities, school boards and voluntary agencies are normally responsible for activities such as conducting local needs assessments, planning collaboratively for service delivery, and sharing responsibility and funding for service delivery.

Monitoring of implementation and service quality is accomplished through a variety of means including self-assessment by agencies, localities and regions; on-site inspection and monitoring by government employees or designees; administering formal assessments (e.g. to measure student's academic progress in schools); auditing of financial records; and conducting research projects. Failure to comply with quality requirements may result in additional training and technical assistance to help address programme shortcomings. Ultimately, failure to comply may result in loss of funding. Quality may be promoted by specifying expected outcomes and setting standards; by requiring local needs assessments; by encouraging service providers to set standards for internal evaluation; and by requiring proposals with quality control plans to be agreed by government and service providers. Additional methods to promote service quality may include the establishment of partnerships and collaborative service agreements so that agencies are relying on one another as well as monitoring each other; fostering in-service training and technical assistance; requiring submission of improvement plans; supporting forums and professional meetings for the exchange of information; and publishing reports on research, evaluations, and cases of best practice.

PREVENTIVE SERVICES

Virtually every country responding to the questionnaire emphasised the importance of adopting preventive approaches and intervening early to identify problems before they escalate and multiply. The reports documented programmes which are preventive in orientation for children in all of the age categories, as well as their families. The report from Finland advanced the notion that "the scope of remedial services is largely explained by the scope of preventive services – when the scope of remedial services is small, the scope of preventive services has to be relatively large, and vice versa". The point is emphasised that, ultimately, provision of preventive measures is considerably less costly for the State than remedial services. In Finland, a large number of programmes and benefits exist for the population as a whole, and a great many are targeted for prevention during the early stages of life, including prenatal and postnatal care which, by their very nature, are preventive in orientation. A case in point is the maternity allowance and benefit programme. As testimony to its success, Finland is able to boast a very low infant mortality rate with over 95 per cent of mothers now attending maternity health centres regularly throughout pregnancy. Programmes such as these, as well as high quality pre-school programmes such as Head Start in the United States, the Better Beginnings, Better Futures Project and the early detection, early intervention orientation of the Integrated Services for Northern Children project in Ontario, Canada, are models of integrated, preventive programmes, in which countries are making investments in the early stages of children's lives with the hope of improving the outlook for these children to become productive members of society.

In analysing and attempting to categorise programmes for older children and families, the question of whether a service is preventive or remedial is an interesting one, in that what is considered remedial and in reaction to a deficiency at one stage, may well be preventive of more serious problems or grave outcomes at another stage. Similarly, assistance which may be primarily remedial for adult family members may well have a preventive effect for children, and therefore, most programmes really combine both preventive and remedial aspects. This should not be misconstrued as an attempt to downplay the importance of preventive measures; quite the contrary, it is to suggest that programmes labelled "remedial" may well have preventive value. For example, in England and Wales, the government is funding an Adult Literacy and Basic Skills initiative, a programme which is at once both remedial and preventive. For adults, it combines a remedial approach to literacy deficiencies with a preventive approach in terms of avoiding problems such as unemployment. For their children, it has a preventive value in improving their chances of achieving literacy.

In another example, by bringing increased resources and a multi-disciplinary approach to areas of high poverty concentration – as for the French *Zones d'éduca-tion prioritaires* (ZEP) programme and the Netherlands' Education Priority Policy programme as well as Italy's and Portugal's programmes of targeting additional resources to priority zones – policy makers have attempted to prevent problems from occurring, to detect problems at an early stage, to improve negative circumstances, and to assist those already manifesting problems. Efforts in Alberta and Saskatchewan, Canada, to develop comprehensive, co-ordinated action plans and programmes for children are supportive of preventive initiatives within the context of an integrated approach. With the adoption of the "Goals 2000" legislation, the United States law requires state school improvement plans to be formulated by a panel of state officials, educational personnel of all levels, parents, community representatives, state and local officials responsible for health, social service and other related services. The law also calls for a focus on prevention and early intervention as well as increasing access to a variety of health and social services.

For youth in transition to work, the programmes providing early career guidance, the apprenticeship and jobs programmes, the drug and alcohol education programmes, and the stay-in-school programmes all have a preventive orientation as they seek to prevent marginalisation of youth and the downward spiral into poverty. Research projects frequently have a preventive orientation such as the government-sponsored youth crime prevention project in England and Wales which explores ways of using schools and youth services to reduce juvenile crime.

Programmes to keep families intact, such as the United States Family Preservation and Family Support Programme, have a preventive orientation in seeking to avoid removing children from their homes. However, an immediate response may be required to remediate or ameliorate specific family crises. In Germany, the concept of youth aid has been expanded to focus on prevention and include support for families in difficulty and family and parent counselling, and local youth aid plans are now obliged to co-ordinate all local provisions.

The subject of crisis intervention raises another important issue related to prevention, namely that of assisting individuals and families only so far as necessary to enable them to help themselves and achieve independence. For example, the Dutch report states that "the Dutch government considers it undesirable that young people should be independently entitled to benefit, arguing that young people should have work instead of benefit". The Netherlands established the Guaranteed Youth Employment Scheme to provide paid work or preparatory training to young people, leaving them only to apply for benefit in exceptional cases.

VOLUNTARY SERVICES

Many countries indicated the integral role that volunteers have played in identifying areas requiring attention, advocating for the creation and extension of services, planning for service delivery, and providing services. Volunteers often sit on national advisory boards and task forces which help inform government policy as well as on community boards of schools and government sponsored or private agencies. In the face of economic problems, volunteers represent a valuable resource to supplement government programmes. In some instances, governments support partnerships with voluntary organisations and sometimes supply funding to help stimulate, support and promote volunteer activities. Indeed, in several countries including Canada, England and Wales, the Netherlands, and the United States, non-governmental, voluntary organisations supply a large volume of voluntary services, and receive virtually all of their support from government funds.

Countries described a number of ways in which volunteers supply services and governments support their efforts. In England and Wales, for example, voluntary providers play a significant role in the government's pre-school education policy. The Welsh Office gives core funding to a voluntary association which supports the Welsh language and provides pre-school education for 14 000 students. In Ontario, Canada, an estimated 75 per cent of child care programmes are non-profit and governed by volunteer boards. In the United States, voluntarism is an integral part of the Head Start Programme, both in terms of securing additional instructional help in the classroom from volunteer aides, and in enlisting the assistance of community professionals to volunteer their services. In the Netherlands, health care services for the 0-4 age group are provided by state-funded, voluntary organisations.

In France, volunteers play an important role, particularly in working with teachers to provide support to children not achieving their potential. On the other hand, in Saskatchewan, Canada, voluntary community service is a part of many schools' curricula, thus involving students, as part of their education, in making a constructive contribution to the community.

In order to address the many and varied problems faced by youth in transition to work, the government in England and Wales gives grants to voluntary youth organisations which contribute to preventive measures such as meeting the needs of young people at risk of drifting into crime. Similarly, in the Netherlands, voluntary organisations provide a large proportion of the services in the area of youth care, youth protection, and youth welfare, and are entirely financed and supported with government funds. Indeed, the success of many of the jobs partnership and apprenticeship programmes hinges on co-operation from the private sector on a voluntary basis. In Germany, the "dual system" relies on participation of the private sector as well, and the welfare system historically has been built on the principle of subsidiarity. Essentially, under this principle, the smaller unit, *i.e.* the family or locality, should provide help and care prior to state agencies and other public bodies. Subsidiarity also favours intervention by private welfare organisations, before public ones, regardless of their size. "This policy (...) is clearly intended to privilege organisations of the churches which play a very important and powerful role in the whole system. The voluntary ('free') sector of youth aid is complemented and administered by public youth aid services."

In Alberta, Canada, included in the regulations for programmes under the Family and Community Support Services Act, is the provision that programmes must "promote, encourage and facilitate voluntarism and the use of volunteers". Programmes may also offer services to encourage and support voluntarism in the community. In Scotland, the government will aim, as a result of a 1992-93 evaluation of government funding of the voluntary sector, to provide greater security and stability in funding to voluntary bodies with regard to social work services.

PARENTAL PARTICIPATION

Virtually all of the countries indicated a positive philosophy on parental participation in legal processes, decision-making and service provision, and stated parents' roles as the primary care-givers and educators of their children. Policies exist to support parents in these roles from the earliest stages of their children's lives. In England and Wales, parents' involvement in running and managing playgroups is seen as a step towards boosting active involvement throughout the school life of their children. The government in England and Wales adopts the premise that parents who gain early confidence in talking to teachers are more likely to maintain involvement and a collaborative approach throughout their child's education. In Ontario, Canada, the Better Beginnings, Better Futures Project requires the presence of 50 per cent of parents or community leaders on every major local committee. Additionally, the Ministry of Community and Social Services is now supporting the implementation of over 60 local planning groups, and each will be requiring membership of at least 30 per cent youth, parents and/or representatives from historically disadvantaged groups. In Portugal, the Basic Law of the Educational System addresses the family's essential role in the education of the child.

The importance attached to establishing a partnership between home and school is reflected in legislation and policies encouraging parental involvement in their child's education. In France, for example, parents are considered partners of the school, and their right to information and expression of their viewpoints is respected. The government pays the costs involved in the participation of delegates from parent organisations in academic meetings and in matters related to the national department of education, such as reimbursement to employers for disruption caused by parents' absence from work. In Quebec, Canada, the first two guidelines for health and social services in the schools state that: "Parents are chiefly responsible for the education and health of their children, [and] parents are key partners for schools and health care institutions in terms of providing health and social services in schools". In England and Wales, parents have the right to choose their children's schools, and thus directly affect funding, since each child enrolled means extra money for the school, thereby encouraging schools to aim for higher standards. Parents can vote for or participate as school governors. In Scotland, parents' rights are included in the Parents' Charter for Scotland and include the right to the best possible education for their children, and to have their views known and taken into account. To ensure that parents' views will be heard, in Ontario, Canada, the Ministry of Education and Training has established an Ontario Parent Council which will advise the Minister on matters relating to education and parent involvement.

Included in the recently adopted United States national education goals is the objective that "every school will promote partnerships that will increase parental involvement and participation in promoting the social, emotional and academic growth of children". This principle has been part of the Head Start Programme for pre-schoolers for more than twenty years. For school aged children in the United States, the proposed re-authorisation of the Chapter One programme of the Elementary and Secondary Education Act would include a provision for supporting the efforts of schools to increase parents' involvement in their children's education. Parents frequently serve in decision-making capacities as members of local boards of education which govern schools. In the school-based management model established in recent amendments to the School Act in Alberta, Canada, parents were given considerably greater authority in determining policies related to programme provision, expenditures, day to day management of the school, and accountability for educational standards. The right of parents to provide a home education programme is also secured. Home education is also an option for parents in the United States.

For youth in the transition to work, parental involvement is similarly encouraged. In England and Wales, careers services are required to keep parents informed of the guidance and services offered in an attempt to gain the involvement and support of parents with respect to their children's career goals.

With regard to legal processes, many countries indicated parents' rights to be informed and present at legal procedures. Their right to be involved in decisions affecting programmes followed by their children in school is also ensured (such as special education placement). For example, in Scotland, parents are guaranteed the right of appeal against education authority's decisions which must, in some cases, be forwarded to the Secretary of State for a final decision. In the Netherlands, under the law, children and adolescents do not have the right to start a legal procedure without their parents, and parents must also be summoned to all legal procedures concerning their children. Parents' legal rights concerning decision-making are specified in the Education Participation Act. Similarly, with regard to youth care, the Youth Care Act gives parents the right to be involved in decisions regarding the form, intensity and need for continued care, and policies on youth protection aim to involve parents as much as possible.

In addition to protecting parents' rights, the matter of ensuring that parents meet their responsibilities to care for and supervise their children was also considered as part of "parental participation". In Alberta, Canada, the Young Offenders Act as well as the policy initiative entitled "Reshaping Child Welfare", being undertaken by Alberta Family and Social Services, holds parents accountable for the care of their children and articulates their responsibilities.

More difficult than securing the right of parents to participate is achieving a high level of parent participation. Countries were not asked to evaluate the degree to which parents actively participate. Further inquiry into the methods which are most successful in engaging parents and actively involving them in the healthy growth and development of their children would be valuable.

CLIENT RIGHTS AND CLIENT CHOICE

With regard to client rights, almost all of the countries stated that clients, including parents, have legal rights regarding complaints. The right of clients to confidentiality was also reiterated as fundamental by virtually all of the countries. Some countries emphasised children's rights along with those of the parents as being protected by the law. For example, in Alberta, Canada, the Child Welfare Act secures the right of children to express an opinion and have it considered in decisions affecting them. In Ontario, Canada, the Child and Family Services Act ensures young people's rights, when under state supervision, to request status and placement reviews. In addition, the Ontario government has passed the Consent to Treatment Act – now replaced by the Health Care Consent Act (1996) and the Substitute Decisions Act (1996) – which codifies the existing common law right to consent to or refuse treatment. A person, regardless of age, has the right to consent to treatment and withdraw consent. Under the act, if a person is deemed to be incapable, a substitute decision-maker may consent to or refuse treatment on his or her behalf, based on the person's prior capable wishes or, if no applicable wishes are known, based on the best interests of the person according to criteria set out in the act. Similarly, in Finland, the Child Welfare Act of 1983 incorporates the statement that the views of children over 12 should be taken into account before any child welfare measures are taken. As in other countries, children in Finland also have the right to be heard and to appeal regarding issues such as achievement, punishment and special education placement. In Alberta, Canada, parents, and where appropriate, the child, must be consulted regarding placement in a special education programme.

In some countries, formal offices or channels have been designated through which clients may register complaints. For example, in Saskatchewan, Canada, clients may appeal to the Human Rights Commission, the Office of the Ombudsman, and the Office of the Child Advocate. Similarly, under the Ombudsman Act in Alberta, Canada, clients may request investigations of actions taken by government employees.

England and Wales has had a long-standing tradition, as set forth in the Education Act of 1944, of protecting parents' right to complain – ultimately to the Secretary of State – if a local education authority or school has acted unreasonably. Parents may also exercise their right to express a preference for the school they wish their child to attend. If their child fails to get a place at the school, they may appeal against the decision to an independent committee. In some circumstances they can take their case to the Commissioner for Local Administration in England and Wales and the Secretary of State. With regard to youth in the transition to work, under the Charters for Further Education, if students, employers or community members are dissatisfied with teaching, training or other services, they may file a complaint directly with the Secretary of State. In Northern Ireland, a Parents' Charter was published in 1992 informing parents of their rights regarding their children's education, including their right to choose a school, to receive information, and to file a complaint. In France, national procedures of appeal exist for parents, as well as means to contest administrative decisions locally. In the United States, parents have the right to complain to local schools and school boards, and ultimately through the court system if they feel their rights are being denied.

Most of the countries explicitly stated that clients have freedom of choice to select those services or benefits which they wish to apply for with no interference from the government. The Finnish report noted that these rights are protected by explicit regulations in Finnish welfare and health legislation. The right of parents to select private instead of public schools is protected in many countries, and depending upon the country, parents may have to pay all or part of the cost involved. In England and Wales, the rights of parents of special education students have been guaranteed in the Education Act of 1993 to include stating a preference for the type of school (maintained or self-governing state school – mainstream or special) they wish their child to attend.

For students in the transition to work, the government in England and Wales has provided a variety of choices, but within the context of some limitations based on students' abilities (as demonstrated by the National Vocational Qualifications and the General National Vocational Qualifications where supervision and guidance are provided to make realistic selections). In the Netherlands, under the Guaranteed Youth Employment Scheme, students have a voice in the type of job in which they are placed but cannot refuse to participate altogether.

One exception to parents' right to choose occurs in serious situations involving youth protection. In these cases, judicial courts often decide on the placement and type of service required.

STATISTICS ON POPULATION AT RISK AND SERVICE PROVISION

Statistics on children and youth at risk are difficult to compare due to inconsistencies among countries as to the definition and therefore the designation of who is at risk. The Finnish report makes the sobering point that "in this respect the population at risk is an invisible class of people". Several countries were unable to estimate the proportion of children and youth at risk in their country because appropriate data were not available. Estimates that were provided by Member countries are reported below.

In Belgium's Flemish community, 1.4 per cent of the Flemish population falls below the legal poverty line specified by the government, but some 22 per cent of the Flemish population are reported to be living in socially insecure conditions.

In Finland, estimates of the population at risk are based on numbers actually utilising services and therefore may somewhat under-represent the total. In Finland, almost 17 000 families use child welfare services annually or approximately 1 per cent of all families with children aged 0-17. Approximately 51 per cent of them are single parent families. The total number of children and youth receiving child welfare has been about 20 000 families annually since 1971. This is 1.7 per cent of all children and youth aged 0-17. Estimates are that 59 000 children and youth, or about 5 per cent of all children and youth, use some kind of psycho-social services annually, including child welfare, child guidance and family counselling, and psychiatric services.

In France, 12 per cent of the students in the *écoles primaires* (primary schools) and 15 per cent in the *collèges* (middle schools) comprise the at risk population served in the ZEP programme.

In the Netherlands, the proportion of young people defined as being "at risk" varies between the Ministry of Education and the Ministry of Welfare, Health and Culture (now the Ministry of Health, Welfare and Sports). For the Ministry of Education following the implementation of the Educational Priority Policy arrangements, nearly half of all primary aged pupils are deemed to be at risk, as a consequence of the way additional expenditure is calculated for disadvantaged families. For Welfare, Health and Culture, however, only 15 per cent are considered as at risk. Mild forms of assistance and extra attention are required for about 10 per cent of all young people, while 5 per cent need more intensive assistance. The Ministry of Education is currently reviewing educational priority policy with the intention of targeting 20-25 per cent of primary school children.

In Ontario, Canada, statistics from the Ontario Child Health Study in 1983 identified approximately 18 per cent of children between the ages of 4 and 16 as having a conduct disorder and at risk of social and academic failure. 10-15 per cent of children have been identified by their school boards as having learning difficulties, and 23 per cent of youth drop out of school.

In Saskatchewan, Canada, an estimated 30 to 40 per cent of children are considered to be at risk. The province reports that it has one of the highest poverty rates in Canada. Almost 1 in 6 children lived in poverty in 1990.

In Slovenia, an estimated 30-40 per cent of school newcomers are considered to be at risk.

In Turkey, an estimated 3 million children need special education and currently only 25 411 are receiving special education services.

In the United States, in 1993, an estimated 33 million persons – 13.3 per cent of the United States population – lived at or below the poverty line. The poorest people in the United States are children with a poverty rate of 20.4 per cent.

CONCLUSIONS

The picture which emerges from a review of the country reports is that most of the countries are devoting considerable attention to services integration as a viable means of improving services for children and youth at risk and their families; as an important strategy towards constructively addressing needs; and ultimately, it is hoped, as an effective approach towards reducing the numbers of those at risk. Services integration is occurring at all levels – national, state, provincial, regional, and local – and it encompasses efforts across the public and private sectors. The reports suggest that countries are making efforts within the context of services integration towards addressing problems more globally and holistically and over-coming fragmentation of efforts. Some of the countries have, to date, undertaken more extensive efforts towards implementing services integration than others, but all of the countries favour the concept on the basis of both humanitarian and economic grounds.

The reports suggest that emphasis on outcomes and goals, early intervention, and preventive activities are valued. However, efforts directed at children and their families when the children are in the earliest stages of life might receive greater attention as an investment in the future. Measures documented by some countries to provide guidance to children at earlier ages, to broaden their vision of realisable career goals and build positive values, seem to be of considerable significance and worthy of further investigation.

Countries are making progress towards addressing barriers to services integration. Laws and policies are being changed to encourage greater co-operation and collaboration by those entrusted with planning and implementing programmes. As indicated in the country reports, policy makers and service providers increasingly recognise that important barriers to services integration have been created by the multiplicity of programmes providing fragmented services. Efforts are being directed towards eliminating the barriers caused by separate financial regulations and funding schemes, varying eligibility requirements, and differing management structures under which ministries and departments operate. Competition continues between institutions for funding, resources and even clients, which leads to a narrow approach to service delivery, but increasingly limited financial and human resources are encouraging greater co-operation. Similarly, attitudes persist amongst professionals that they are being side-tracked from their main purpose when they are asked to deal with the multitude of problems presented by children and families at risk. However, gradually these views appear to be changing. Other barriers including confidentiality requirements, lack of training in co-operation and collaboration, and entrenched cultural traditions, also continue to inhibit services integration. However, they are widely recognised and creative solutions are being sought and implemented.

Finally, while significant progress is clear from the country reports, quantitative indicators of change and measures of programme effectiveness and relative costs are needed. Evaluation of ongoing and new programmes is necessary to ensure that the potential benefits of services integration both from a humanitarian and an economic perspective are being realised. Additional attention is needed by countries to develop methodologies to evaluate programmes. Measures of services delivery and effectiveness are needed to help target resources most effectively and to encourage greater co-operation. Hope for the future which pervades the commitment of all those who work to help children and youth at risk must be matched by clear indicators of the effectiveness of differing approaches to improve outcomes on behalf of children and families and to build more effective services systems.

4

STRATEGIC, OPERATIONAL AND FIELD LEVELS: THE THEORETICAL AND PRACTICAL DIMENSIONS OF INTEGRATED SERVICES

by

Philippa Hurrell and Peter Evans

In the previous chapter a synthesis of developments at the mandating level of laws and policies in participating countries was given based on country reports prepared by them. In the following three chapters a synthesis, based on case studies carried out by experts, covering strategic, operational and field levels extracts common and generalisable issues. Vignettes of the full case studies on which these chapters are based are given in Part II.

As we have seen, from the work already described, many in the human services field have shown a strong interest in identifying different "models" of services integration and discerning which work best. However it is evident from the work carried out during the course of this study, that the concept of services integration is so complex, and in practice can take so many different forms (see in particular the case study of integrated services in California), that it is difficult to identify a distinct and limited range of "model types". Attempts have been made to set out different models of integration on the basis of: the location of services; how integration is instituted; and the nature of facilitating structures and mechanisms (Kagan, 1993). However, frequently they mix these dimensions and the results have been muddled.

PROPOSED DIMENSIONS OF SERVICES INTEGRATION

Therefore, for the purposes of human services providers, it seems to make sense to separate out some of the most useful dimensions in thinking about services integration and to use these. On the basis of the CERI research, it is proposed that the most salient aspects of services integration relate to:

- the actors involved (*e.g.* education, health or social welfare professionals);
- the structures in place (*e.g.* co-operative agreements, co-ordinating bodies);

– the mechanisms which operate (*e.g.* case conferences); and

– the physical location of the actors and structures (*e.g.* inside or outside of schools).

Using these criteria empirical examples of services integration can be typified. Equally they can be used to assist in the planning of new integrated programmes.

The actors

In considering the actors involved in integrated services, it is important to identify *who* participates and *at what level*. To answer the "who" question, it is necessary to map out all of the different kinds of agencies that (or individuals who) are involved in a programme. These might include:

- Public sector:
  - Education services
  - Health services
  - Social services
  - Youth services
  - Employment services
  - Housing services
  - Criminal justice services
  - Police services

- Private sector:
  - Education services
  - Health services
  - Social services
  - Youth services
  - Employment services
  - Housing services

- Companies
- Community people
- Parents of children at risk

In contrast, to answer the "at what level" question, consideration is needed of the position in the services hierarchy – mandating, strategic, operational or field – at which integration takes place. To take public education services as an example, integration at the mandating level might involve national government administrators; at the strategic level, regional government administrators; at the operational level, local government administrators; and at the field level, teachers. Clearly, their involvement would imply collaboration around different activities – specifically, legislating, strategic planning, local planning and organisation, and service delivery. In an "ideal", fully integrated network all agencies or individuals, at all levels in the services hierarchy would be working together with both horizontal (between agency) and vertical (between level) linkages.

In practice, some of the best examples of integrated services involve a (nearly) complete set of the different agencies required to fulfil programme goals, including representatives from different levels in the services hierarchy. Without integration at the "top" and "bottom" of this hierarchy, barriers to integrated services delivery can arise. Classically, the creation of separate funding streams at the mandating level can prevent the development of co-ordinated programmes, which need to share resources, on the ground.

The following three examples, taken from Finland, the United States and Australia, indicate how integrated services can be conceptualised in terms of the actors involved, more specifically, "who" and "at what level". All three are considered to represent good practice in providing services for pre-school children (Finland), school children (the United States) or youth in the transition to work (Australia).

In Finland, public sector health and social welfare services co-ordinate their activities to provide high quality services for mothers, babies and infants. This collaboration is the product of an administrative arrangement in which health and social welfare departments are combined in one ministry, the Ministry of Social Affairs and Health. Central government gave municipal governments the option to link their social welfare and health departments too. Like many other towns, Jyväskylä embraced this option, and the new Municipal Social Services and Health Board now runs local Social Welfare and Health Centres.

In New York City in the United States, the Children's Aid Society (CAS), a private organisation, has formed a partnership with the Board of School District 6 to provide a range of community services to three neighbourhood populations plagued by poverty, drugs and crime. Provided at local public schools, these services include "extended day" and "Saturday" programmes, medical and dental care, and adult education.

In New South Wales, Australia, on the other hand, South Sydney Youth Services draws on the support of a wide array of public and private organisations and individuals to help teenagers and young adults who can be in dire situations – caught up in drugs, homeless, or even suicidal. These include community people, a community based Management Committee, an Interagency (made up of 25 youth service providers), the Central Sydney Community Health Centre, Maruba Central Employment Services, the Central Sydney Youth Access Centre, the Department of

Social Security Youth Services Unit, and Upstart Graphics (a small business which South Sydney Youth Services set up).

These examples are fairly typical insofar as they reflect the tendency for social welfare and health services to gravitate towards each other for pre-school child care; for schools to collaborate with social welfare and health agencies (which provide services on-site); and for youth services to collaborate very widely indeed.

Some general country differences exist in terms of the collaborators involved in integrated services. Most importantly, in many European countries, integrated networks often are almost exclusively made up of public sector agencies, whereas in the United States co-operation between public and private agencies, and private organisations alone, is more common. Clearly this reflects the greater importance given to private sector provision in the United States. Integrated programmes in the United States also seem to place more emphasis on community participation – a pattern clearly linked to the notion of limited state intervention and self-help. Interestingly, this emphasis also exists in Canada, where community support for government initiatives is viewed as important. The dynamism linked to some private initiatives, and the benefits of local involvement to pinpoint real community needs, are two aspects of the "American" approach from which other countries could learn. However, equally, the United States may wish to reflect on its patchwork of (often exemplary) integrated programmes, and consider the benefits of comprehensive, public sector support.

The structures

Integrated services can also be conceptualised in terms of the structures – legislative or organisational – that have been put in place to facilitate co-ordination.

Integration may be promoted by legislation which provides for the merging of ministries, introduces joint, inter-ministerial programmes, or requires different ministries to align their administrative procedures. Other initiatives of this type, at the departmental or agency level, may be instituted through formal "agreements". The fusion in 1995 of the British Department of Employment, and the Department for Education, to form a new Department for Education and Employment is an example of policy making in this area.

At the mandating, strategic and operational levels organisational structures promoting integration may include inter-ministerial, inter-departmental or inter-agency committees, councils, boards or administrative bodies. South Australia's State Interagency Committee, which is made up of senior ministry directors, and which has endorsed an Interagency Referral Process to cater for children with multiple problems, is an excellent example. At the field level, professional networks, co-ordinating agencies, multi-disciplinary case management teams or co-ordinators are more likely to be the norm. In the Huchting area of Bremen, Germany, for instance, the interagency District Committee has appointed a co-ordinator to liaise between the different layers of organisation, to build local networks, and to keep abreast of the problems facing Huchting's disadvantaged population.

Inter-agency or multi-disciplinary organisational structures play an important role in facilitating integration in different countries: they provide a formal context in which joint planning and discussion can take place. Frequently, informal structures – especially multi-professional groups – are set up at the grassroots. However, without the administrative and funding support of higher levels of government, members can find it difficult to "make time" for regular collaboration.

The mechanisms

The recruitment of appropriate "actors" and the creation of necessary "structures" are insufficient on their own to ensure successful collaboration. Agreed mechanisms also need to be in place. These, too, can be used to typify the nature of integrated programmes.

Different mechanisms (or means to achieve integration) can be found at different levels in the services hierarchy – and some may exist at more than one level. At the mandating level, integration is achieved through implementing legislation jointly, or in co-ordination with, other ministries or departments. For example, Finland's 1992 Planning and State Subsidies for Welfare Act sets out common rules for the planning and funding of health and social welfare services.

At the strategic level, co-ordinated activities tend to centre around joint planning, programming, budgeting and administration. In Ontario, Canada, for instance, the inter-ministerial Better Beginnings, Better Futures Programme for disadvantaged children has involved extensive collaboration in planning and administration between the Ministries of Health, Education and Training, and Community and Social Services, and the federal department of Indian and Northern Affairs.

At the operational level, collaborative activities tend to be more varied. They may include joint planning, programming, budgeting, and administration, or, equally, the sharing of personnel and services. In Hämeenlinna, Finland, for example, the municipal departments of Education, Social Welfare and Youth lend each other personnel and building space to create a comprehensive and seamless array of human services to meet clients' needs.

Field level mechanisms to achieve integration are rather different. These include joint case management (including case assessment, plan development, review, and monitoring); sharing intake and assessment procedures; sharing information; sharing resources and equipment (e.g. fax machines and photocopiers), and conducting joint training research and evaluation. The St. Charles Employment Office in St. Louis, Missouri (United States) combines many of these strategies to provide employment, education, training and social welfare services in a "one-stop-shop". Normally, one agency takes the lead in case management, while the others provide non-duplicative backup. A joint intake form is currently being developed, and there are plans to share an automated data system with information on clients.

Joint planning, joint programming and case management are common features of integrated provision in different countries. However, according to a number of countries, pooling funding for joint projects, sharing client information, and training professionals to work in multi-disciplinary settings, are strategies which need to be used more extensively than at present. Equally, our case study research suggests that while field level workers often co-operate "naturally" (out of necessity or because they recognise obvious benefits for clients), professionals at higher levels in the services hierarchy are sometimes less aware of the need to do so, and do not always deliver the necessary backup (*e.g.* pooled funding) to make integration possible. The same research also reveals that teachers are amongst the poorest field level "co-operators", although appropriate pre-service training (New South Wales, Australia), or desperation in response to severe student problems (Missouri, United States), can make them more able or willing to do so.

The location

Integrated services can also be conceptualised according to their location. Most mandating and strategic efforts to co-ordinate programmes take place in the confines of government ministries or departments. However, attempts to integrate services "vertically" can take government administrators out into the field. In Alberta, Canada, as part of the Co-ordination of Services for Children programme, a small group of officials have been assigned to five integrated services sites where they attend inter-agency meetings on a regular basis. In doing so, they provide a useful link between workers on the ground and administrators at the Assistant Deputy Minister level.

At the operational and field levels, integrated services may be located in a community building or within a particular agency serving that community. Community-based services often are provided by a multi-disciplinary team of professionals or local people who work out of the same office. In St. Louis, Missouri, for example, Grace Hill Neighbourhood Services, which provides education, health, social, housing, and employment support, is located in a former church. Agency-based integrated services may either be provided in one of a network of separately located agencies (for example, a school), or at a single site where they are co-located (the classic "one-stop-shop"). The Latokartano Health and Social Services Centre in Helsinki, which provides general health, maternity, child health, dental, community care, intoxicant abuse and social security services, is a good example of the latter.

In most countries, integrated services for pre-school children tend to centre around child care centres or primary schools, services for school aged children are normally located in schools, and services for youth in the transition to work, in schools or employment offices. Schools tend to be a particularly popular choice because they are accessible and most children attend them. However, country differences exist. Portugal and the United States, for example, either have quite limited school-based services, or ones that are not provided universally. By contrast, the services offered in Finnish schools are both full and comprehensive, although public spending cuts are leading to reductions in provision.

CONCLUDING COMMENT AND AN EXAMPLE OF AN IMPLEMENTATION STRATEGY

In conclusion, it is suggested that defining integrated services according to actors, structures, mechanisms and location is useful for conceptual thought and also for practical action. Using these dimensions, human service providers can, if they wish, consider the various options under each "heading" to aid them in programme planning to meet government goals. We believe that considering the different dimensions of services integration is superior to recommending particular "models" because models which work in one setting may not work in another (*i.e.* they are culturally specific) and integrated services need to be designed according to the particular goals the government has in mind in the context of local needs.

However, readers may find it of interest to be familiarised with at least a small number of fully developed strategies to integrate services for children and youth at risk. To this end, in Part II of this report we have provided fifteen descriptive summaries of national or state level initiatives to integrate services. Also, summarised below is a full account of a proposed strategy to integrate services for school children with social and behavioural problems in South Australia. It was recommended for implementation in 1988.

The strategy is set out in the Stratmann Report (Stratmann, 1988), and incorporates the following:

- Agreement to be reached at the Chief Executive level as to the range and extent of services to be provided by each agency at the local level.

- Inter-agency networks (school response teams) relating to specific clusters of schools be formally identified and effectively maintained.

- To facilitate inter-agency co-ordination, clusters of schools be identified which are as compatible as possible with the Health and Welfare Sector boundaries, and with the clusters of schools being identified as a base for Superintendents within the Education Department.

- Multi-disciplinary, district based Student Support Teams be established in the Education Department. (A model has been proposed in which these teams would initially incorporate existing personnel in the Education Department from project teams and support services, guidance officers, social workers, attendance officers, etc. They would offer services to students referred from the same cluster of schools referred to above. The team managers of these teams would have a major role in the maintenance of the inter-agency networks referred to above, as well as being the points of contact for school based personnel and accepting responsibility for case management plans for individuals.)
- Specific programmes enhancing teacher skills in behaviour management to be developed.
- At least one form of withdrawal facility or programme be available in each Education Department Area, on the basis that it is used also as a vehicle for staff development and as a catalyst for change within the referring schools.
- More joint welfare and education intensive personal supervision for some students be provided through the Department for Community Welfare Intensive Adolescent Supervision Program, in close association with Education Department personnel.
- Expansion of specialist CAMHS (Child and Adolescent Mental Health Services) and DCW (Department for Community Welfare) personnel, deployed specifically to support school children with social and behavioural problems.
- The co-location of community health, education and welfare services be formally adopted as policy in the Department for Community Welfare, Education Department and Health Commission, and every effort be made to identify school premises which could be made available for co-locating services (on a permanent or visiting basis). This would provide a service base for clusters of schools and, where possible, might provide the site for a withdrawal facility (Stratmann, 1988, p. 4-5).

Clearly, this plan includes many of the different actors, structures and mechanisms discussed earlier, but has the strength of bringing them together in a cohesive whole.

5

STRATEGIC, OPERATIONAL AND FIELD LEVELS: THE MAIN OUTCOMES

by

Philippa Hurrell and Peter Evans

This chapter describes the main outcomes of the study considered mainly from the point of view of those working at the strategic, operational and field levels, although some reference is made to the mandating level where relevant.

WHAT KIND OF EVALUATIONS OF SERVICES INTEGRATION EXIST, AND WHAT ARE THE RESULTS?

Five, inter-related aspects of integrated services have been evaluated: in terms of client outcomes (of various types); outcomes for agencies and professionals; financial costs; cost-effectiveness (outcomes in relation to costs); and the process of services integration. Most studies carried out by countries examine client outcomes; however, a small number look at outcomes for agencies and professionals, financial costs, cost-effectiveness and the integration process.

Client outcomes: a very large amount of information was provided by countries on client outcomes. This related primarily to school attendance, school achievement, employment and health, and to a lesser extent, to levels of client satisfaction. A particularly high proportion of integrated programmes in the United States and Canada are evaluated, and it is common for assessment to be a requirement for funding. Evaluation of programmes appears to be less common in European countries like Finland, Germany and Portugal although it is being utilised increasingly. Almost without exception, evaluations of the exemplary programmes we visited have identified positive outcomes. While encouraging, they give little indication of whether programme success is the result of integration, increased funding, charismatic leadership, or any other factor. One of the best examples of data collection on client outcomes can be found in Duisburg, Germany. Here, the results of integrated efforts to improve the employment chances of young people are recorded on a yearly basis by the city's Statistics Office. The information collected by the Office reportedly shows that "transition counselling" and special care for youth at risk works successfully to reduce Duisburg's youth unemployment.

Outcomes for agencies and professionals: a very small number of studies have explored the effects of initiatives promoting integration on local agencies and professionals. These studies recognise the importance of support from the field level for the effective implementation of integrated programmes. In Australia, an evaluation of Youth Access Centres (YACs) (Waller, 1992), discovered both positive and negative outcomes. Some agencies found the inter-agency meetings and information sharing activities organised by YACs very useful; on the other hand, it was discovered that there was some confusion, uncertainty, suspicion, and even resentment, connected with YACs' role in co-ordination.

Financial costs: Very few of the countries visited reported analyses of the financial costs of integrated services. Some of the best information gathered came from the Children's Aid Society which runs an integrated programme in public school IS 218 in New York City. The Society reported that by using the school's buildings free of charge, rather than paying to use a community centre, it could spend 90 cents of every dollar on programme activities. It spends around $850 per child, per year on these activities, compared with the $6 000 spent by School District 6 on their education.

In California, under the Healthy Start (HS) programme, planning grants for integrated school-linked services of $50 000, three-year operational grants of $300 000 and start-up costs of $100 000 can be awarded. In the years 1991-93, 65 operational grants to 210 schools were given. Evaluations (Wagner *et al.*, 1994) demonstrated that this funding approach had been successful in bringing together new partners and supporting on-going school-linked services.

Cost-effectiveness: very little information was received from countries on the cost-effectiveness of integrated services. However, in the Netherlands, in particular, important work is being developed in this area (Daudey and Oosterbeek, 1995). The importance of developing cost-effectiveness was noted by Stallings in her presidential adress to the American Education Research Association (AREA) meeting, in 1995, concerning teaching and learning in the next century (Stallings, 1995).

The process of services integration: a number of studies, particularly in the United States, Canada and the Netherlands try to identify processes and practices which facilitate or inhibit integration. These studies are helpful in determining what needs to happen, given certain initial inputs, to achieve desired outcomes. In public school IS 183 in New York City, for example, an evaluation team from Mirand Research Associates Inc. (1993) found that the following factors were associated with the successful implementation of additional social and educational pro-grammes to prevent drug use:

- Substantial, widespread agreement about the need for change and the actions needed to bring it about.

- Observable and sustainable change in the structure of the school or organisation.

- Widespread participation in efforts to bring about change.

- Leadership which encourages contributions from others and offers them the chance to take on leadership roles.

- Time to develop new types of funding mechanisms which cut across existing agency boundaries.

In California, the philosophy behind the implementation of Healthy Start is that each community must tailor its programme to respond to citizens' needs and expectations, and to build on local strengths. Within this approach four basic models of service delivery emerged: school site family resource centres; satellite family service centres; family service co-ordination teams; and youth service programmes.

Evaluations of each of these models showed that they had their own individual strengths and weaknesses. For instance school site centres provided the broadest array of services; satellite services produced significant improvements in clients' mental health; service co-ordination teams stressed academic services and school related counselling; and youth services led to a significant increase in clients' employment status. A full account is given in the California case study report.

The Dutch have described and evaluated, processes and practices connected with three different models of services integration (Geelen *et al.,* 1994). These have been implemented as part of national Educational Priority Policy to support schools in disadvantaged areas:

"The governing bodies of the participating schools and institutions draw up a formal co-operation agreement. The role of central government is limited. A specially appointed administrative body sets out general policies, divides government subsidies between the participants, and monitors closely how co-operation between the participants develops. Quite often, the participants appoint an executive board with well-defined powers. The executive body appoints managers, who establish working groups at the field level (including neighbourhood level). The model generally has limited power to implement change, because the participants retain a relatively high degree of autonomy. The model is often used in the initial phase of a change process, to gain the confidence of institutions and people.

The governing bodies of the participating schools and institutions draw up a co-operation agreement in which the main lines of policy are described. Much of the responsibility for the implementation of policies is left to the co-ordinator (or co-ordinating team), who gives account to the participants of what has been achieved. This model is frequently used (Maastricht); it is more powerful in implementing change than the one described above, but it places stronger demands on the qualities of the managers. The influence managers are able to exert on institutions is of particular importance. In the educational priority areas, special training is provided for managers to ensure improvement of quality. These models often involve strengthening the ties with local authorities with a view to influencing policy making.

The governing bodies of the participating schools and institutions give up part of their autonomy and their powers to a specially established foundation whose task is to prepare policies. In this way, relatively small but powerful "innovation bureaux" are created, representing various sectors. One problem in this model is the justification of interventions at the field level; here a great deal depends on the qualities of the co-ordinators and the means they have at their disposal to ensure the commitment of staff working at the field level. Although still fairly uncommon, this model is gradually gaining ground (Rotterdam, Emmen)."

To date, evaluations of the process of services integration perhaps have been the most informative. Client outcome assessments have been useful in informing us that many "good" examples of integrated programmes achieve positive results in at least some areas, although they do not tell us exactly why. Research on costs, cost-effectiveness, and outcomes for agencies and professionals, simply is quite rare.

Most work on costs is conducted by staff at the mandating, strategic and operational levels; in contrast, most work on processes and outcomes is carried out at the field level. More research on integrative processes at higher levels in the services hierarchy would be informative as it is often at these levels that significant problems (such as negative competition between department heads) can arise.

Evaluations of integrated services for pre-school children, school children and youth in the transition to work differ primarily according to the client outcomes they measure. Evaluations of pre-school programmes often examine the academic achievement of children once they have started school; evaluations of school programmes look at outcomes such as attendance, drop-out and graduation rates; while evaluations of "transition" programmes focus on success in gaining employment.

North America without doubt leads the field in this area – particularly in relation to client outcome evaluation. However, as stated earlier, this kind of evaluation cannot always tell us why a particular programme is successful, and if "good" programmes are to be replicated this is vital. The Caring Communities programme in St. Louis, Missouri, illustrates this point very well. While it has proved successful, the state government is uncertain whether this is because of its integrated nature, or because it has an unusually charismatic leader. Only the replication of the programme elsewhere, under different supervision, can reveal how important the particular brand of leadership present in the "parent" programme is. In fact, the Missouri government has decided to provide funding for "clone" programmes and will monitor their success.

WHAT ARE THE PERCEIVED ADVANTAGES AND DISADVANTAGES OF SERVICES INTEGRATION?

Since many quantitative evaluations of integrated services are unable to tell us what role integration plays in achieving specific outcomes, programmes are open to the criticism that it is not the fact that they are co-ordinated which makes them work, but some other reason. However, lacking "hard" empirical evidence, it is useful to turn to "softer", more qualitative data which reflects professionals' perceptions and attitudes, and deserves more attention than it is sometimes given by decision-makers.

In this section we shall explore the perceived advantages and disadvantages of integration from the perspective of administrators (at the mandating and strategic levels), managers and professionals (at the operational and field levels), and clients.

Advantages

The benefits of services integration emphasised by government administrators in different countries primarily relate to staff morale and cost-effectiveness.

- *Morale:* some administrators are strongly motivated and enthused by integrated working methods. In Kansas City, Missouri, for example, members of the Local Investment Commission (LINC) say they are excited by ongoing efforts to integrate services (and this is reflected in their dynamism).

- *Costs and effects:* administrators believe that services integration has the potential to reduce costs and improve client outcomes. This viewpoint was shared by administrators in all of the countries visited.

Middle managers and professionals, on the other hand, are able to report a broader range of perceived advantages (although in policy terms they may not be as significant as those mentioned by administrators). These can be divided into

personal/professional benefits, and benefits for clients. Personal/professional benefits can be classified under the following headings:

– *Professional satisfaction:* professionals regard work in integrated settings as
  more satisfying, interesting, enjoyable and motivating, and less stressful.
  They believe that an integrated approach allows them to reach more clients
  and to achieve better results. Teachers, in particular, benefit from improvements in students "readiness to learn" as teaching is easier. By participating
  in activities which are not strictly educational like New York City's "extended
  day programmes" they are also able to develop more well-rounded relationships with students.

– *Relationships with other professionals:* professionals report that through co-
  ordinated activities they are able to develop a better understanding of the
  roles and perspectives of other professionals, learn useful strategies and
  techniques from them, and benefit from their support. In addition, they are
  able to share information, and improve their relationships with individuals
  and departments. In Huchting, Bremen (Germany), for example, mutual support amongst professionals from different agencies has led to the creation of
  a powerful and cohesive human services network.

– *Community involvement:* professionals who staff community-based integrated programmes say that they benefit from community participation and
  support, good relationships with community members, and an increased
  ability to understand and adapt programmes to community needs. Workers
  involved in Portugal's Anti-poverty Trap Project 3 in Porto, for example,
  report a high level of local support for the programme as well as increased
  dynamism in the community.

– *Costs and effects:* middle managers and professionals believe that integrated
  working practices achieve better outcomes for clients, reduce costs, and
  provide more scope for prevention. For instance, staff at the St. Charles
  Employment Office, a one-stop-shop in St. Louis, Missouri, claim that "we
  can stretch the dollar and our resources because we can tap into what
  everyone has".

Perceived client benefits, by contrast, can be classified as follows:

– *Better services resulting from case management:* professionals believe that,
  by using a case management approach involving a multi-disciplinary team,
  clients can benefit in several ways. They are more likely to get all of the
  services they need and to get them before a crisis point is reached. They are
  more likely to have a single and continuous contact point and to receive
  consistent advice. In addition, if the case manager is a "generalist", they are
  also less likely to be stigmatised than they would be if they received help

from a specialist. These points were emphasised particularly strongly in Finland.

– *Better services resulting from the creation of one-stop-shops:* one-stop-shops are viewed by professionals as being more accessible and convenient for clients because they provide a single entry point for receiving information, making applications, and getting services. Field workers can also allocate clients the services they need more quickly and efficiently. Again, these points emerged most strongly from the Finnish case studies.

– *Community involvement:* professionals believe that local involvement in integrated programmes can increase community power and influence in the design of activities. Parents can benefit from integrated projects by taking advantage of their resources (*e.g.* school facilities), improving their knowledge and self-esteem (*e.g.* through contact with professionals), and obtaining employment as members of staff. Parents can use skills learnt from training courses to socialise and educate their children, who thus also benefit. In Kansas City, Missouri, for example, parent classes in child development offered by the Family Focus Centre have reportedly led to improvements in the way parents interact with their offspring.

– *Outcomes or "effects":* professionals believe that clients are more satisfied with integrated than fragmented care, and benefit from it to a greater extent.

Hence, administrative and field level workers perceive integrated provision to be advantageous in many different ways. However, in line with a more client-focused approach to services provision, it is important to ask, "what do clients think about integrated services?". While fewer clients than administrative and field workers were interviewed, those we did talk to, or received information about, generally indicated that they were very satisfied with the services they received. For example, two "graduates" from Kansas City's Women's Employment Network (WEN) (in Missouri), which collaborates with other agencies to help young women find employment, write:

"Currently on SOC SSI [Social Security Supplemental Security Income] benefits, but not forever. I thank God for women like yourself and others reaching out to those that want more. I can make it. I am enough."

"I feel great since WEN and I have a good job. Back in school and my life is fine. Thank you all for your help in getting me back on my feet."

Disadvantages

On the whole, administrators, middle managers, professionals and clients were more positive than negative about integrated working practices. However, some disadvantages were mentioned and, indeed, point to problems which may need to be addressed by governments to ensure that policies promoting services integration are implemented effectively.

The concerns emphasised by different administrators in respect of integrated services are:

- that the development of integrated programmes and structures will lead to an increase (rather than a decrease as one might expect) in the layers of bureaucracy;
- that organisers of integrated community programmes will refuse, or not have the time, to co-operate with other local services (perhaps leading to duplication in services provision);
- that different professionals in the same multi-disciplinary team may demand greater equality in status and remuneration; and
- that services integration will require a re-alignment of service structures, leading to a significant increase in workload.

On the other hand, the concerns of middle managers and professionals are:

- that integration will lead to disempowerment;
- that integration will result in a loss of professional identity;
- that integration will necessitate a reduction in specialisation;
- that integration of various kinds (e.g. departmental or agency mergers) will lead to funding reductions and job losses;
- that inter-professional communication and relations will be difficult;
- that collaborative activities will increase workloads during the normal working day, as well as overtime; and
- that human and financial resources will be insufficient to achieve integration easily.

Clients occasionally said that they were not happy with the services they received, or the effect they had. However, these comments seldom were linked to the fact that they were integrated, as opposed to "separate", services.

Overall then, administrators in different countries seem fairly convinced that services integration can save money and improve outcomes. The perceived money saving aspect of services integration seems particularly attractive to them, and can be linked to the current economic climate. Those working at the field level appear to be much more appreciative of the fact that integration can make their job easier, and that they can see real improvements in client outcomes. In spite of slightly contrasting reasons for supporting services integration, what is interesting is that professionals at all levels of the services hierarchy (as well as clients) find it useful. This observation holds for most, if not all, of the countries visited.

The fact that many professionals who collaborate enjoy it, and find it motivating, suggests that integration can help to improve staff morale (although, self selection may partially explain this pattern). Similarly, the fact that a significant proportion of professionals believe that collaboration helps to improve client outcomes, suggests that there may be a causal link between the two (although, again, this is difficult to prove).

The perceived disadvantages of services integration need to be considered carefully. Certainly, this approach may introduce unintended "problems". For example, a proliferation in the layers of bureaucracy, linked to the setting up of various interagency committees, could make decision-making slower and more complicated. Problems like this need to be weighed against the advantages of integration (interagency committees, for example, might be able to erase unnecessary duplication in services provision). Other problems, such as relational difficulties between key individuals, may be unjustifiable but equally real, and may also require serious attention.

Interestingly, while services integration generally is seen as a money saving strategy, this is not always the case. Sometimes, it is seen as representing an additional cost, either in terms of human or financial resources. This may be because services integration saves money in some areas, but incurs additional costs in others. Equally, it may be because the lack of empirical research on the subject makes the whole area rather a grey one: no-one knows for sure what the exact nature of the relationship between integration and costs is.

Few differences in the perceived advantages and disadvantages of services integration are evident amongst professionals working in services for pre-school children, school children, and youth in the transition to work. Country differences are also slight. However, greater community participation in integrated services in the United States and Canada is reflected in a more pronounced tendency for service providers to view community support and participation as an important advantage of collaboration.

WHAT ARE THE FACTORS THAT FACILITATE OR INHIBIT SERVICES INTEGRATION?

The preceding section suggests that integrating services is desirable. If this conclusion is accepted, then it becomes important to consider what factors facilitate or inhibit it. These will provide the key to ensuring that integration is achieved successfully.

Analysing facilitating and inhibiting factors is difficult because they are by their very nature inter-linked. If pooled funding, for example, is perceived to facilitate integration, then the "flip-side" is that separate funding streams will be considered to inhibit it. Often, professionals in the field give more emphasis to inhibiting factors, as these are the ones that cause them obvious difficulties. The following analysis will consider facilitating and inhibiting factors together, as opposite sides of the same coin, while trying to reflect whether professionals tend to express them primarily as one or the other.

Facilitating and inhibiting factors tend to be rather similar at different levels in the services hierarchy although some small differences are evident. At the mandating and strategic levels facilitating and inhibiting factors articulated by professionals in different countries can be grouped under the following headings.

- *Political support:* strong political support for integration at both administrative and grassroots levels is viewed as important. Co-ordinating committees or co-ordinators need to be given sufficient political power to institute change. Tough and bold leadership is required to achieve real shifts in policy direction. In Kansas City, Missouri, strong leadership and support for services integration is provided by the Local Investment Commission which has instituted wide ranging change in services provision.

- *Legislation and administration:* services integration can be facilitated by waiving legislation which impedes co-operation between services. In contrast, integration can be inhibited by too much red-tape and rigidity, differing departmental rules and regulations, and inflexible service delivery mandates. In Missouri, rigid bureaucracy and red-tape at times have been overcome by breaking obstructive rules. However, the removal of these rules would make this action unnecessary.

- *Funding:* special funding mechanisms can be used to promote the co-ordination of services. For example, in California, school districts are encouraged to identify school medical services which can be reimbursed through the federal government's Medicaid programme. On the other hand, integration reportedly can be inhibited by separate, "stove-pipe" funding of services, a lack of special funding to set up co-ordinated initiatives (which require "start-up" money), and a lack of general or long-term funding.

- *Communication.* services integration can be promoted by horizontal communication between department and agency representatives, and professionals, as well as vertical communication between senior officials, middle managers and field workers. It can be impeded by differing professional terminologies or "languages" – a problem made explicit by those involved in collaborative activities in Alberta (Canada) and Finland, and also elsewhere.

- *Structures and mechanisms:* the co-ordination of services can be facilitated by the institution of appropriate structures and mechanisms (see earlier discussion on the "dimensions" of integrated services).

- *Research and consultancy:* quantitative and qualitative research, and the skills of outside experts, can be employed to promote services integration. In

Finland, for example, political support for a multi-service centre in Latokartano, Helsinki, was won by a client survey which showed that while only a small proportion of clients used several services, they were heavy consumers. Later on, the results of a survey concerning staff perspectives on working patterns was used by a consultant, in collaboration with staff, to develop a "joint operating model".

– *Training and experience:* integration is facilitated by multi-disciplinary training which prepares teachers and other professionals to work as part of a team. Collaboration appears to come more easily to professionals who work in systems which have a long history of co-operation. In Finland, for example, school health services have been in operation for around 100 years, and this tradition appears to be reflected in the harmony with which health workers collaborate with other school staff.

– *Attitudes and relationships:* a dynamic, bold and positive outlook towards services integration, combined with a refusal to let deeply entrenched traditions triumph over innovation, can (sometimes) help efforts to integrate services. These traits are particularly characteristic of North American service providers. Integration reportedly can also be facilitated by employing "the right kind of people"; more specifically, those with diverse previous experience or with "co-operative personalities". On the other hand, it can be restricted by rigid, hierarchical or old-fashioned attitudes; poor or competitive relationships between particular departments, agencies or individuals; and fears amongst workers that integration may lead to job cuts.

A similar set of facilitating and inhibiting factors are present at the operational and field levels although they impinge on different working contexts. However, some factors come into play to a greater extent at these levels. For example, at both levels, the co-location of services and sharing of geographic areas of responsibility are perceived as useful in facilitating integration. The sharing by services of a joint data management system is also perceived as helpful. And integration on a limited scale (such as in a small town setting) is seen by some as easier than efforts to co-ordinate services over a wide area. By contrast, a lack of time to engage in teamwork, differing terminologies, principles and practices, professional prejudices, and professional specialisation (at the expense of a more inter-disciplinary knowledge), are regarded by some field workers as significant impediments to collaboration.

The facilitating and inhibiting factors articulated by professionals differ little according to the age group they serve – specifically, pre-school children, school children or youth in the transition to work. Indeed, the general pattern is one of similarity rather than difference for these three age groups.

Interestingly, some of the best examples of facilitating factors and worst examples of inhibiting factors are to be found in the United States. More specifically, the three States visited in this country were remarkable for at least two (if not more) of the following:

- the clarity and depth of political support;
- the flexible use of legislative waivers;
- the dynamic approach to policy implementation;
- the boldness of service leaders;

but also:

- the high level of negative competition between public and/or private agencies; and
- the complexity and fragmentation of the services system.

Finland, Canada and Australia can also be regarded, to some extent, as "exceptional" countries in terms of the facilitating factors which operate in them. Finland has a remarkably long tradition of providing high quality school-linked services for children at risk; the three provinces visited in Canada make significant use of community resources, support and opinion to implement integrated programmes; and the three States visited in Australia have employed teachers who appear to be particularly open to co-operation with other professionals.

CONCLUDING COMMENT

For many countries, services integration is clearly seen as a major step forward in helping to prevent and overcome many of the more intractable problems faced by today's educational systems. The advantages are visible across a wide range of actors. However, implementing reforms of this scale is a different matter which involves developments across the four levels of the system that have been examined. Account must be taken, both of the factors which may serve to derail the effort and of the need to develop training policies and evaluation methods.

6

PRINCIPAL CONCLUSIONS
AND POLICY CHALLENGES

by

Peter Evans and Philippa Hurrell

The previous chapters have provided an introduction to the concept of integrated services and its development and a summary of the main outcomes of the study. In this chapter the main conclusions and policy implications will be drawn out for the mandating, strategic, operational and field levels. Although the research investigated services provided during the pre-school, school and transition to work periods, this categorisation is not used in this chapter since differences that exist are ones of degree and not of kind. However, it is worth noting, that the complexity, intensity and difficulty of the effort needed to support older students who are failing, sometimes with limited success, is very striking, and this of itself argues for more support in the earlier stages of education.

CONCLUSIONS

The holistic support of children

Changes in the socio-economic structures of many Member countries and the global recognition of children's rights are focusing attention, more strongly than before, on the social-emotional adaptation and educational progress of all children. There is growing acceptance that these two elements of a child's development cannot be separated and it is the dislocation of structures involved with the nurturing of children's social, emotional, motivational and cognitive development which is at the root of the failure to adapt responsibly to the demands of our present social order.

The balanced development of children is increasingly seen holistically. It is embedded in and emerges from a balanced social support system. An effective system is nurturing, and by this token, preventative in nature.

New service systems are required

In the past, when education, health and social services structures were elaborated, the support they offered was frequently mediated through families and communities. In the 1990s, family and community structures, for many children, no longer exert their presence in the same way as in former times. Education systems, which are heavily reliant on family involvement for success, are being pressed everywhere to improve standards for all children and are, at the same time, becoming increasingly hard-pressed to cope with growing disruption. This significantly affects the education and development of school children. It is the extent of the problem being experienced by schools, allied to new educational demands, which are forcing education systems into a new alliance with other services and agencies. That is, a new piece of social machinery is being forged to replace designs that are either worn out or simply non-existent. The design is intended to prevent damaging environmental conditions (physical, psychological and sociological) from arising and to provide remedial support when necessary.

In addition, different legal frameworks operate for different professsionals, such as teachers and social workers, and these themselves may produce conflict. The education system was frequently identified as being an unwilling collaborator in efforts to co-ordinate services.

The narrow categorical organisation of services is inadequate to meet either the extent or the nature of the present demands. New comprehensive integrated and preventive systems are required.

Integrating services – a clear way forward

It is significant to note that these observations transcend many features of the cultures and socio-economic status of nations. From an advanced welfare state system such as Finland to the market economy of the United States, or from a relative large GDP, Germany, to a relatively small GDP, Portugal or for countries which are intermediate (Australia, Canada, the Netherlands), changes in the way statutory services are organised and regulated can be seen. Furthermore, these changes are in one direction: towards greater co-ordination and even integration. However a great deal more evaluative work still needs to be carried out to identify the elements of the integration process which are most strongly related to the apparent improvement in service provision.

The work of CERI reveals the nature of the problems encountered as well as the complexity of effective solutions being proposed. While there are many variations on offer, it is clear that the co-ordinated efforts of education, health, social and employment services and justice departments acting in concert with community initiatives and interest (for example, from voluntary organisations, foundations, families and business), are at the heart of the necessary and sufficient conditions for effective change. The main differences between a categorical service delivery model and an integrated one are itemised in Table 3.

Integrating services and co-ordinating the work of other agencies to meet the needs of children and families at risk is the most promising comprehensive solution on offer. It extends across many different cultures and economies.

Table 3.   **Summary of the identified differences between old style "non-integrated services" and new style "integrated services"**

New system	Old system
• is customer driven	• is focused on agencies
• is family-oriented	• is individually focused
• is outcomes driven	• is input driven
• seeks balance between prevention and intervention	• is crisis-oriented
• is decentralised	• is centralised
• uses multi-agency funding including private sources	• uses formal service delivery
• provides integrated services	• provides categorical services
• is evaluated by outcomes	• is evaluated by compliance to rules and regulations
• is community based	• sees clients in agency offices
• services are delivered through teams of professionals, parents and non-professionals	• services are delivered through credentialed professionals
• seeks institutional change	• funds isolated projects

Note: The differences are not trivial and indicate the extent of conceptual change required and subsequent reforms needed.
Source: Chynoweth, 1994.

Decentralisation is a key component

Where national responses to this development have involved supporting services integration there have been changes in the law (*e.g.* relating to confidentiality), and decentralisation of the administration of services. While cynics may argue that decentralisation takes away the blame for service failure from central government it carries several advantages. It reduces the inhibiting impact on change of the different structures and practices that exist in government departments or ministries. It allows for the development of ownership, empowerment, response flexibility and increased resource input through community involvement. In addition it opens the way to some reduction in political involvement unnecessarily influenced by the electoral cycle. In these ways, decentralisation may well help in implementing changes which require long term resource investment if they are to take root. It remains unlikely that all decision-making can be decentralised. Central government will have to maintain control of the steering elements of policy implementation as well as of accountability issues. Formulation of national policies for professional training and development and the maintenance of standards are also functions that would probably best stay at central government level.

Decentralisation is key to creating the conditions for effective services integration. Changes in the law may also be necessary.

Evaluation is in need of development

Evaluation of integrated services was clearly identified in the study as a weak point. Although evaluations, both our own and others, demonstrate moves towards services integration supported by consistent evidence of beneficial outcomes for a wide range of actors, separating out the critical elements of an integrated approach will require much more empirical work.

The decision to sample information vertically in a service structure using the mandating, strategic, operational and field levels was justified, since changes in the system were described at all of these levels with different levels revealing different changes. For instance at the mandating level, there were changes in laws and policies; at the strategic, changes in steering function, evaluation/accountability needs, training, and enthusiasm; at the operational level, changes in implementation methods, locations, and organisation; and at the field level, changes in practices and outcomes.

There are a number of key issues which are not well addressed in the evaluation literature and which will present serious problems in developing an evaluation framework that will be sensitive to change and suitable for the purposes of accountability.

First, community based change does not follow any simple set of rules or paths. These systems by their very nature are multi-dimensional. Change in a system may appear at any point in that system, depending on input variables that make up a local system, on the point of development of that system, and already established patterns of practice. Because of this, different community developments will have different strengths and weaknesses and indicators of change will most likely be different in different locations. An evaluation methodology will need to be sensitive to these differences and thus be broad in conception and sensitive to the dynamics of change over time. This requires the existence of a descriptive model or theory of services integration from which indicators can be derived. Any agreement on such a model or methodology is conspicuously absent at present.

But in the context of evaluating and understanding the process and providing a further analytic grip when planning implementations, the system describing integrating services in terms of the actors, the structures, the mechanisms and the location – or who is involved, in what structures, in what ways and where – seems useful.

Informal evaluations have noted and argued for the "cost-effectiveness" of integrated services. With the exception of the "Head Start programmes", no formal cost-effectiveness evaluations were identified, although the work reported that has considered this approach supports its potential.

Substantial development is needed in the area of evaluation methods to capture and stimulate the changes taking place in complex systems on the ground. These methods will need to be developed for the purposes of accountability along with cost-effectiveness analyses.

Funding issues

The re-organisation of services involves a change in their resourcing. Changes have often been implemented with no increases in the funding base although arrangements for additional short-term support in the form, for instance, of start-up funding or consultants have been made. Necessary increased workloads in implementing system change has been absorbed within the human resources available.

The issue of equity in funding is an important one and models of distribution need developing which ensure that funds available match local needs. This should include an assessment of the proportion of clients needing access to a full set of co-ordinated services and those needing only partial access. There is some evidence that full access is only required by some 5 per cent of a country's school aged population.

Models for the equitable distribution of funds both across regions and client types will need to be developed.

Training of professionals

One of the main inhibiting factors in integrated service settings is the failure of professionals and administrators, at all levels of the system, to understand each other's working practices. The recognition of the changing roles of all involved is essential. The importance of training for professionals was recognised at the outset of the study. The need for national strategies to develop interdisciplinary training has been identified as a clear weakness. Policy academies have been developed in the United States to meet the training needs of the actors involved at all levels of the system.

The development of trans-disciplinary training is urgent and of the essence.

Policy implications

Webb and Wistow (1982) have identified a number of categories relevant to policy considerations which are of significance to this study and which have been identified as providing barriers to services integration particularly at central government level in the United Kingdom.

Policy ownership refers to the specialisation between government departments in relation to clients and types of services and the ways in which these may act to prevent effective co-ordination.

Policy streams relating to service policies, resourcing policies and governance policies are also relevant. Service policies refer to policies about needs and services as institutionalised in the professions and in the policy divisions of social policy departments. Resourcing policies involve committing the means to achieve policy goals. If supply side policies dominate decision-making and service policies, then strategic planning becomes de-emphasised when future funding is unpredictable. Governance policies refer to policies about government and can be key if for instance that policy is one of decentralisation. Different departments may not interpret their role in decentralisation in the same way, and hence their relationships with local government may vary.

It seems clear that all of these issues are highly relevant to the question of developing effective integrated services on the ground. Noting the policy classification described above, some challenges can be identified.

Policy challenges

Ownership: clearly central government departments which are funding and responsible for services will wish to "own" the policies relating to them. But community based developments will be "owned" by the communities.

Service policies: policies that are tied to the professions and their unionised and professional interests may become out of step with the needs of the customers of integrated services on the ground.

Resource policies: supply led resource policies, which discourage long-term planning, may be incompatible with the development of new integrated services which will need substantial support over the short-, medium- and long-term to reap benefits.

Governance policies: decentralisation appears to be a *sine qua non* of effective customer driven integrated services. This will affect policy implementation, and the implied relationship between central and local government will require changes in the ways central government departments communicate with local service providers and respond to local variation.

This CERI research has provided examples relevant to these policy challenges as integrated services have been implemented and developed on the ground. As indicated above, governments will need to work out for themselves how to manage turf disputes, joint long term funding, relationships with professionals, the means of effective evaluation and short-, medium- and long-term accountability mechanisms, if they wish to introduce and steer, what is seen by some, as the only currently available and practicable solution to the problem of children and youth at risk.

FINAL SUMMARISING COMMENT

The extent and complexity of the problems presented by children and youth at risk and their families is clearly mismatched with the services available. This mismatch is in both the type and extent of services. Countries have therefore begun the process of reforming their services structure in a way that can at least in principle best meet the needs of customers or clients on the ground. This has been achieved through decentralisation and integration with the main goals of:

- prevention in contrast to crisis management;

- the attainment of greater flexibility of provision; and

- improved effectiveness and greater economy.

The development of integrated services is a major reform which requires changes in the ways central governments function *vis-à-vis* local governments and community arrangements. This will involve confronting the policy issues that have been identified above of ownership, service, resourcing, and governance, as well as implementation. There is a great urgency for the development of new evaluation methods and instruments in order to provide accountability mechanisms which are sensitive to local reforms as they are taking place and the many levels of system change identified. In addition, for the development of the "new" service model, trans-disciplinary training for all actors will be needed that is complementary and sensitive to the skills, attitudes and experience of the professionals, administrators and managers involved.

At the end of the day, integrating services is a key element in achieving equity and in creating the conditions for access to education and lifelong learning for all. It is the most promising comprehensive solution on offer.

Part II

CASE STUDY ABSTRACTS

Section 1

CASE STUDY ABSTRACTS CARRIED OUT BY OECD EXPERTS

GERMANY
The human services underpinnings
of Europe's economic giant

by

Philippa Hurrell and Peter Evans

INTRODUCTION AND SUMMARY

By far the most significant event in Germany over the last five years has been its dramatic and long-awaited re-unification. With a current population of 81 million people (OECD, 1995b), the "new" Germany is easily the largest country in western Europe. Achieving a gross domestic product of over 2 billion dollars in 1994, it is also the biggest economy. However, world-wide recession, and the introduction of new technologies in "old" industries, have made it difficult for poorly qualified Germans to secure jobs. For this reason, the provision of vocational training for disadvantaged youth is one of the government's top concerns.

The combined forces of re-unification and recession have had an important impact on human services in Germany. Following re-unification, the old system of educational and social welfare provision in eastern Germany was over-turned, and replaced with services based on the western German model. Such radical change has created instability and insecurity, but has also allowed useful innovation, including efforts to integrate services. Recently, western German programmes, which have developed close-knit agency networks, have been transplanted to eastern Germany with some success. Recession, however, has reduced the amount of public money available to set up integrated networks, and threatens agencies' ability to form effective partnerships.

CHILDREN AT RISK IN GERMANY

In Germany, both children who leave school early, and children who leave school without qualifications, are deemed to be at risk. This reflects Germany's concern that all of its young people have some skill or training experience that will enable them to become fully integrated into the workforce. Many of these children are from disadvantaged backgrounds, and a high proportion of these, in turn, are from ethnic minority groups.

Germany is populated by around 1.9 million Turks and 1 million immigrants from the former Yugoslavia. All other nationalities (especially Italians, Greeks, and Poles) make up less than 10 per cent of the ethnic population. Many of these immigrants are classified as "guest workers" and, as a result, do not enjoy the same rights as German nationals. Moreover, they are threatened by the extreme racism of a minority, reflected in attacks on immigrant hostels. This has been a source of growing concern for the government.

Many immigrants are ghetto-ised in run-down communities – although to some extent this is by choice as they endeavour to maintain their cultural identity. Their children not only experience racism and poverty, but also frequently find themselves caught between traditional and German cultures.

POLICIES PROMOTING SERVICES INTEGRATION

The concept of "integration" in Germany first came to the fore in discussions concerning human services provision in the late 1960s. Over the next twenty years, changes in philosophy, particularly in Germany's social services, led to the promotion of "model" integrated projects. These tended to be client focused and analysed individual's problems in their social context. More recently, a new impulse has been given to services integration by the Children and Youth Services Act, and German re-unification in 1990.

Enacted in 1990, in the new *Länder* (eastern German States), and in 1991 in the old *Länder* (western German States), the Children and Youth Services Act includes several sections which promote the concept of services integration:

- Section 4 compels public agencies to co-operate with other "free" (voluntary) agencies that offer youth services.

- Section 36.2 states that in cases where educational support has to be provided over a long period of time, public agencies must elaborate a support plan. This "ought to be" worked out in collaboration with any other agencies who might be involved in its implementation.

- Section 72.1 recommends that, where necessary, professionals from different social welfare disciplines "should" work together to determine the most adequate form of support or therapy for an individual.

- Section 78 summons public youth agencies to establish with free agencies working groups to harmonise their programmes and make them complementary.

- Section 80.3 states that free agencies "ought to be" involved in youth welfare planning by public agencies.

– Section 81 requires youth welfare agencies to co-operate with organisations like schools, training agencies and public health services, to provide remedial youth care.

While the act undoubtedly promotes services integration, public services are under little legal obligation to do so. The "ought tos" and "shoulds" in many sections, leave public agencies free to decide whether or not they wish to adopt the act's recommendations. Another weakness is the one-sidedness of the legislation, which is only directed towards public agencies and does not require free agencies to co-operate.

Recent evaluations of the Children and Youth Services Act suggest that, in the context of economic cutbacks, youth services are unlikely to initiate new approaches to services provision unless required to by law. However, there is some hope that in the new *Länder*, where social services are growing quite rapidly, the lack of traditional structure and hierarchy will allow services integration to spread more easily.

EXAMPLES OF BEST PRACTICE IN INTEGRATED SERVICES FOR PRE-SCHOOL CHILDREN

Social services in Huchting, Bremen

Unlike other parts of Germany where human services are provided at different locations, Bremen City-State has organised joint health, youth and social welfare centres for its population. This "integrated" approach was the result of research conducted in the 1970s and 1980s which showed that traditional human services structures were not working effectively.

Two broad principles lie behind the re-organisation of human services in Bremen: a neighbourhood approach to care, and professional specialisation for different demographic groups. In accordance with the "neighbourhood" principle, Bremen's Office for Health, Youth and Social Welfare is divided into four regional departments, for North, South, East and West Bremen. These in turn are divided into districts and, at a lower level still, into neighbourhoods of 5 000 to 10 000 people. Demographic specialisation is achieved through the division of the four regional departments into *Bezirkssozialdienste*, or specialised units, for children and their families, youth and their families, adults and the elderly.

The re-organisation of social services in Bremen is well exemplified by Huchting, which is one of the most disadvantaged areas of Bremen, with 25 per cent of its families on benefits. In Huchting, regional and district level committees operate to co-ordinate the different services which work there. The Regional Committee is made up of the director of the regional office, and the directors of the *Bezirkssozialdienste*. The District Committee includes the social educators from the welfare department, and one representative from each of the welfare organisations operating in the district (namely its kindergartens, youth organisations, leisure clubs, the City Farm, the Social Services Centre, the local council, psychological services, health services and non-profit organisations).

A central function of the District Committee is to get all of the providers of social services in Huchting around the table, and to establish a forum for discussion and co-operation to improve local services. Although the committee only has an advisory role towards the local council and state ministries, it has become very influential, providing important vertical links between field level activities and higher levels of the administration. These links have been fortified by the appointment of a co-ordinator, whose function is to liaise between the different layers of organisation, to build local networks, and to keep abreast of the problems facing Huchting's population. To improve vertical channels of communication, he attends the public sessions of the local council and its committees. This helps to facilitate communication between council officials and field level workers. As a result of these efforts, a recognisable human services network has developed in Huchting.

The development of this network was supported by a workshop, initiated by the directors of local kindergartens in 1991, on "Children in Huchting". A specific aim of this workshop was to analyse data on children and families in the area. It found that significant gaps existed in the provision of services, and that around 50 per cent of family problems required multi-faceted care. As a follow-up to the meeting, a planning group of local agency representatives was set up to consider all aspects of service provision in Huchting. This has helped to identify new services which are required, and to reduce existing competition between agencies offering similar services.

Several of Huchting's social services are housed under one roof at the Social Services Centre, a "one-stop shop". This arrangement has also assisted in improving inter-agency and inter-professional relations.

Unfortunately, due to national public funding cuts, social services networks like the one in Huchting are under threat. Indeed, the federal government has already asked Bremen to reduce current levels of social services provision.

EXAMPLES OF BEST PRACTICE IN INTEGRATED SERVICES FOR SCHOOL CHILDREN

The RAA, Leipzig

The RAA in Leipzig is a local branch of the national voluntary organisation, *Regionale Arbeitsstellen zur Förderung Ausländischer Kinder und Jugendlicher* (Regional Centre for Foreign Children and Youth). The main aim of this organisation is to help foreign youth to become integrated into German society, and to combat negative attitudes towards foreigners amongst German young people. Originally founded by the Freudenburg Foundation in 1980, the RAA now has 18 regional centres in west German, and 11 in east German, cities.

The city of Leipzig is populated by a total of 15 000 foreigners, of which only around 200 are children. Most of the adults are Eastern Europeans who came to study at the University of Leipzig, and never left the city. Although their numbers are small, they face a disproportionate amount of hostility which reportedly exceeds levels found in western Germany.

The RAA office in Leipzig opened in 1993, with funding from the Freudenburg Foundation, the municipal government, the Federal Conference of Ministries for Culture and Education, and the Saxony Ministry of Education. It functions in two different ways, either co-operating directly with other agencies, or acting as a catalyst to bring other organisations together to co-operate with each other as part of a network. It has, for example, collaborated with the city on a special project, called "Schools Without Violence", which addresses the problems faced by immigrants in several municipal middle schools. It has also helped fuse co-operative relationships between schools and free associations, as part of which the latter provide out-of-school leisure activities. While the RAA normally seeks out schools with immigrant children to encourage collaboration first, occasionally schools themselves take the initiative.

The potential to develop inter-agency collaboration in Leipzig is large, because of the recent change and innovation resulting from German unification. Human services are in the process of dramatic re-structuring and have yet to develop the rigidity and hierarchy associated with older organisations. However, at the professional level, competition and lack of understanding between school teachers and social workers (who are a relatively "new" professional group in eastern Germany) seem likely to emerge as important barriers to successful collaboration.

EXAMPLES OF BEST PRACTICE IN INTEGRATED SERVICES FOR YOUTH IN THE TRANSITION TO WORK

Youth services in Duisburg, Northrhine-Westphalia

Over the last decade the city of Duisburg has put vocational training for disadvantaged youth at the top of its list of priorities. Demographic change in the age structure of the population, economic recession, and the decline of the coal and steel industry (on which Duisburg's early prosperity was based), have widened the gap between the demand for vocational training and the supply of apprenticeship positions, leaving many young people unoccupied.

To combat the problem of youth unemployment, the city has created three special committees: the Youth Unemployment Committee, the Vocational Help

Group for Young People, and a Co-ordinating Committee (to integrate efforts, and to advise the Youth Unemployment Committee). They have attempted to build a network of services in Duisburg to meet the multi-faceted needs of its most disadvantaged and poorly qualified young people.

One of the principle agencies in the network is Duisburg's Youth Office. This is the city's umbrella organisation for all youth services, and has links with representatives from public, private and political bodies with whom it plans services. Two of its closest partners are the Employment Office and the Duisburg branch of the RAA (mentioned earlier). The Employment Office co-operates with many other stakeholders in the network through both formal and informal agreements. While its closest partner is the Youth Office, it also liaises extensively with free associations which run programmes to facilitate the transition to work. The RAA in Duisburg has extended its role beyond its normal one – namely addressing the problems of foreign youth – to deal with the city's youth unemployment. It plays a significant part in building bridges between educational, social and employment services. Its social educators and teachers are important providers of vocational counselling, and have found a special niche in dealing with youth at risk of dropping out of school early, and unemployed youth who have been out of school for several months. The RAA meets regularly with other stakeholders in the network for service planning and case management, and also to maintain a shared database. One of its closest partners is the Vocational Counselling Service, although at times their relationship is considered rather too close as their work can overlap.

Typical of the schools visited by the RAA's staff is the Berthold Brecht Vocational School in Duisburg. This school provides the kind of dual training, including vocational education and apprenticeship experience, for which Germany is famous. However, more unusually, it also provides full-time vocational education for those who cannot obtain an apprenticeship (an adaptation to the declining local economy), and a "general" or academic education for those who might wish to go to university. The school works closely with the Youth Office, the Youth Unemployment Committee and local companies. For disadvantaged young people who are unable to cope in a normal vocational institution, Duisburg also has a Vocational Training Centre. Youth attending the centre spend some of their time in a normal vocational school and in job placements, but also receive special training in social skills. In addition to vocational teachers, the centre also employs social educators who can address both the educational and social welfare needs of students, and are specially selected for their interpersonal and communication abilities. Key partners of the centre are local vocational schools, companies, and the Employment Office which makes every effort to find its students work.

Cohesion amongst the partners in Duisburg's youth services network has been promoted by the huge need for support amongst under-qualified young people, and by the sharing of a common goal – to ensure that all young people make a successful transition to work. The traditional reluctance of school teachers to co-operate with social welfare agencies has been overcome by employing other teachers to perform social work functions. However, competition between agencies with similar roles has at times weakened inter-agency relationships.

The outcomes of Duisburg's efforts to integrate its youth services are reflected in a comprehensive annual report on education and employment by the Statistics Office which tracks students destinations after leaving school. All agencies involved in the network co-operate in producing the Office's database. Statistics show that the number of children dropping out of school in Duisburg has declined. Duisburg has also proved itself successful in reducing youth unemployment.

CONCLUSION

Germany has succeeded in creating some rather sophisticated examples of human services networks. These networks have been facilitated by the development of co-ordinating organisations, by the setting up of co-ordinating committees, and by the appointment of special co-ordinators. In Leipzig, the RAA provides a good example of how a relatively small organisation can bring together, and harness the efforts of other agencies, to improve the conditions in multi-ethnic schools. Both Bremen and Duisburg have created powerful committees to co-ordinate the activities of a wide range of agencies. Bremen additionally has employed a local co-ordinator to develop important vertical and horizontal links between agencies and their administrations.

The networks in all three cities, feature partnerships between public agencies, and co-operation with private agencies. According to the German policy of subsidiarity, free associations are given priority over public bodies. The principle behind this is that responsibility for social welfare should rest with the smallest possible social unit, starting with the family and working upwards to the State. Therefore government agencies often are obliged to fund private organisations, and treat them as important partners.

In both Leipzig and Duisburg, the important "hybrid" role of Germany's social educators is exemplified. These professionals, armed with both pedagogic and social welfare skills, are highly effective in meeting the needs of students who have both educational and social difficulties. Not only are they helpful in addressing the problems of disadvantaged "clients", but they also are effective mediators, who are able to communicate well with both education and social welfare professionals.

As in other OECD countries, the negative attitudes of teachers towards social workers and other professionals, and unconstructive friction between competing agencies, are two significant barriers to German services integration. However, important efforts are being made to overcome these problems.

2

FINLAND
A "safety net" approach
to integrated services provision

by

Philippa Hurrell and Peter Evans

INTRODUCTION AND SUMMARY

Finland ranks amongst the top four OECD countries for spending on education, health and social security and welfare as a percentage of GDP (OECD, 1995b). This investment is reflected in a human services system which is of a high quality. Generous social security benefits mean that real poverty hardly exists, and human services form a dense, all-encompassing safety net through which few people fall. Educationally disadvantaged young people have, until recently, been protected from social marginalisation by laws requiring municipalities to provide all youth with further education or employment after compulsory schooling. However, this legislation has been suspended because of the severe recession in Finland – one that is also threatening the existence of many publicly funded services.

In this economic environment, services integration has been seen as a means to provide better services more cost-effectively. Initiatives emanating from central government have encouraged municipal services, and in particular social welfare and health bodies, to function in a more co-ordinated way. Collaboration has been facilitated by a long tradition of co-operation between public agencies, notably in schools, and is evolving gradually throughout the human services system. At the same time, important barriers to collaboration, such as over-strict confidentiality rules and inflexible funding slowly are being eroded by legislative changes.

CHILDREN AT RISK IN FINLAND

The Finnish government recently used the provision of psycho-social support as a criterion to determine the proportion of children at risk of school failure in the total population. Employing 1988 figures, it estimated that 5 per cent of children aged 0 to 17 years were at risk. This estimate is low compared to many other OECD countries (although the criteria they use tend to differ). One of the most significant risk factors for Finland's youth is alcohol abuse, with around 17 per cent of boys and 11 per cent of girls aged 16 consuming alcohol weekly. Also threatening to young people's successful participation in society is the substantial level of youth unemployment – as high as 25 per cent in 1994.

During the 1990s, the problems experienced by children and youth in Finland reportedly have become more numerous and complex than they were in the 1980s boom years.

POLICIES PROMOTING SERVICES INTEGRATION

Support for human services integration was a reaction to the proliferation of health and social services in the 1970s and 1980s, precipitated by the National Health Care Act of 1972 and the Social Welfare Act of 1984. The service system became increasingly complex and specialised, making it difficult to use, and ineffective as a provider of holistic care. In the last few years, several pieces of legislation have been passed which have impacted significantly on the ability of human services to function in a co-ordinated way.

- Since the 1970s and 1980s, the maintenance of consistency in health and social welfare policy has been a guiding principle. More recently, the 1992 Planning and State Subsidies for Welfare Act set out common rules for the planning and funding of health and social welfare services to strengthen this approach.

- In 1993, aiming to improve the accessibility of human services, Parliament passed an Integrated Customer Services Act which removed obstacles preventing public authorities from providing integrated services in joint, "front-line" offices.

- Implemented in early 1993, State Subsidy Reform has given municipalities greater flexibility in the way they can use central government funding. The State now provides the municipalities with a lump sum – based on total population, age structure and local tax revenues – which they can allocate to social and health services as they choose. While they are bound by legislation to provide basic services, money can be used flexibly to purchase services from various agencies according to different funding arrangements. This means that there is more potential to finance integrated service programmes.

- Although secrecy concerning client information is emphasised in Finnish social welfare and health policy, the last few years have seen an easing of legislation on confidentiality in order to facilitate discussion between professionals concerning shared clients.

- Following a successful piloting programme between 1989 and 1992, a policy of "Local Population Responsibility" (LPR) has been adopted state-wide. According to this principle a multi-professional team of social welfare and health professionals is given responsibility to serve a small geographically defined area of 2 000 to 4 000 people. The aim is to improve the co-ordination, functioning and accessibility of services to better meet the needs of service users. The National Research and Development Centre for Welfare and Health is assessing the outcome of LPR.

EXAMPLES OF BEST PRACTICE IN INTEGRATED SERVICES FOR PRE-SCHOOL CHILDREN

The Nenäinniemi Elementary School and Day Care Centre, Jyväskylä

Nenäinniemi is a new residential area with a socio-economically mixed population including a number of families with serious problems. The Nenäinniemi Elementary School and Day Centre provides day care services and primary school education to children between 1 and 8 years of age on one site. The standard pattern in Finland is to provide these services separately, although joint provision has frequently been debated at the national level.

Initial support for the development of the centre came from a group of key individuals in the Municipal Education and Social Services departments who succeeded in securing both the agreement and financing to set it up. Current funding for the centre comes from two different budgets: the School is supported by the Education Department and the Day Care Centre by the Social Services Department.

From the start, a key feature of the combined facility has been its effort to be accepted by, and integrated, into the local community. Even before building started, questionnaires were sent to local inhabitants to discover their expectations of the project and their willingness to participate in it on a voluntary basis. Staff make every effort to get to know parents and to involve them in the centre's activities, and locals are encouraged to use the facility for community meetings. Several other "community" services also operate out of the centre including home day care, medical and social welfare assistance, and meals-on-wheels.

While no formal evaluation of the services of the combined school and centre has been undertaken, the municipality judges the facility to be efficient and economic in providing several services in one building.

The Oulunkylä Home for Mothers and Children, Helsinki

This home was opened in 1990, and is part of a five-year experimental programme funded by the Federation of Homes and Centres for Mothers and Children, a voluntary organisation. It provides accommodation for up to six pregnant or new mothers who have problems with alcohol or other intoxicants. Additional funding comes from the Association of Slot Machine Charities, and the Municipal Social Welfare Department which "buys" its services on a client-by-client basis. Government funding of voluntary agencies is fairly common in Finland.

At the Oulunkylä Home for Mothers and Children collaboration with the client is given a high priority. The client's decision to accept treatment has to be voluntary, at which point they are asked to sign an "agreement" indicating their willingness to receive help. Clients are active partners in decision-making and are also required to sign a mutually agreed treatment plan which is evaluated every two months. Family and friends are regarded as an important part of the client's support system and are encouraged to visit the home and to attend its social events.

Intense collaboration efforts are made by staff when mothers are due to leave the home. Child care, housing and other services are liaised with as necessary to provide on-going support. The home itself, offers professional help for six months following a client's departure and continues to invite them to social functions for up to two years. Every effort is made to ensure that mothers and children receive adequate "post-treatment" care and guidance.

Around 30 per cent of mothers are successful in returning to a normal life-style once they have left the home. However, up to a quarter continue to have serious problems which may result in their child going into local authority care.

EXAMPLES OF BEST PRACTICE IN INTEGRATED SERVICES FOR SCHOOL CHILDREN

The Huhtasuo Social Welfare and Health Centre, Jyväskylä

The Huhtasuo Social Welfare and Health Centre illustrates Jyväskylä's approach to Local Population Responsibility, combining social welfare and health services at one neighbourhood site. The centre, set up in the late 1980s, serves around 9 365 people who live in a socio-economically disadvantaged area. It is located next door to the local comprehensive school, and also to a special school for children with cerebral palsy and motor disabilities. The facility is run by a combined Municipal Social Services and Health Board which was created as a result of the merging of the two separate administrations in 1993. Services provided by the centre include health counselling, medical care, home nursing, school health care, day care, social welfare support and home help.

Following the unification of Finland's social welfare and health administrations into one Ministry of Social Affairs and Health, the central government gave provincial and municipal governments the option to make parallel changes at the regional and local levels. In Jyväskylä, both levels of administration decided to arrange mergers. While the impetus for this change came from central government, it occurred largely as a result of a perceived need on the ground. Administrators and managers from the different services recognised that they were often serving the same clients, and that a united approach to care would be more efficient and cost-effective.

The Huhtasuo Social Welfare and Health Centre's professional staff are organised into four mixed teams, each of which serves a population of around 3 000 people in the Huhtasuo area. Co-operation with local schools is high. One of the centre's eight social workers participates in Student Welfare Groups (see also below) which meet every other week in Jyväskylä's schools. Similarly, one of its public health nurses is responsible for comprehensive pupils' health care. The centre also invites teachers to its general monthly meetings.

The centre's staff are very positive about the benefits of their professional teamwork. They believe that they are better able to provide co-ordinated care and to prevent crises, and that clients benefit from being able to access services at one location. They have also increased their understanding of the roles of other disciplines and, professionally, feel more satisfied.

The Mannerheim League for Child Welfare, Jyväskylä

The Mannerheim League for Child Welfare was founded in 1920 to safeguard the rights of children and to promote the interests of families. It initiated many of Finland's public human services, starting with voluntary provision and then advocating government "take-overs" to make services available nationwide. It is a powerful organisation with 63 000 members and 480 local organisations. Many of its initiatives have a preventive bias.

Representatives of the League in Jyväskylä provided three examples of programmes it runs which have strong collaborative components. The League's 21-year-old Peer Counselling Programme provides support for students throughout Finland. A total of 500 peer counsellors especially trained by the League aim to make classrooms safer and more comfortable, to address the problem of violence, to provide friendship and hospitality, and to offer voluntary help to staff. In Jyväskylä, teams of two to four peer counsellors can be found in each class in 90 per cent of its schools. The League's 20-year-old Home Help Programme serves to supplement municipal provision in this area. Day care is provided to families in need by a team of around 80 volunteers (some unemployed) for a small hourly fee. The programme accepts people's requests for help without question, and is even willing to provide day care for couples who want a few hours away from their children to relax. Established in 1980, the League's Telephone Counselling Service provides help and guidance to individuals in crisis situations in eleven out of Finland's twelve provinces. Anyone can dial the service's national number for the price of a local call. Callers are encouraged to seek help from local welfare agencies, and are provided with relevant information concerning them.

EXAMPLES OF BEST PRACTICE IN INTEGRATED SERVICES FOR YOUTH IN THE TRANSITION TO WORK

Hämeenlinna Vocational Institute, Hämeenlinna

The Hämeenlinna Vocational Institute is owned and maintained by a consortium of eleven municipalities who supply two-thirds of its funding; the last third comes from the State. It provides vocational education for youth aged 16 to 19 years and an increasing amount of adult education. As one of the biggest institutions of its kind in Finland, it offers almost 30 vocational courses to 1 085 students from around 100 municipalities.

The institute provides a range of special services for its pupils, with two social workers, two special teachers, a doctor (part-time) and a public health nurse (full-time) on its staff. It also has three "student" counsellors who play an instrumental role in advising students on further studies and careers, and providing a link with employment agencies and the business community. These professional groups co-operate in the Institute's Student Welfare Group, which is also attended by the two vice principals. The group meets on a regular basis to discuss general problems such as violence, unsociable behaviour and drug abuse, and also to address crisis situations involving individual students.

Collaborative efforts for students at risk are particularly strong during the transitional phases from lower secondary school to the institute, and from the institute to employment. Specifically, the institute offers a one year preparatory course for students with learning difficulties and under-achievers which gives them an introduction to vocational education in a non-pressurised environment. Lower secondary school and vocational teachers, as well as student counsellors and employers, collaborate to place students on this course and to give them the opportunity to experience the world of work. Once students have completed their vocational education, a successful transition into employment is facilitated by the institute's student counsellors and outside vocational inspectors. The latter negotiate apprenticeship programmes with employers, give students vocational advice, and interview them for apprenticeship positions on-site.

Links are maintained with employers through the institute's work placement scheme. In addition, businesses are represented on Vocational Advisory Committees, and often offer small gifts to students who have successfully completed courses. However, in general business involvement is not particularly strong.

The role of the local Employment Office's vocational counsellors in the school-to-work transition has lessened since student counsellors have been employed.

Nonetheless, they often play an important part in helping students who are in the process of dropping out of school, or who have definitively left. Educationally disadvantaged young people are directed by them to the Employment Office's special unit for unskilled youth, or to its specialist psychologist for youth with special educational needs.

In terms of "results", there has been a decline in the rate of drop-out from 15 per cent in 1989-90 to 6.7 per cent in 1992-93. However, it is still a significant problem amongst students "at risk": in 1992-93, 35.1 per cent failed to complete their courses. News of students' employment status is gathered by the institute through a questionnaire sent out six months after they have left. Many male students go straight into the Army to complete their National Service and therefore are not available for work. In 1993, of those students who were available, only 30 per cent managed to find employment – a lower percentage than usual.

CONCLUSION

At the national level, services integration is most obviously enshrined in Local Population Responsibility, involving co-operation between health and social welfare workers, and in educational establishments which are the hub of multi-disciplinary activities to support children at risk. School professionals have been particularly effective in facilitating the transition to work of their students, although national economic difficulties have made this process harder. Increased links with local businesses may be one of the best means to improve students' employment opportunities.

While most nationwide services are public, and Finland's voluntary sector is relatively small compared to other OECD countries, a small number of powerful private agencies exist. The Mannerheim League, in particular, has played a signifi-cant role in initiating new kinds of services which it later proposes for government take-overs. In this way successful private services have been made public (although it should be emphasised that the more general trend is now government privatisa-tion). Like other voluntary institutions, the league has a symbiotic and harmonious relationship with government services, supplementing comprehensive public provision.

One-off projects such as the Nenäinniemi Elementary School and Day Care Centre and the Oulunkylä Home for Mothers and Children have exemplary charac-teristics from which other services can learn. In Nenäinniemi, the full involvement of the local community in the planning and day-to-day functioning of the centre is a feature apparently rare in other human services in Finland. In the Home for Mothers and Children, the most striking characteristic is its policy to include clients in all decision-making processes. This approach seems to be slightly more common although it is by no means standard practice.

Rigorous evaluation of individual human services programmes is not heavily emphasised in Finland, Local Population Responsibility being a notable exception. However, taken as a whole the human services system clearly functions rather well: international studies by the OECD have shown that Finland has one of the lowest infant mortality rates in the world and exceptionally high levels of educational achievement and participation.

3

PORTUGAL
Integrating services in the context
of socio-economic change

by

Philippa Hurrell and Peter Evans

INTRODUCTION AND SUMMARY

Although catching up fast through rapid socio-economic change, Portugal remains one of western Europe's poorest countries. Its population is also relatively uneducated: around one million people over the age of ten are illiterate, and many young teenagers of school age work in exploitative, low paid jobs. Now, the Portuguese government ensures that all children receive a basic education, and is working to up-grade social support structures.

Several of Portugal's most exemplary integrated services are funded by the European Union. This support makes it possible to develop sophisticated programmes which are superior to other locally funded projects, and are equally impressive by international standards. Many human services programmes are underpinned by public-private sector partnership, and the government is keen to hand more management control of social services to Portugal's Private Social Solidarity Institutions. Partnership with business appears to be less common, although, where it does exist, it can be done rather well. Evaluation of integrated programmes is not uncommon, but is not as comprehensive, perhaps, as in North America.

Rigidity and red-tape are two important problems experienced by human services agencies in their "vertical" relations with ministries. On the other hand, schools often seem to lack the motivation and ability to collaborate "horizontally" with other agencies.

CHILDREN AT RISK IN PORTUGAL

With the third lowest gross domestic product amongst OECD countries (OECD, 1995b), poverty is still a major problem in Portugal. Indeed, around 30 per cent of the population was recently classified as "poor" (Vasconcelos, 1993). The economic difficulties facing many families, combined with insufficient social support, has impacted significantly on the well being of many of Portugal's children. In addition, rapid social change has weakened traditional family structures, leading to an increase in the rate of divorce and separation (of 139 per cent between 1981 and 1991) and a rise in the number of single parent families.

A significant number of children in Portugal's cities are left out on the streets while their parents are out at work, and many "street children" are homeless. Other children, often from immigrant families, live in makeshift settlements called "barracas". Lack of proper sanitation, poor shelter and criminal activity, including drug dealing, make these settlements unsafe for habitation and make it difficult for "barracas" children to attend school.

POLICIES PROMOTING SERVICES INTEGRATION

Efforts to promote the integration of human services in Portugal have been based on a combination of inter-ministerial co-ordination, and co-operation with the private sector. The Portuguese Ministries of Education, and Employment and Social Security, for example, have joined forces to provide a network of pre-school educational institutions and child welfare centres for young children. The Ministry of Employment and Social Security has also developed a collaborative arrangement with Private Institutions of Social Solidarity (IPSS) in which they have been given responsibility for the management of some child welfare centres.

While there are many small-scale programmes to integrate services in Portugal, the biggest impact has been achieved by just four: the Interministerial Programme for the Promotion of Educational Success (PIPSE); the Education Programme for All (PEPT 2000); Projecto Vida; and the European Poverty Programme.

Launched in December 1987, the main goal of the PIPSE Programme was to reduce academic failure amongst Portuguese students by targeting public resources on the first four years (or primary cycle) of education. Using a multi-sectoral approach, several state ministries – including Education, Planning and Territorial Administration, Agriculture, Fisheries and Food, Health, Employment and Social Security – grouped together to plan the programme. This collaboration was co-ordinated by the Ministry of Education. Together they identified ten broad areas for action:

- nutrition;
- health care provision, including prevention and diagnosis;
- pre-school education;
- special education;
- support to families;
- leisure activities and sport;

- transport provision;

- supply of school materials;

- psychological and pedagogical support; and

- professional and initial training.

Following several years of implementation, the programme officially terminated in 1991-92. While initial evaluations were promising (OECD, 1995a), the final evaluation is still awaited. It was originally envisaged that lessons learned from the collaboration would be transferred to all departments of the participating ministries at the regional and local levels. It is not yet clear to what extent this aim has been realised.

PIPSE has now been superseded by PEPT 2000 which was launched in 1991 and will continue into the year 2000. Its purpose is to ensure that all children receive nine years of compulsory schooling and also have access to another three years of post-compulsory education if they want it. By encouraging organisational, curricular and pedagogical reforms in schools, the government hopes that PEPT will help reduce school failure and drop-out, so that all children are able to receive a basic education. While the programme is largely school based, the development of links with the local community is also considered important, and it is in this area that co-operation is particularly strong.

The government's Projecto Vida involves the Ministries of Health, Education, Employment and Social Security and Internal Administration, who have worked together in an attempt to combat alcohol and drug abuse. As part of a joint initiative, they are awarding special funding grants and equipment to voluntary organisations to set up prevention programmes, day centres and hostels for addicts.

The European Poverty Programme, on the other hand, has provided European Union financing for small scale, multi-disciplinary projects. In Lisbon, for example, money has been used to set up an agency, staffed by social workers, educators and other professionals, for the city's street children (see below).

EXAMPLES OF BEST PRACTICE IN INTEGRATED SERVICES FOR PRE-SCHOOL CHILDREN

Anti-poverty Trap Project 3, Porto

This project was set up to foster urban renewal, and social, cultural and educational development, in two of the poorest areas of Porto – Sé and São Nicolau – both of which are in the old part of the city. It is one of eleven Anti-poverty Trap programmes in the Porto District, and is part of a nationwide scheme to combat poverty.

A recent study of the quality of housing in Sé and Sãn Nicolau by the Centre for Community Information and Assistance revealed that around two-thirds of families were living in seriously dilapidated housing, and that approximately 60 per cent lacked a bathroom. In addition, it was discovered that around 50 per cent of young people left school without completing compulsory schooling, and nearly 25 per cent started working at the age of 14 or below. Overcrowding, family break up, violence, poverty, prostitution and drug addiction are all part of the context in which these families live.

The Anti-poverty Trap Project is managed by the Foundation for the Development of Old Porto. Sitting on the management committee, are representatives of the Regional Social Security Centre, the local council, and several charitable organisations. Of the total budget, 55 per cent come from the European Social Fund and the other 45 per cent mainly from central and local institutions. Pre-school activities are focused around a centre in Sãn Nicolau which provides day care for children aged between three months and six years, and also provides some services for school aged children and the elderly. The centre's efforts are directed mainly towards education and social welfare issues. In general, however, the project is concerned to meet all of the client's needs – including housing and employment – and to pool the resources of participating organisations to achieve this aim.

An evaluation of the project in 1993 reported that its benefits could be seen in improved housing, the development of family self help and management skills, higher incomes, client acquisition of technical, vocational and social skills, and improvements in self-image. Community involvement in the project has also led to a new dynamism in the area. However, the reluctance of educational establishments to develop links with the project has been a disappointment.

In 1994, all Anti-poverty Trap Projects, including this one, were due to be handed over to Private Social Solidarity Institutions for management, thus accomplishing their privatisation.

EXAMPLES OF BEST PRACTICE IN INTEGRATED SERVICES FOR SCHOOL CHILDREN

The Street Children Project, Lisbon

This project is run by the Institute for the Support of Children, a Private Social Solidarity Institution set up in 1983 to support children through co-ordinated, community activities. The institute started the Street Children Project in 1989 as part of a programme to fight poverty in Lisbon. It also enjoys the status of being a pilot project for the European Union's Third Poverty Programme.

The project's main backing at the national level comes from the Ministries of Employment and Social Security, and Education. The former has provided the project's central headquarters which acts both as a reception and emergency centre. The latter, on the other hand, has seconded teaching staff to work "on the streets" within the structure of the TEJO club, a street school which aims to facilitate children's social and educational integration. The institute also has arranged special agreements with several ministries (including Employment and Social Security, Education, Health, Justice and Youth), enterprises (such as the local zoo) and local authorities (specifically, the Townhall of Lisbon, the Prefecture and the *Junta de Freguesia*). As a consequence, it is well connected with strategic level bodies and has enhanced political strength.

In addition to its teaching staff, the project also employs several social workers and part-time health professionals. Their responsibility is to seek out and help young street children, who have been abandoned or have run away from home, and to re-integrate them back into their families or community homes. An additional goal, is to assist them in returning to school, or if they are older, in finding a suitable job. The project's social workers and teachers meet daily to plan activities and twice yearly to evaluate their progress. They also invite representatives from other institutions to these meetings, including the courts, Misericordia (another Private Social Solidarity Organisation) and Casa Pia (a local institution providing schooling to children at risk, described below). The project's health workers inform children of the health services which are available to them, and how to use them. Unfortunately, some local hospitals refuse to accept children who are not in their catchment area. Another problem faced by all staff has been the rigid hierarchy and red-tape linked with the Ministries of Education and Health. Schools have also been found to be difficult partners, particularly in their unwillingness to try new methods to address children's problems.

The project has been evaluated by both internal and external agencies who have focused on both process and outcomes. Findings have pointed to the need to develop further partnerships with enterprises and to improve co-operative working arrangements. In addition, they have shown that the number of street children in Lisbon has been reduced.

EXAMPLES OF BEST PRACTICE IN INTEGRATED SERVICES FOR YOUTH IN THE TRANSITION TO WORK

Pina Manique School, Lisbon

Pina Manique is a semi-independent school which provides a high quality vocational education for children aged 9 to 18 years. It is one of a group of seven institutions, for children at risk of all ages, collectively called Casa Pia de Lisboa. Funding for Casa Pia is mixed. Three-quarters come from the Ministry of Employment and Social Security, and most of the rest from its own patrimonial resources (derived from the renting of land and property, and commercial interests). Some funding also comes from the European Union which is, for example, supporting an extensive building renovation programme at Pina Manique. Pina Manique is in many ways a "model" institution, and is not representative of the Portuguese education system as a whole. It is housed in impressive and beautiful old buildings, and boasts the latest mechanical equipment and information technology.

As laid down in national policy, the school co-operates with many government services including the courts, social services and health services. It also has its own welfare staff, including three social workers and three psychologists. By Portuguese, and even international standards, this quota, for a student population of 1 400, is large. These professionals work closely with each other, liaise with staff from other Casa Pia institutions, and have some links with outside agencies, including state social services and the Mental Health Centre in the local hospital. However, the most striking feature of Pina Manique is the relationship it enjoys with the employment and business sector in Lisbon.

Through Casa Pia, it enjoys co-operative relationships, set out in formal agreements, with the Ford Car Company, the Swiss Watch Makers Federation, Le Grand (a French electrical company), Graphic Arts, the Portuguese-German Chamber of Commerce and the Institute of Employment and Vocational Training. The school's agreement with Ford is typical, signed by the Director of Casa Pia and the Director of Ford following an approach made by the car maker. As part of the agreement, Ford provides technical input to the school and contributes to courses. Along with the Ministry of Education, the Institute of Employment and Vocational Training, the unions and representatives from Casa Pia, local businesses are also involved in examining courses, although company demands for payment for this work has made co-operation in this area problematic. Additional input into the school comes from the Portuguese-German Chamber of Commerce which organises an administration course there.

The school's links with business have resulted in improved job opportunities for all its students. Pupils following administration, commerce and mechanics courses regularly work for companies with whom the school has agreements during the summer holidays. Once they have graduated from school these companies often offer them full-time jobs. While firms may approach the school when they are looking to fill a position, the relationship is two-way, and school co-ordinators (senior teachers) frequently approach them. Indeed, this is one of their stated responsibilities.

Co-ordinators' approaches to establishing relationships with companies differ. One of the most enterprising members of staff is an administration teacher who developed school-business links through writing to companies listed in the telephone directory, and maintains them through contacting firms to secure her pupils summer placements. She also helps students to secure permanent jobs if they ask for her assistance. Her efforts are rewarded by an annual employment rate of close to 100 per cent amongst graduating students. However, she and others involved in the school believe that companies themselves should play a more active role in initiating school-business relationships.

Several of the companies which presently co-operate with the school have "old boys" (or girls) on their staff, and are knowledgeable of the superior vocational preparation provided by Pina Manique. The wealth of teaching resources at the school's disposal gives it an important competitive edge over other local schools which are less well funded.

CONCLUSION

Reflecting Portugal's position as a net recipient of European Union funds, many of its best examples of integrated services are supported by European money. The Anti-poverty Trap Project, the Street Children Project and Pina Manique School all benefit from international support to a greater or lesser extent. Targeted at some of the poorest and most disadvantaged children in Portugal, European funding is playing an important role in reducing national and international inequalities. It is also being used to support "integrated" programmes. The Anti-poverty Trap Project is perhaps one of its strongest examples of inter-disciplinary collaboration, addressing in one attempt the issues of education, social welfare, housing and employment.

Like many other OECD countries, the Portuguese government provides a significant amount of support to voluntary initiatives, and in some areas is pushing towards the privatisation of public sector agencies. Public-private sector partnership is common. The Foundation for the Development of Old Porto, which runs the Anti-poverty Trap Project, is made up both of government agencies and charitable organisations. The Street Children Project, while being run by a private sector institution, also has backing from two of the government's key ministries, and special agreements with several others. Likewise, Pina Manique School, while having its own private resources and independent history, receives significant funding from the Ministry of Employment and Social Security.

Pina Manique provides a fairly glowing example of what schools can do to build links with local business. Specified in co-ordinators' job contracts, liaison with companies is formally one of their responsibilities. What is more, they often (voluntarily) go to great efforts to secure their students work, both by writing to and telephoning prospective employers. School links with local businesses are also solidified in special agreements which ensure an on-going and two-way relationship. The school benefits from technical support and donations of equipment; businesses benefit from the opportunity to recruit students with high quality and specialised skills. However, companies reportedly have been rather slow to adopt an active role in developing school-business relationships themselves.

MISSOURI, UNITED STATES
Integrating services through public-private sector partnership

Philippa Hurrell and Peter Evans

INTRODUCTION AND SUMMARY

Missouri's social problems, including teenage pregnancy, gang violence and poverty amongst full-time workers, are typical of those in America as a whole. The emphasis on economic solutions to social problems in the United States is reflected in the non-uniform nature of public social welfare and health provision (leaving many people without access to basic services). Widespread belief in self-sufficiency and limited government in any case makes many public agencies unpopular.

One of the most common types of "integration" seen in Missouri is combined public and private sector funding and support for individual projects. Pooling financial resources offers a means through which different organisations with limited budgets can develop good quality, holistic services. On occasions, over-specific and inflexible funding rules have made this practice difficult. However, key public and private figures in Missouri often have been prepared to cut red-tape and bend rules to provide communities with the services they need.

CHILDREN AT RISK IN MISSOURI

The Partnership for Children's Annual Report Card on the status of children in Kansas City, one of Missouri's largest agglomerations, gave it a D+ (for "seriously deficient") in 1994. Compared to the national average Kansas City was rated as "worse" in several areas including violent crime, child abuse and neglect, number of teenage births, and alcohol and drug use. Gang violence is a major problem in several of Missouri's large towns. Indeed, "urban warfare" is probably not too strong a term to describe the territorial disputes and drive-by shootings common in many disadvantaged neighbourhoods. A significant proportion of the population, many of them Afro-American, are either without jobs, or in jobs which do not pay an

135

adequate wage. They are Missouri's "working poor". Many who live in these neighbourhoods are without jobs or in jobs that do not pay a "liveable wage". Self-sufficiency plays a significant role in a child's success and safety, whether a family lives in an urban or rural setting.

ADMINISTRATIVE STRUCTURES AND POLICIES PROMOTING SERVICES INTEGRATION

Several state and municipal level structures have been developed in Missouri to push through, and implement, policies which support services integration. In general, these structures must include representatives from the public, private and community sections.

At the forefront of Missouri's efforts to promote services integration is the Family Investment Trust which is the main conduit for Human Service. Created in 1993, by Governor Carnahan, the Trust is a partnership of private sector leaders and Cabinet level directors of the Education, Health, Mental Health and Social Services departments, and Labour/Industrial Relations. One of its central goals is to replace "fragmented bureaucratic systems" and "red-tape" with collaboration between public and private agencies, flexible funding, and local design. In connection with federal Family Preservation and Family Support legislation, it is also looking at ways to increase collaboration between maternal, child and mental health services to prevent family break up.

At the municipal level, the most dynamic agency for human services reform is Kansas City's Local Investment Commission (LINC). Created by the Department of Social Services, LINC is made up of an impressive array of local representatives: business and civic leaders, social service professionals, service participants and private citizens. One of LINC's stated goals is to develop integrated and locally governed services which achieve "measurable results" and successful outcomes. To this end, it brings together community partners to establish common goals, jointly plan and implement services, pool financial resources, and arrange evaluation. Charismatic, bold and sometimes rule-bending leadership from two individuals, the Director of Social Services and a powerful local businessman, has made LINC a formidable agent of change in Kansas City.

The Commission oversees two job-related programmes which focus heavily on services integration. The 21st Century Communities initiative, which is being piloted for the first time in Kansas City, emphasises a comprehensive approach to the development of low income, urban communities. Government, private and local community organisations are working together in the areas of job creation, wage supplementation and work skills development, learning readiness of children, and family and neighbourhood support. By addressing the economic, education and social concerns of disadvantaged communities concurrently (and over an extensive period of time), it is hoped that real change will be achieved in the lives of local families. Missouri's FUTURES initiative draws its funding from the Job Opportunities and Basic Skills Programme (JOBS) and State General Revenues. FUTURES provides education and job training exclusively to adults who are receiving Aid to Families with Dependent Children (AFDC). Once again, the initiative draws on the resources of a mind-boggling array of public and private services to provide for its clients. These include social welfare, education, mental health, employment and economic development services of various kinds. Both programmes have strong evaluation components which reflect Missouri's (valid) preoccupation with getting measurable results and successful outcomes.

EXAMPLES OF BEST PRACTICE IN INTEGRATED SERVICES FOR PRE-SCHOOL CHILDREN

New Start, Kansas City

New Start was developed by the KCMC (Karing for Children is our Main Concern) Child Development Corporation which is the grantee of the (federal) Head Start programme in Kansas City. In contrast to normal Head Start programmes which provide half-day services, New Start offers all-day, year-round child care. In partnership with other agencies, such as FUTURES and the Full Employment Council, it also provides educational and employment services for parents. Low income families who are working, in education, or in a job training programme, are eligible for this programme. Its main aim is to help families to achieve self-sufficiency through adequate employment. Initial funding for New Start came from a variety of federal, state and private sources. On-going financial support is provided by Head Start and the Department of Social Services, with parent co-payments.

One of the organisations providing New Start services is the Goppert Child Development Centre in Kansas City. The centre provides high quality child care and education to up to 100 children between the hours of 6.30am and 6pm (maximum of ten hours per child). Breakfast, lunch and afternoon snacks are provided to all children free of charge, and extensive health, dental and mental health services are also available. Parents are encouraged to be involved in the programme's educational activities – including visits to museums, theatres and zoos – as much as possible. They are also invited to provide input into programme planning through monthly parents' meetings. A family advocate, with a social work background, is available to help families with practical problems and, where necessary, to direct them to appropriate services. The advocate also has a small budget to buy minor items which can improve families situations; for example, an alarm clock so that a parent can get to work on time, or some laundry soap so that a mother can wash her child's school clothes.

While child care and education are being provided on the ground floor of the centre, on the first floor parent education is on offer. This is organised by the federal/state funded FUTURES programme. Most parents work through self-study – guided by an adult education teacher – towards their GED (General Education Development certificate, the equivalent of a high school diploma). Parents who study for more than 20 hours a week are entitled to a $25 a week incentive payment. On average 15 or 16 parents attend the programme each day, or whom around 9 or 10 have children attending New Start. Many of these parents provide occasional help to the staff who are caring for their children downstairs.

FUTURES also collaborates with the Full Employment Council to provide parents with relevant job training and employment counselling. In addition, each parent is provided with a FUTURES advocate (also with a social work background) who meets with them weekly to discuss problems, to provide advice and to help them in transition to full self-sufficiency.

The centre is required to meet or exceed a child attendance rate of 85 per cent. In fact, attendance has been very good and the programme is popular with parents. An evaluation of the first three years of the New Start programme, completed in 1993, found "compelling evidence of New Start's impact as a provider of high quality, developmentally appropriate child care designed to prepare children for school while offering comprehensive services to support families". The evaluation discovered that, because of the full-time day care provided by the programme, parents experienced increased job productivity, could work longer hours, and took home higher incomes.

EXAMPLES OF BEST PRACTICE IN INTEGRATED SERVICES FOR SCHOOL CHILDREN

William Herron Health Centre, Southeast Health Professions Magnet High School, Kansas City

One of LINC's first service delivery initiatives was to create health clinics in schools in the Kansas City area, the aim being to address the high rate of preventable health conditions amongst Kansas City's children. At present, four clinics are functioning, one of which is located at Southeast High School.

Southeast High School is a health professions magnet school situated in a low income area of Kansas City. It rather resembles a prison with only one unlocked entrance at which a metal detector operates. Many of the children come from ethnic minority, low income or single parent families (with no medical insurance). The rate of teenage pregnancy is high. The social problems of pupils have put increasing pressure on the school's teachers who are close to breaking point. They appreciate that pupils' social and health problems need to be addressed before they can learn properly.

The clinic's original funding has been exhausted. Therefore LINC has developed a new funding partnership, with the Missouri Department of Social Services, the Kansas City School District, and foundations to keep the clinic operational and to prevent it from closing. The Swope Parkway Health Centre has been operating the clinic as a "satellite" facility – and is negotiating with the committee for reimbursement.

The health clinic delivers services through a multi-disciplinary team including a nurse, medical assistant, social worker and intake worker. The assistance of other health workers is available through co-operation with the Swope Parkway Health Centre (although the latter is unhappy about providing services for the many children "bussed" in from other districts to attend the school as part of a school desegregation plan). The main services provided by the clinic are health assessments, laboratory screenings, medical treatment, and counselling in several areas including nutrition, sexuality, pregnancy and drug abuse.

To become a member of the clinic, pupils' parents are required to complete a special consent form which States that they are agreeable to their child receiving health care on the school premises, and to pay a $5 fee. Some parents are unwilling to sign these forms because of a deep-seated distrust of government intervention which they feel impinges on their right to freedom. Others feel that the health clinic will distract their children from attending school classes.

About 70 per cent of pupils have become members of the health clinic. The school's Head reported that the clinic had led to lower rates of absenteeism because pupils can be treated for ailments at school. He also reported lower suicide rates. However, pregnancy rates have remained similar.

Caring Communities, Walbridge, St. Louis

The Caring Communities programme in Walbridge is a locally organised initiative tailored to meet the very serious needs of the Walbridge area. The physical environment in Walbridge clearly reflects the magnitude of its social problems: sophisticated graffiti marks out gang territory; ex-crack houses have been boarded up by the police; and an unusually quiet street is the location of frequent homicides. Set up in 1989, Caring Communities' community-centred approach was considered visionary – indicative of a new state willingness to delegate responsibility. A local Afro-American man, of particular charisma, vision and intelligence, was chosen to develop and implement the programme. Funding for the initiative is provided by the Danforth Foundation (the catalyst organisation) and various government agencies, including the state departments of Mental Health, Education, Health and Social Services, and St. Louis School District.

Caring Communities provides a range of school-linked and school-based programmes aimed at meeting the social and health needs of the neighbourhood creating a real sense of community empowerment. These services include after-school tutoring, latchkey programme, pre-employment counselling and job placement, a teen drop-in centre and a "respite night" programme (whereby children can spend up to four nights per year at school to give their parents a break). Remedial services include an anti-drug and anti-gang task force, a case management programme, a Families First (family preservation) programme, day-time treatment services, and drug and alcohol counselling. Collaboration amongst the programme's professionals is nurtured by special training in co-operative techniques and Team Treatment Meetings. Efforts are also made to build links with other agencies. Caring Communities works primarily with the Walbridge Elementary School (in which it has offices), but also receives referrals from the Division of Family Services and the juvenile courts. Community involvement and respect are heavily emphasised: local residents are represented on an Advisory Board; services are provided on "their turf" if they so wish; and a sense of empowerment is nurtured through various activities such as organised drug marches against local gangs.

Preliminary evaluation results for the Walbridge programme show large and consistent improvements in the academic performance of children receiving Families First and case management services. Because of the success of this concept the governor recommended $21 million in funding and expanding to 64 more sites across the State.

EXAMPLES OF BEST PRACTICE IN INTEGRATED SERVICES FOR YOUTH IN THE TRANSITION TO WORK

The St. Charles Employment Office, Greater St. Louis area

The St. Charles Employment Office is situated in one of 15 service delivery districts which receive Job Training Partnership Act (JTPA) funding from the federal Department of Labour. The use of JTPA funding has been strongly influenced by the Missouri Governor's Co-ordination and Special Services Plan which, amongst other things, sets the goal "to assure co-ordination of Missouri's employment and training activities through public/private partnerships so that services are provided in an efficient and cost-effective manner".

At the St. Charles Employment Office, this aim is facilitated by the co-location of JTPA staff, and representatives of the Division of Family Services, FUTURES, the Division of Employment Security, Adult Basic Education, and the St. Charles County Community College. Hence the Office functions as a "one-stop-shop" through which residents can access the services of several, co-ordinated agencies in one trip. Co-location of employment services is not standard in Missouri, and was only realised at St. Charles through strong lobbying by the Office's Director. The governor has recommended expansion of the one-stop-shop concept across the State.

Day-to-day co-operation between the agencies located in the Employment Office is at a high level. JTPA and FUTURES case management is co-ordinated to decide who should take the leading role in client support, and to arrange non-duplicative backup by the other agency. If one agency has insufficient resources to meet a client's needs – such as child care or transportation – they refer them to the other. Current efforts to develop a joint intake form will facilitate this process. Administrative resources and information are shared by all co-located agencies, and they are jointly utilising an automated data system between the Division of Employment Security and the Department of Social Services.

The Employment Office tracks participants, monitors outcomes, and sets yearly goals. Quantitative data shows that over 60 per cent of participants who complete the JTPA programme find jobs. In a qualitative sense, staff reported that "we can do more together than we could alone", that "co-operation allows us to reach more people", and that "we can stretch the dollar, and our resources, because we can tap into what everybody has".

CONCLUSION

At the administrative level, LINC is one of the most dynamic and impressive engines of human services reform in Missouri. With strong, charismatic leadership, and varied support from public and private agencies, local businesses and the community, it has succeeded in fusing public-private sector alliances of many kinds in the Kansas City area.

Public-private sector partnership is, indeed, found throughout the State of Missouri and is particularly common in funding arrangements. Both the William Herron Health Centre and Caring Communities, for example, get significant financial support from private foundations and the state partnerships also exist between public agencies where they have a shared goal – as seen in the St. Charles Employment Centre where employment, education and social welfare services have joined caring communities forces to help the unemployed. Another form of partnership which is emphasised in Missouri is that with local communities. The Caring Communities programme exemplifies very well how local people can be involved in designing and implementing projects which are intended to address their own needs.

Special human services programmes in Missouri are frequently very intensive and provide high quality services, the New Start programme being a case in point. However, while one neighbourhood may benefit from these services, those around it may receive very little support. In other words, some of Missouri's human services are delivered in a patchwork pattern with "well-served" and "poorly-served" areas. "Well-served" areas often benefit from services which are admired internationally, and are frequently copied. On the other hand, some would be considered "standard" by other nations. The William Herron (school-based) Health Centre, for example, is seen as an important innovation in Missouri whereas in other OECD countries school health care is well established.

Evaluation of new programmes in Missouri is the norm and, indeed, it is difficult to get funding for a project without incorporating an assessment component. While many "integrated" programmes report positive results, it is not always clear what contribution has been made by co-ordinated work practices. However, anecdotal evidence suggests that integration can improve outcomes.

5

NEW YORK CITY, UNITED STATES
Co-ordinating services in a multi-ethnic metropolis

by

Philippa Hurrell and Peter Evans

INTRODUCTION AND SUMMARY

The fact that there has been widespread middle class "flight" from New York's public schools is indicative of the serious problems facing its education system. As many as one third of the city's children now attend private institutions, and there is little evidence of a reversal in this trend.

Broadly speaking, municipal schools' main priority is to provide basic education services to their students. However, against a backdrop of poverty, crime and violence, children in many schools are unable to reach their full potential without additional support. Many private agencies have recognised this "gap" in provision and are attempting to fill it through social welfare and health programmes. At the same time they are developing selected schools as "hubs" of local community life. Both private agencies and schools appreciate the mutual financial and practical benefits of their relationship. However, the mixture of professionals from different sectors and disciplines in schools has at times created tensions.

CHILDREN AT RISK IN NEW YORK CITY

Attracted by its cosmopolitan atmosphere, family ties and perceived economic opportunities, New York City is the chosen destination of many recent immigrants and refugees. This has led to an ethnically diverse school population with over 50 languages being spoken in urban classrooms. More than half of the children in New York City live in poverty, and many reside in neighbourhoods where ethnic tensions and other social problems – including drug use, serious crime and violence – are rife. These conditions impact significantly on children's performance in school and hence on their ability to break free from their disadvantaged roots.

MUNICIPAL LEVEL POLICIES PROMOTING SERVICES INTEGRATION AND PRE-SCHOOL EXAMPLES

Perhaps significantly, responsibility for the organisation of the OECD visit to New York City was given to the private sector. As a result, little was learnt about public sector efforts to integrate services. Integrated services for pre-school children were not included in the itinerary of the visit.

EXAMPLES OF BEST PRACTICE IN INTEGRATED SERVICES FOR SCHOOL CHILDREN

Community School IS 218

IS 218 is located in Washington Heights, an extremely deprived area in North Manhattan. The community has the highest poverty rate in New York City, with around 40 per cent of families on incomes below $10 000 a year. Washington Heights-Inwood police precinct has the highest levels of drug addiction and crime, including murder, of all police precincts in the city. Around 86 per cent of students in School District 6 are Latino, many of whom are recent immigrants with poor English proficiency.

The Children's Aid Society (CAS) of New York City has a long history of providing community centres in deprived neighbourhoods, and identified Washington Heights as an area which could benefit from its support. To this end, the CAS forged a partnership with the Board of Education and the Board of School District 6 to develop their community schools in the locality. They decided that these schools would provide a full range of educational, recreational, medical and mental health services for children and adults, and would open 15 hours a day, six days a week, all the year round. The cost is borne by CAS but there is hope that government will eventually support the efforts.

As soon as the building of IS 218 began, the CAS became active in the Washington Heights Community, communicating to community groups the nature and purposes of the new project, and providing an initial range of small-scale social services. This helped it to win local support and to gain people's trust. IS 218 eventually opened in 1992.

CAS staff presently work out of their own offices in the school and have engaged regular teachers at the school, parents in the neighbourhood, and other professionals to provide extra-curricular programmes. Current activities and facilities include:

- An Extended Day Programme for school children which operates from 7am to 9am and 3pm to 6pm. This offers many courses, some of which are extensions of school activities (for example, basic English, maths, computer games, sports and music). The CAS also offers business courses and has provided some students with "seed money" to start up their own companies. Around half of the school's 1 200 students are enrolled in this programme.

- A Saturday Programme for school children which is open to all children in the local community and organises various activities (gym and computer classes, day trips, etc.) from 10am to 3pm throughout the school year.

- A Teen Programme for 14- to 18-year-olds which provides activities, such as sports, arts and crafts, and workshops (on AIDs, violence, pregnancy prevention, etc.), two evenings a week.

- A Medical Centre providing health and dental services, and a Social Services Unit offering mental health services.

- A Family Resources Centre which offers, classes, workshops and services to adults in the community from 6 pm to 10 pm. The classes and services offered are usually a response to community demands. English as a second language and computer classes have been particularly popular. Special rooms are also made available for community meetings and activities.

The financial benefits of using IS 218 to provide community services are clear-cut: the annual cost of the CAS programmes per child is only $850. This figure would be much higher if the CAS had to pay for its own facilities. The students benefit from medical, dental and social services, teachers are able to concentrate on their main task of teaching, and parents benefit from educational and recreational programmes.

Project HighRoad in school IS 183

Project HighRoad is a drugs prevention programme funded by the Fund for New York Public Education and the United Way (both voluntary organisations), and is currently operating in three public schools in the city of New York. The Project HighRoad model is the product of extensive research into preventive strategies to aid disadvantaged communities, and has been tested and evaluated at other sites.

The Project HighRoad approach involves recruiting a community-based organisation (CBO) near each target school. CBOs are entrusted to select project staff and to establish a local advisory committee made up of representatives from the school, housing management, parents' and tenants' associations, police and other CBOs. Local advisory committees are responsible for assessing community needs and planning services to "reduce risk" among middle school youth and their families.

They are asked to follow ten guiding principles, of which four relate to co-ordinating activities: they must devise a memorandum of understanding between the school, the lead CBO and other partners; a clear mechanism must exist to ensure the co-ordination of programme activities; key partners must receive training to establish a common understanding of project goals and activities; and parents, students and the wider community must be involved in programme design and implementation.

One of the current Project HighRoad schools is IS 183 in the Mott Haven district of South Bronx. Mott Haven is a poor, high crime area with a thriving drugs market. It accounts for 10 per cent of New York city's population, but 17 per cent of drug-related arrests, 18 per cent of drug-related deaths, and 19 per cent of AIDs related deaths due to intravenous drug use. Around 56 per cent of the student population is Hispanic and 44 per cent, Afro-American. IS 183 offers a range of Project HighRoad programmes which aim to keep students out of Mott Haven's all-pervading drugs culture. These include:

– an After-school Programme which operates from 3pm to 6pm and provides teaching in basic school subjects and recreational activities;

– a Summer Programme (held at the school), and regular weekend activities;

– a Youth Leadership Programme for around 35 eighth grade students per year. Following a rigorous selection process, successful students receive training and orientation to the "World of Work" in after-school workshops, and are then placed in part-time supervised jobs with local businesses (for which they receive a $30 a week stipend);

– workshops on drug and alcohol abuse for all school pupils; and

– various community programmes, such as neighbourhood policing to rid the area of drug sellers.

As yet there has been no evaluation of the success of Project HighRoad in preventing drug abuse amongst IS 183 students. The evaluation so far has concentrated on "process" and how to improve collaboration between partners. In this respect certain tensions between education and other professionals have been noted.

The Decatur-Clearpool School and Camp Clearpool

In 1990, Camp Clearpool (a summer camp), the Edwin Gould Foundation, and Community School District 16, formed a partnership to develop the Decatur-Clearpool School (a junior high school) and Camp Clearpool as a year round, split-site educational establishment. They brought together various stakeholders, including administrators, teachers, parents and business people, to design a new organisational structure and programme for the school, with additional help from Yale University's School Development Programme (SDP). The "Clearpool Model" which was articulated during this planning stage emphasised strong parental involvement and co-ordinated decision-making involving all major stakeholders in the school.

Opened in 1992, the new school features many of the structures recommended by Yale University's School Development Programme. These include:

- A School Management and Planning Team, involving parents, teachers, administrators, paraprofessionals, unions, health and family centre staff, and extended day staff, to formulate school policy.

- A Leadership Team, composed of senior education, health and social welfare staff in the school, which ensures that the policies determined by the School Management and Planning Team are implemented, and that co-ordination exists between school-based and outside agencies.

- A Mental Health Team which co-ordinates the work of all mental and physical health staff in the school.

- A Parent Programme incorporating the Parent-Teachers Association and a Parent Class Representative scheme whereby two parents per class are selected to act as links between other parents and school decision-making bodies.

In spite of the complexity of decision-making involving all stakeholders, and tensions connected with inter-professional collaboration, measured outcomes of the Clearpool approach suggest that it is working. The attendance rate at the school is 93 per cent which places it in the top 3 per cent for attendance in New York City, and standardised test results have improved. Anecdotal evidence from teachers also suggests that students are more willing to learn.

EXAMPLES OF BEST PRACTICE IN INTEGRATED SERVICES FOR YOUTH IN THE TRANSITION TO WORK

The Door

The Door is an open access centre which offers a range of educational, recreational and medical facilities for young people aged 12 to 21. Started in 1971 by a mixed group of professionals – including street-workers, dancers and artists – it brings together expertise in the arts, law, education, and physical and mental health. Its goal is to help young people to side-step the bureaucracy, fragmentation and red-tape of public provision by offering co-ordinated services on one site. One aspect of co-operation is the joint intake system and shared set of forms used by the Door's various services.

The centre currently occupies four floors of a six-storey condominium building, and has a paid staff of 145 and over 100 volunteers. Facilities available include a health clinic, library, crèche, cookery room, art and pottery studios, gymnasium and a central meeting place. Funding for the Door comes from a wide array of sources: nine government bodies, 78 foundations and corporate founders, and several individual donors.

The centre is open in the afternoons and evenings up until 9.30pm from Monday to Friday, and an average of 250 young people visit it each day. Various programmes are provided to facilitate the transition of disadvantaged youth into employment or higher education. In addition to teaching basic English and maths and preparing young people for General Educational Development (GED), a high school diploma equivalent, the Door also offers the following:

– Employability Skills training to help young people to develop their social abilities.

– Career Exploration which offers opportunities for job shadowing, voluntary work and entrepreneurial work within the Door.

– Youth Apprenticeship, a scheme which uses volunteer companies to provide Door members with training and hands-on experience of the business world.

– College Preparation which aims to increase young people's awareness of the post-secondary options open to them, helps with college applications, and offers some financial assistance to those who are successful.

In 1993, 75 members of the Door achieved their GED and 70 enrolled in college. The success of the centre in helping young people to make the transition to work has been recognised elsewhere, and its approach has been copied in numerous American towns and cities, and abroad.

CONCLUSION

A common trend in New York City is for private agencies to form partnerships with municipal schools, and to supplement basic public education services with health and social welfare programmes. Private agencies function in a symbiotic relationship with school "hosts", benefiting financially from the use of their facilities, but providing important services in return. IS 218, IS 183 and (the less impersonal sounding) Decatur-Clearpool School have all opened their doors to private initiatives which, in turn, have placed little demand on the public purse.

The three schools, in co-operation with their private sector partners, have also made every effort to remove barriers to the community. Community involvement in decision-making, the provision of community programmes on-site, and the employment of parents in project activities, have all contributed to making these schools like miniature "villages" which serve several different social functions.

IS 183 and the Decatur-Clearpool School both have clearly articulated strategies to co-ordinate services, and the latter in particular has set up an impressive array of organisational structures to ensure that collaboration takes place. The strong interest shown by New York's private agencies in applying exemplary and replicable "models" in schools – such as those developed by Project HighRoad and Yale University – is one that can be found throughout the United States.

Like IS 218, IS 183 and the Decatur-Clearpool School, the Door offers a broad and impressive range of services, funded to a large extent by private agencies. While all of these initiatives are commendable, the existence of so many largely voluntary programmes in New York City, at times providing (arguably) essential services, must bring into question the rather weak role played by the State.

6

CALIFORNIA, UNITED STATES
Moving towards integration
in America's "honeypot" state

by

Philippa Hurrell and Peter Evans

INTRODUCTION AND SUMMARY

In recent years, California has been in the grip of a sharp recession. Loss of jobs through closure of military bases and downsizing of businesses, especially defence-related industries had devastating effect upon the California economy and employment opportunities. Depleted state revenue has led to deep cuts in human services budgets and a decline in the intensity of services provision. As a result, increasing antagonism has been felt towards California's illegal immigrants, and a recent state vote favoured making them ineligible for most education, welfare and medical services. However, this referendum was challenged by the San Diego Independent School District, and others in the Federal Court System as being unconstitutional and therefore has not yet become law.

California has used imaginative and creative policy making to promote cooperation amongst its human services agencies. In addition, to making available special grants and waivers, it has changed confidentiality laws, provided training, and exploited federal funding mechanisms to encourage interagency collaboration. However, the long term funding of integrated projects, and the existence of destructive competition between agencies, are two issues which need to be addressed.

CHILDREN AT RISK IN CALIFORNIA

In recognising the gravity of the situation of many children in California, the State has taken an important first step towards addressing their needs. A recent act reported that:

> "The condition of California's children is in sharp decline. In 1991, 1.8 million or 22.3 per cent of California's children lived in poverty, 200 000 more than in 1988. Over the last four years, the birth rate for teenage mothers has risen by 25 per cent. Child abuse and neglect reports rose from 63.5 to 70.5 per thou-

sand children between 1988 and 1991. In 1992, 10 per thousand children were separated from their parents and were living in foster care. California's performance was worse than national data on 83 per cent of measures of children's welfare included on a 1992 state-wide 'report card'" (California Legislature, AB 1741, 1993a).

California is also a leading destination of illegal immigrants to the United States, especially from Mexico. Their children are at particular risk of social and educational disadvantage.

STATE AND COUNTY LEVEL POLICIES PROMOTING SERVICES INTEGRATION

In the last five or six years, California has introduced several initiatives to stimulate services integration state-wide. The push towards integration has not been without difficulty, and at each step of the way the State has been forced to find solutions to emerging problems. However, both the public and private sector still see services integration as the best approach to addressing the needs of disadvantaged children in California.

The Presley Brown Interagency Children's Services Act of 1989 (California Legislature, 1989) authorised counties to establish Interagency Children and Youth Service Councils to co-ordinate local services for children. The law prescribed that these councils should include representatives from education, social welfare, housing and legal services, and the private sector. It allows counties who meet stated requirements to obtain waivers against state regulations that inhibit services co-ordination. In order to qualify, counties must have an approved interagency council in place and have developed a three-year plan for establishing a system of co-ordinated services (including an evaluation component). In 1991, Chang et al. reported that while several councils had been set up, not one had achieved a waiver. This was blamed on the over-exacting requirement for a detailed, medium-term plan. In the same year, the State enacted SB 786 (California Legislature, 1991a) to overcome some of the problems associated with the earlier legislation. This allowed councils to enter into "negotiated contracts" with the State, to enable them to combine resources from different agencies for joint projects. However, three years later, DeLapp (1994) reported that none of the councils had taken advantage of this legislation either.

Enacted by state legislation in 1991, the Healthy Start Programme was California's first comprehensive effort to bring public and private sector social welfare, health and educational support services together at the school site. The programme awards planning grants ($50 000), start-up grants ($100 000), and three year's worth of funding ($300 000), to groups composed of local government, community agency, school and parent representatives, for school-linked projects.

Funding decisions are made by the state Department of Education. In order to qualify, schools must have a high percentage of children either living in poverty or with English as a second language. They must also be able to match state funding with a 25 per cent contribution in cash or in kind, and must offer at least four different support services. During 1991-1993, a total of 65 operational grants and 163 planning grants were awarded to individual schools or school "consortiums" (most of which were elementary).

An interim evaluation of the first year of the Healthy Start initiative revealed the utilisation, at different sites, of four contrasting service delivery structures or programmes:

- School-based Family Resource Centres (to which teachers, other service providers or a services co-ordination team could refer pupils, or of which families could make voluntary use). These were associated with: providing the broadest array of services to meet the diverse needs of families; significant reductions in families' unmet basic needs; significant improvements in clients' use of health care for illness or injury and reductions in health care access problems; and significant improvements in clients' mental health.

- Satellite Family Service Centres (providing a range of services at an out-of-school site). These were associated with: serving the least clients, delivering the least services, and providing those services least intensively (although they were the most active in providing basic needs assistance); significant reductions in families' unmet basic needs; significant increases in access to dental care (although no other significant health benefits were noted); and significant improvements in clients' mental health.

- Family Service Co-ordination Teams (mainly school personnel, without a physical base, but working together to develop service strategies for pupils at risk). These were associated with: a greater emphasis on academic services, and school-related counselling, accompanied by significant gains in students' educational performance; and significant increases in access to dental care and physical examinations (although no other significant health benefits were noted).

- Youth Service Programmes (addressing the health, education and social welfare needs of adolescents, and generally either school-based or in a school-linked health clinic). These were associated with: the strongest emphasis on health screenings and medical services, consistent with the utilisation of school-based or school-linked health clinics; significant improvements in clients' employment status, with a significant proportion of teenagers acquiring part-time jobs; and significant reductions in health care access problems (Wagner *et al.*, 1994).

In spite of differences in outcomes, the evaluators concluded that none of these initiatives could be labelled as "the best" on the basis of their research.

In 1992, 17 locally based foundations set up the Foundation Consortium for School-linked Services. They shared the conviction that comprehensive, integrated, school-linked services had the potential to be more powerful in meeting children's needs than existing (and fragmented) services. They also believed that by pooling their resources they could achieve more than by acting separately. An open outlook towards the public sector led to the setting up, in January 1992, of a special "partnership" between the Foundation Consortium and the State. Three shared objectives under-pinned their alliance: to create and support models of comprehensive, school-linked services; to develop stable financing mechanisms so that these services could continue when foundation grant money ended; and to initiate significant, sustained, state-wide changes in the way services are provided. To this end, the Foundation Consortium's main role is to provide private financing, support and evaluation; the State's is to provide assistance in kind, to make available state moneys (through Healthy Start), and to apply for relevant federal funding.

Also in 1992, the federal government for the first time approved school districts as official Medicaid providers. Medicaid is a federal medical assistance programme for very poor individuals who qualify for Aid to Families with Dependent Children (AFDC) and Supplemental Security Income (SSI). In order to create on-going support for school-linked services funded by Healthy Start, school districts are encouraged to identify medical services being provided in schools whose costs can be reimbursed by Medicaid (through a federal-state, 50-50, matching funding formula). Any federal money they attract must be re-invested in additional "Healthy Start like" services. However, DeLapp (1994) reported that this "billing option" was not being heavily utilised, and that some Healthy Start sites are in their third year of funding without having secured long-term financial support. In any case, Medicaid money alone is insufficient to maintain school-linked services.

The success of the "billing option" has been impaired by the State's decision to require counties to provide managed health care for all recipients of Aid to Families with Dependent Children. Managed health care structures, or "Health Maintenance Organisations" (HMOs) provide beneficiaries with access to a stable, continuing relationship with a primary care physician, and offer services up to a prepaid financial limit. The problem is that children enrolled in a prepaid managed health care plan may not be eligible for school district health services. In addition, some HMOs may view schools providing health services as competitors for funding, thus inhibiting co-operation. The Foundation Consortium has attempted to address this situation by developing three pilot projects to create and implement strategies that can be used to integrate managed care and school-linked services. To this end, each project has been given an incentive grant of $50 000 for the year 1994-95.

Act AB 1741 (California Legislature, 1993*a*) permits up to five counties selected by the Governor to combine a portion of state funds for child and family services over a period of five years, starting in 1995. The blended funds, which will be freed from state categorical restrictions, must be used for comprehensive, integrated services for low income families with multiple problems. At least four different human services must be involved. Participating counties must appoint broadly representative child and family interagency co-ordinating councils to plan, implement and evaluate their chosen initiatives.

Because of the practical difficulties involved in cross-agency information sharing, Healthy Start's field office provides technical assistance to help Healthy Start programmes to make important distinctions between what is or is not confidential, and to establish how to facilitate exchange of information while respecting clients' rights. In addition, the Californian legislature has taken steps to make the sharing of information between integrated agencies easier. AB 2184 (California Legislature, 1991*b*) permits multi-disciplinary teams of two or more persons to share relevant information if they have received the signed consent of a parent or legal guardian. Later, AB 3491 (California Legislature, 1992) expanded the possibility to pool information by authorising counties to establish a computerised database containing data from specified agencies relating to child abuse and neglect. Furthermore, SB 931 (California Legislature, 1993*b*) authorised the exchange of information between housing and public assistance agencies to determine individual's eligibility for services.

Realising that state legislation and funding options were not always sufficient to overcome important barriers to collaboration (such as confidentiality concerns, leadership styles and ambivalent attitudes to resource sharing), the Foundation Consortium and State decided to adopt a strategy, devised by Chynoweth (1994), called the Policy Academy. This is an approach which develops collaborative teams and engages them in planning and implementing specific policy objectives. Experts and facilitator-coaches work with the teams at intensive retreats and provide one-to-one training on-site. The application in California has brought together top level county decision-makers and leaders of the State's human services agencies. The Academy is viewed as a twelve-month process, and includes two three-day work sessions held off-site for county collaborative teams. The initiative began with eight counties selected through a competitive process, and it is anticipated that they will serve as resources to other counties who have not been through Academy training.

Perhaps the most widely publicised county level initiative to integrate services is San Diego's New Beginnings Programme. This was started in 1988 by the Director of the County Department of Social Services and the Superintendent of San Diego City Schools who recognised that schools needed to co-operate with social welfare services who were in contact with their students. In partnership with over 20 other public agencies, a New Beginnings Council was set up to discuss collaborative ways to help children in several areas of mutual concern, including school attendance, teenage pregnancy, and the health needs of children in City Heights, a disadvantaged neighbourhood. Eventually, a six-month feasibility study, funded jointly by the Stuart Foundation and in kind contributions from partners, was undertaken in Hamilton Elementary School. Its purpose was to determine the need for school-linked integrated services and what resources each participant could provide. Enrolment data from the school were matched electronically with caseload data from several programmes of the Department of Social Services, such as AFDC, food stamps and Medicaid. This study showed that over 60 per cent of students' families were served by at least one partner's programme and that 10 per cent were known to four or more programmes. It was also discovered that these agencies seldom collaborated with each other.

EXAMPLES OF BEST PRACTICE IN INTEGRATED SERVICES FOR SCHOOL CHILDREN

The OECD site visit to California focused specifically on school aged children, and did not include comprehensive visits to services for pre-school children or youth in the transition to work. The New Beginnings Programme was a main focus of the study visit to San Diego.

The New Beginnings Centre at Hamilton Elementary School

After two years of planning, New Beginnings opened a demonstration centre in September 1991 in Hamilton Elementary School. The school is located in an area with the highest crime rate and second highest child abuse rate in San Diego. It enrols 1 300 students from kindergarten to grade five, 40 per cent of whom are Hispanic, 30 per cent Indochinese, 20 per cent Afro-American, and 10 per cent from other ethnic backgrounds.

The centre was located in three portable classrooms donated by the school district and refitted with funding from the County Health Services and local foundations. Funding for the first year of the operation included $225 260 in grants and $347 980 in institutional funding. The intention in the long term is to replace all grant contributions with regular agency money. All participating agencies were asked to provide staff, furniture, supplies and equipment for the new centre, as well as supporting agency-based personnel ("extended teams") to back up professionals on-site.

The school's teachers participate in the initiative through intensive training on problem identification, supportive techniques, the roles and services of other agency staff, and referral processes. In addition, a Task Force including New Beginnings professionals, teachers and parents meets twice a month to facilitate communication and co-ordination.

Families are introduced to the initiative on school registration days, when the New Beginnings project is explained to them, a list of local support services is distributed, and they are offered an initial assessment of their service needs. The most extensive case management services are targeted at the 250 plus students who are deemed "at risk" according to the school district's academic criteria, and who are known by at least three different agency programmes. There is less intensive assessment – and referral when necessary to the "extended teams" – for the 600 to 800 students who are known only to AFDC, Medicaid and/or the free and reduced price lunch programmes (New Beginnings, 1990). Co-operation between several (although not all) of the participating agencies has been facilitated by the use of a shared screening form. Efforts are also being made to develop a joint Management Information System to provide data on agency programmes and clients, while at the same time maintaining confidentiality.

In 1993, New Beginning's Institute for Collaborative Management – which is charged to "institutionalise collaboration among the partner agencies (...) through an ongoing training process" – held a training conference for 123 upper level executives and directors from various human services agencies in the county. The conference was very successful and another is planned for middle managers. The United States Department of Health and Human Services has recently given San Diego Department of Social Services a two-year grant of $400 000 to facilitate the expansion of New Beginnings to three other communities in the county. New Beginnings has also been given the responsibility for co-ordinating Healthy Start grants in San Diego.

CONCLUSION

The State of California has played an active role in promoting the creation of interagency groups, with varying success. The Presley-Brown Interagency Child Services Act authorised counties to set up interagency councils, although the "carrot" of specified waivers against state regulations was seldom delivered because of over-exacting eligibility requirements. Similarly, the State's Healthy Start Programme has encouraged the creation of interagency groups to set up school-linked services. While this initiative has been more successful than the Presley-Brown one, the long-term survival of many school-linked services is precarious because of lack of on-going funding.

In implementing its integrated services policies, the State has met with a number of problems; however, it also has been flexible and resourceful in finding solutions to them. Following the failure of interagency councils to qualify for "Presley-Brown" waivers, for instance, the State turned to another strategy to help agencies to co-operate instead. Unfortunately, though, its efforts to set up "negoti-ated contracts" also failed to attract take-up by interagency councils. In another example, efforts to develop integrated school-linked services using Medicaid money were hampered by managed health care policies which made some children ineligi-ble for school health care. Working in partnership with the State, the Foundation Consortium has attempted to address this problem through pilot projects aiming to integrate managed health care and school-linked services.

State policies clearly point to the school as a favourite site for providing integrated services. Like public sector administrators, private organisations such as the Foundation Consortium also view the school as the optimal place to encourage co-operation. This is reflected in the special partnership it has formed with the State to promote school-linked provision. The Healthy Start initiative has focused on bringing together both public and voluntary organisations to provide services in schools. Other school-based initiatives, such as New Beginnings, are oriented more specifically towards the public sector.

The State of California has shown great imagination in the variety of approaches it has employed to achieve services integration. The use of financial mechanisms (such as the Medicaid "billing option"), changes in confidentiality laws, and efforts to provide relevant training to senior administrators (notably through the Policy Academy approach) have enabled California to move further down the path towards state-wide integrated services. However, predicted and unforeseen barriers have still to be overcome.

7

SASKATCHEWAN, CANADA
United efforts to integrate services from the top-down and bottom-up

by

Philippa Hurrell and Peter Evans

INTRODUCTION AND SUMMARY

Patterns of government spending on human services in Canada bear a close resemblance to those in Nordic countries. For public expenditure on education as a percentage of GDP, it is grouped in a tight cluster with Denmark, Finland and Sweden, all of whom invest heavily in their education systems. Canada's spending on health as a percentage of GDP is second only to the United States, with the Nordic countries a few percentage points behind (OECD, 1995b). Investment in its people has earned Canada one of the lowest infant mortality rates in the world, and one of the highest life expectancies for both men and women.

Control for education, health and social services in Canada is delegated largely to the provinces. The province of Saskatchewan (from the Cree Indian word "kisis-katchewan" meaning "the river that flows swiftly") has, in turn, devolved authority to its regions. However, there is a strong push from the provincial level to encourage municipalities to adopt integrated working practices, and a concomitant drive to involve community people in all levels of decision-making. Provincial government concerns to provide co-ordinated and holistic services are often found to be synchronised with grassroots initiatives, although senior administrators believe that there is yet to be "a critical mass of people working in a collaborative way". Lack of available time to collaborate, insufficient training in collaborative practices, and restrictive confidentiality laws, may go some way towards explaining this.

CHILDREN AT RISK IN SASKATCHEWAN

As in western Europe, global recession has forced upwards the rate of unemployment and the number of families living in poverty in Saskatchewan, albeit from a fairly low level. This has caused considerable concern in the provincial government. These worries have been intensified by a recent study in Ontario which showed that poor children are more than twice as likely as other children to suffer from emotional and behavioural disorders, and to perform badly in school.

With a weakened cultural and economic heritage resulting from early colonisation by Europeans, many of Saskatchewan's 80 000 aboriginal people, and 40 000 mixed race "Métis", live in disadvantaged situations. Created to satisfy legitimate demands for the "return" of land, a large proportion of them live on special reserves. Unfortunately, the scope for economic activity in these communities is often limited. This, in part, explains why around one third of all social welfare recipients have aboriginal backgrounds.

Other important recipients of social welfare benefits are single and teenage mothers. Teenage mothers are a particular concern because their offspring are more likely to be premature, to have a low birth weight, to exhibit developmental delays, and to be subject to abuse. In 1992, a total of 1 624 babies were born to young women between the ages of 10 and 19.

POLICIES PROMOTING SERVICES INTEGRATION

One of the most striking features of efforts to integrate services in Saskatchewan is that not only are they explicit at the strategic (government) level, but they are also much in evidence on the ground. Top-down policies to promote integration often have been equalled by grassroots initiatives to do the same. However, in some areas, the collaborative culture embraced by the government has yet to filter downwards as far as administrators would like.

The provincial government's concern to co-ordinate its human services arose from a series of tragic deaths – reported in the Ombudsman's Report of 1992 – of children who died from neglect or abuse. Following the publication of this report, the finger was pointed at the province's human services who were seen as partly responsible. The next year, the Department of Education, Training and Employment responded to this report by launching a discussion paper entitled "Children First: An Invitation to Work Together". This proposed a common approach to addressing children's problems and a set of provincial goals to improve their well-being. As a follow-up to this paper, an Interdepartmental Steering Committee was set up, including provincial and regional staff from several different departments, to review planning proposals and provide recommendations. Also created were two Health and Education councils, and a Council on Children, made up of various community representatives. These were amongst the first products of Saskatchewan's newly devised "Action Plan for Children".

Under the umbrella of the Action Plan, the provincial government also set up a school focused programme, called "Working Together to Address Barriers to Learning: Integrated School-linked Services for Children and Youth at Risk". Several government bodies – including Education, Training and Employment, Health, Social Services, Justice, Indian and Métis Affairs, and Municipal Government – have joined together to support this programme, and 20 pilot projects have been set up (with evaluation components). Mirroring the strategic level, these projects have involved a mix of local organisations, including companies, churches, community associations, non-government agencies and aboriginal groups. They also emphasise a set of formally identified principles, amongst which co-operation, the provision of holistic and comprehensive services, and community involvement are key. Developing school-linked services is seen as a process in which all stakeholders should participate, from provincial departments to schools to parents. To this end, regional directors play an important role, sitting on interagency committees, and working with other stakeholders to implement integrated approaches. Integration also has been facilitated by teacher training involving other agencies in a multi-disciplinary effort.

The provincial government believes that schools are an ideal location for integrated services efforts because the majority of children are required by law to attend them. However, some believe that, for this policy to be successful, more money needs to be put into collaboration (because it is not cheap), and efforts need to be made to reduce differences between professional cultures.

While not explicitly referring to integration, an important precedent to the concept of school-linked services, was that of the "community school". The first of these schools was set in North York, Toronto in 1966, and they have since been instituted all over Canada, including Saskatchewan. Three central aims embraced by the community school model are the involvement of the community in school affairs and policy making, the provision of education services for adults, and assistance by the school in making the local environment safe for children. Racial and cultural understanding is also emphasised. To achieve these goals, each school takes on additional staff, including a community school co-ordinator, nutrition co-ordinator and aboriginal teaching associates. Schools must conform to several criteria of disadvantage to gain "community" status and the funding related to it. This enables them to bring together, and collaborate with, a wide variety of health, welfare, recreational and educational agencies for local people's benefit.

The examples of best practice in integrated services which were visited by the OECD experts were extremely comprehensive and, as such, spanned provision for pre-school children, school children and youth in the transition to work. However, since the Prince Albert visit focused on pre-school children and the Saskatoon visit on school aged children, they are discussed separately under these headings.

EXAMPLES OF BEST PRACTICE IN INTEGRATED SERVICES FOR PRE-SCHOOL CHILDREN

West Flat Citizens Group, Prince Albert

Prince Albert is a town of 33 000 inhabitants located in a relatively remote part of Saskatchewan north of its capital, Regina. Around one third of its population is of aboriginal descent. Many of these people live in one of the poorest parts of Prince Albert, known as the "West Flat" area. In this neighbourhood, unemployment rates are high, housing is substandard, many families are single parent, and alcohol abuse and crime are widespread. Matters are made worse by alcoholic and violent forays into the area at weekends by young men from rural areas.

Up until recently, these problems generated anger, frustration and a sense of hopelessness amongst West Flat citizens. However, in 1991, a small group of women who were concerned by the frequency of crime in the neighbourhood, and the fact that many pensioners had become too frightened to leave their homes after dark, decided to try to change the community. Following their first meeting – humorously referred to as a "bitch tea party" – they conducted a community survey to gather information on local population needs and to encourage local involvement. Support for their efforts came from the provincial Education, Training and Employment, Health and Social Services departments who agreed to provide funding, for integrated and community based services, under the province's Action Plan for Children. To administer this money, the West Flat Citizens Group was set up. An additional boost to the group came from the City of Prince Albert which acquired and renovated a former school for its use.

The Citizens Group has organised four different types of programme – education, recreation, housing and policing – to meet the needs of locals pinpointed by the survey. The education component includes pre-school care for 3- and 4-year-olds, an "EAGLE" programme for youth between the ages of 15 and 18 who cannot cope in regular school, parent education, advice on health and nutrition, and speech and language services. The recreation programme includes various sports and social activities for young people, including skating, swimming and teenage dances. Housing efforts are focused on low cost repairs for pensioners and low income families, and policing revolves around a neighbourhood police office, manned by Citizens Club staff, and voluntary night patrols.

Collaboration is at its greatest in the pre-school, EAGLE programme, and in community policing. The staff at the pre-school includes a director, family support worker, four teachers and five volunteer parents. Additional support is provided by a public health nurse and a dental nurse who screen children for problems, and a nutritionist who prepares breakfast for them twice a week. A pre-school committee, which includes representatives from the Citizens Group, social services, health and education, co-ordinates the work of these professionals.

Most of the 73 children currently enrolled in the programme have aboriginal backgrounds. Anecdotal evidence suggests that their parents are very satisfied with its services, and that the children's language abilities and social skills have improved.

The EAGLE (for "Education: A Good Learning Experience") programme provides a mixture of education, life skills, and employment training, with a staff of one teacher and one social worker. These professionals collaborate to a large degree with the local high school, which allows "EAGLE" children to use its computers and sports facilities, and works with them to achieve their successful integration back into normal school. The teacher and social worker also liaise with health professionals who provide health checks and nutrition courses. Up to 15 young people can be accommodated by this programme. Attendance amongst the nine children who were participating in 1994 was an impressive 98 per cent.

Collaboration in the Citizens Group's policing efforts takes the form of partnership between local community members and the city's professional police service. A community liaison officer has trained around 60 volunteers in the legal aspects of community policing, and they take turns manning a police substation, and patrolling the streets in their own cars. This arrangement has assisted the professional police force, which was unable to provide adequate cover because of limited funding, and has improved local residents' sense of security.

The efforts of the West Flat Citizens Group have been strongly boosted by the province's philosophical support for integrated projects, and provincial money linked to the Action Plan for Children. In addition, the enthusiasm of the community, and its small size (allowing close ties to develop between service providers), have been significant for the group's success. Barriers to co-operation, however, have included the reluctance of certain bureaucracies to collaborate, the lack of time for liaison, and over-strict data protection laws.

EXAMPLES OF BEST PRACTICE IN INTEGRATED SERVICES FOR SCHOOL CHILDREN

Princess Alexandra Community School, Saskatoon

With a population of 194 000, Saskatoon is Saskatchewan's largest city. While the city as a whole enjoys a high standard of living, it still has some pockets of poverty. One of these is in the Riversdale neighbourhood, where the average family income is the lowest in Saskatoon, many families are single parent, 80 per cent of inhabitants have aboriginal ancestry, and 40 per cent do not have English as their first language. A massive 80 per cent have direct involvement with the social services or the justice system, and 60 per cent are on welfare benefits.

Aware of the problems in neighbourhoods such as Riversdale, the Saskatoon Board of Education held a symposium in 1990 to develop a "Concept Plan for Inner City Elementary Schools", with the goal of improving educational achievement and empowering disadvantaged communities. One of the four schools which eventually qualified for funding under this plan was the Princess Alexandra Community School. Its eligibility was ensured by the high level of student turnover in the school, low levels of self-esteem and educational achievement, and child delinquency, prostitution and "street wandering" in the local neighbourhood.

The school runs several programmes in which collaboration is an important component. One of these is a pre-school which has been set up on the school premises. Overseen by a board made up of the principal, community workers and parents, the pre-school provides child care for 3- and 4-year-olds three days per week. Three quarters of its funding comes from the government, while the rest comes from its own fund raising activities. Local churches and other services have been active in supporting its efforts. However, to date, attempts to make the pre-school culturally relevant to local aboriginal people, by organising regular "healing circles" (or group discussions), have failed to attract many parents and children.

The school's Re-entry Programme, for children who are in danger of dropping out of school or have already done so, is organised in partnership with Radius Tutoring, which runs a Community Centre for Education and Employment Training. The centre attempts to change students' behavioural patterns and to teach them individual responsibility. At any one time up to 20 places are available to children from Princess Alexandra. Funding for these places comes from the federal "Stay in School Initiative", the Saskatoon Board of Education, the Saskatoon Social Services Branch, and private donors.

Princess Alexandra has also formed a triumvirate with Nutana College and the Star Phoenix newspaper, to organise art and drama exchanges between the two schools which are advertised by the paper. Princess Alexandra additionally co-operates with Star Phoenix through a role model and tutorship scheme in which newspaper employees provide guidance to selected students from the school. Links with the business world have been extended by the organisation of student art exhibitions in which paintings are sold with the aid of local companies.

The general needs of the local community are addressed by the school through an Extended Day Programme, whereby it remains open from 7.30am to 11pm, five days a week. In addition to providing breakfast and lunch, the school also provides leisure and educational activities including art, craft and cookery classes, adult literacy courses, and aboriginal Hoop Dance lessons. A Hoop Dance Troop has been formed by the school with the aim of developing community pride in the aboriginal culture.

Poor relations between local people and the police in Riversdale, prompted the Police Department's education unit to arrange "friendly" police visits to Princess Alexandra to help reduce the antagonism felt towards them. They have also set up a Community and Police Help Centre where locals are able to report crimes, but can also benefit from computer literacy classes. Open from 9am to 9pm every day, the centre is jointly manned with "community partners" (or volunteers). It is also connected to a locally organised "Zero Tolerance Group" which has attempted to reduce prostitution by arranging exposés of embarrassed clients. This enterprising example of police-school-community partnership is formally known as the Inner City Police Liaison Programme.

Another prong to Saskatoon's efforts to improve conditions has been its nomination of Riversdale as a Business Improvement District. Efforts have been made to improve local shops, and two local pubs which were the focus of "trouble" have been taken over by new management. In addition, a Clean Sweep programme has been set up to keep the pavements rubbish-free, and wall paintings have been commissioned to improve the environment. These efforts have helped to reduce the local problems of vandalism, gang activity and "street wandering".

The outcomes of these various efforts have been positive. Staff report improvements in pupils' social skills, increased pride in and commitment to the school, reduced truancy and crime rates, and a general feeling that they are doing a good job. They believe that collaboration has been facilitated by regular meetings between staff and with the community, staff dedication, and the dynamism and commitment of the school's principal. However, lack of training on collaborative processes and staff exhaustion resulting from intense extra-curricular activities have emerged as problems.

CONCLUSION

Both Prince Albert and Saskatoon provide excellent examples of how strategic level and grassroots initiatives can be married to create effective integrated services systems. The provincial government's Action Plan for Children provided vital support for the West Flat initiative, created by a small group of dynamic local women. Similarly, Saskatoon's "Concept Plan for Inner City Elementary Schools" provided important backing to the efforts of the Princess Alexandra School's charismatic head and devoted staff.

They also reflect the provincial government's concern with community involvement and empowerment, symbolised at the strategic level by the Council on Children. In Prince Albert, the West Flat Citizens Group by definition is controlled and run by ordinary community members. In Saskatoon, parental involvement in the Princess Alexandra School, as well as in local policing, is evidence of the strong bias towards community participation.

The clear aim of Saskatchewan's provincial and local governments is to develop integrated services in the fullest sense of the term. Both the West Flat and Riversdale networks, incorporate co-operation between education, social welfare, health and police services, as well as addressing environmental needs. In contrast to the United States, network participation comes largely from the public sector, with little private sector involvement. On the other hand, an emphasis on community involvement in integrated services is something that Saskatchewan shares with its southern neighbour.

8

ALBERTA, CANADA
Radical change towards services integration

by

Philippa Hurrell and Peter Evans

INTRODUCTION AND SUMMARY

While Alberta ranks as one of Canada's richest provinces, it still has important socio-economic problems. Federal funding for social programmes has been in decline since 1992, and at the time of the visit (1994) there was a large budget deficit, with unemployment at around 10 per cent.* In reaction to these difficulties, the Alberta government has decided to institute deep public spending cuts. However, it still wishes to maintain, and even improve, human services provision. Services integration is seen as key to achieving these apparently conflicting goals.

Recognising that Alberta's human services system is fragmented, the government has marked out integration as a top priority. Its "Co-ordination of Services for Children" programme has encouraged an unusual degree of "vertical" collaboration between senior officials, service providers and the community, in addition to "horizontal" collaboration between different departments at all levels. Co-operation has developed in the context of limited funding – but this has been balanced by a profound determination amongst administrators and professionals to implement desired changes.

Lack of flexibility in funding mechanisms and service delivery mandates, and inter-professional communication difficulties on the ground, are two important barriers to integration which the government has yet to fully overcome.

CHILDREN AND YOUTH AT RISK IN ALBERTA

As in Sakatchewan, the historical disempowerment of Alberta's aboriginal people – which until the late 1960s meant that their children were being sent forcibly to residential schools – has impacted significantly on their social well being. While

---

* However, in 1996 the budget deficit has been eliminated and unemployment has fallen substantially.

only 5.5 per cent of Alberta's population is aboriginal, around 45 per cent of children requiring child welfare services, and 31 per cent of children known to the justice system, are of native descent. What is more, cultural differences and language difficulties, have contributed to a high drop-out rate from school, and the aboriginal unemployment rate, at 20 per cent, is double the national average. Clearly then, these children are at serious risk of becoming marginalised in Canadian society – although the success of many aborigines in their careers is witness to the fact that they can and do "get on".

Also at risk, are children from low income families and broken homes. An increasing number of these children are exhibiting serious behavioural problems, and are becoming alienated from school. These difficulties are reflected in growing levels of crime and violence in Alberta's cities.

POLICIES PROMOTING SERVICES INTEGRATION

The concomitant need to reduce the province's budget deficit, and to improve the quality of inaccessible and duplicative services, has driven the Alberta government to instigate massive and far-reaching changes in its policies. These changes are linked to a three-year plan which is intended to bring government spending into line with the resources that are available. Three of the main aims of this plan are to eliminate waste and duplication in services provision; to encourage teamwork and innovation; and to create more scope for private sector involvement. The goal is to integrate and improve services at no extra cost (and to reduce staffing at the administrative and field levels).

Several government departments are involved in the reform effort, including Education, Health, Justice and Social Services. To support the process of change, an office of the Commissioner of Services for Children was set up in 1993 after extensive community consultation and approval by government. This Commissioner was asked to focus on integrated, readily accessible and community managed service delivery. Its recommendations – expected to be directed heavily towards decentralisation – were implemented in 1995.

Before the Commissioner of Services for Children was created, four government ministries (Education, Health, Justice and Social Services) grouped together to launch a joint programme christened "Co-ordination of Services for Children". It was conceived as an experiment to look at how officials in central government could work with local communities to introduce integrated approaches to service delivery, and to remove administrative barriers which might stand in the way.

The high priority given to this project was reflected in the decision to set up a working committee at the Assistant Deputy Minister level, of two representatives from each ministry involved. In mixed pairs delegated staff from the four ministries, worked closely with the five selected pilot sites – Calgary, Edmonton, Lethbridge,

Wabasca-Demarais and Wetaskiwin. One of each pair takes responsibility for attending all inter-service meetings, while the other provides support for evaluation activities. In practice, they act as important intermediaries between field level workers and senior administrators, and often serve as advocates for their adopted sites.

"Vertical" collaboration of this kind was also encouraged by a Forum, held in the autumn of 1993, where the pilot sites were brought together with senior government officials to share their ideas, and the problems they had experienced in project planning. This gave motivation and encouragement to everyone involved.

A sub-committee of the central working group has drawn up a draft survey for interim evaluation purposes. This will take stock of working methods and action affecting service planning and delivery, both at the provincial and local levels. It will also explore clients' views on the services they receive and how they compare with earlier provision. The questionnaire is geared towards internal evaluation, and the pilot sites are free to adapt it. Three ministerial departments – Education, Health and Social Services – are providing C$100 000 per annum to fund the evaluation (as well as consultation, facilitation and planning at the sites).

Of the five pilot sites, the three visited by OECD experts are part of the Commissioner of Services initiative and are described below. All of them cater for children, youth and their families, and therefore are grouped together under this heading. It is interesting to note that the New Beginnings programme in San Diego (described earlier) was drawn upon as a model of integrated services delivery in planning projects at the sites.

EXAMPLES OF BEST PRACTICE IN INTEGRATED SERVICES FOR CHILDREN, YOUTH AND THEIR FAMILIES

The Opening Doors Project, Calgary

Thanks to its thriving oil industry, Calgary is a prosperous city in which the majority of the population enjoys a good standard of living and education. However, around 10 per cent of its inhabitants are unemployed – and their children are at particular risk.

Calgary's Opening Doors Project is an attempt to improve linkages between different service providers, managers and administrators, and to involve the community in planning its own services. The project began in 1991, following the publication of a report which revealed a large number of gaps in the services system, as well as room for improvement in communication between service providers and the public. The report also emphasised public discontent with the way in which services responded to their needs. Parents and children found it hard to access services, and felt that they were excluded from decision-making when they did. In response, the Board of Education and the ministry held a meeting with services in Calgary dealing with families "at risk", and soon afterwards the Opening Doors Project was set up. In 1993, following the launch of the province's "Co-ordination of Services for Children" initiative, Calgary was invited to become one of its five pilot sites.

While enjoying the political support of senior level officials, Opening Doors receives no special funding to implement an integrated approach to services delivery. Resources are simply redistributed. For instance, the mental health service "lends" three specialists to schools to assist teachers and pupils, and two members of staff from the health service. Joint training is regarded as important for successful collaboration, and specialists from Alberta's paediatric hospital have already taught school auxiliaries how to deal with disabled children. However, the Opening Doors team believes that more training of this kind is needed.

The Opening Doors Steering Committee includes representatives of government agencies that provide city-wide services, including Education, Social Services, Health, and Justice. A decision was made to support a neighbourhood-based, interagency, multidisciplinary collaboration that would include schools as major partners. One goal was to find a way to merge bottom-up and top-down efforts to achieve better service integration. The Huntingdon Hills district of Calgary was selected as a pilot site, based upon criteria of identified needs of residents, agency willingness to participate, and community willingness to be involved. In this neighbourhood there are nine schools attempting to provide services to individual students, many of whom have complex needs. Nearly every school has a Resources Group which is able to resolve service needs of children and families where only one outside agency's services are needed. However, a Pupil Resources Group often can not negotiate needed services from several different agencies.

A Professional Resources Group (PRG) was constituted to provide direct services to these children and families. At the time of the site visit, it consisted of a public health nurse, a police officer, a mental health worker, a public school itinerant behavioural resource teacher, a child welfare worker, a financial benefits and client support services worker from the Alberta Family and Social Services Department, and a single parent worker from the City of Calgary Social Services Department. Most of the individuals chosen to be members of the PRG were already involved in this community. The PRG meets for one half-day per week to identify children and families appropriate to receive their services, to develop collaborative roles and strategies for serving them, and to gain better understanding of the resources, policies, programmes, and philosophies of the agencies involved. The PRG meets every six weeks with the Steering Committee in order to provide front-line information relevant to priority setting, confidentiality concerns, and liaising with other organisations.

A Supervisors Group consists of the individuals who have supervisory responsibility for the direct service workers. It meets monthly. The Steering Committee recognised the importance of constructing such a group in order to deal with the changing roles and functions of a PRG as compared with regular agency-based work, to identify personnel training needs, to resolve conflicts, and address confidentiality issues.

As in other cities, Calgary's keen efforts to integrate services have been hindered by certain problems. At the administrative level, the most important has been rigidity in methods of funding and mandates for service delivery (so that agencies are unable to pool resources to serve the same set of clients). At the grassroots level, relational and communication difficulties between different professional groups have been cause for concern. However, the early signs are that Opening Doors is beginning to achieve at least some of its initial goals: families seem to appreciate having a single point of access to services; local people are becoming more involved in services provision; and the police have improved their relations with the community.

The Lethbridge Project, Lethbridge

Lethbridge is a small city of 63 000 people in the south of Alberta. However, its size does not prevent it from being a major business centre for the local agricultural industry. Its population includes a wide range of cultural and ethnic groupings, and two aboriginal reserves are located nearby.

Having started an integration drive as far back as 1978, Lethbridge has a long history of services co-ordination. Indeed, it was the city's reputation as an innovator in this area which led the provincial government to invite it to become a pilot site. Lethbridge decided to focus its collaborative efforts on three separate projects: the fusion of its Family and Community Development Programme (FCDP) and "Parent's Place", an organisation providing parental support; the amalgamation of its Pre-school Assessment and Treatment Centre (PATC) and Paediatric Neuro-muscular Unit (PNMU); and the development of an Outreach Programme to provide young people aged 15 to 24 with support in training, employment and personal development.

The fusion of the FCDP and Parent's Place is in its early stages, although they have been working informally together for many years. So far, the FCDP has allocated one-fifth of a psychologist's post to Parent's Place, and they have arranged several planning meetings. The two organisations have yet to develop a joint case management system, and to be housed under one roof. When the merger does happen, the new organisation will provide an interesting example of services integration at the secondary level, since the existing FCDP is itself a product of joint activity by Alberta's social services, the town of Lethbridge and two school districts. The future for the FCDP-Parent's Place partnership looks bright because both share a strong client-oriented outlook.

The amalgamation of the PATC and the PNMU (currently located in a hospital) is still being planned. While the PATC has already agreed to provide child psychological monitoring services to the PNMU, they have yet to be relocated in a shared building. The new body will be financed by a community fund, and specialised equipment required by the PNMU will be financed by voluntary contributions. PATC already co-ordinates its activities with other services, including a speech therapy department and a public health unit, and a committee is working on how to enhance its co-ordination with the PNMU. Joint training sessions between PATC and PNMU staff relating to the care of disabled children seem likely to help this process.

The Outreach Project is located on the ground floor of a business centre, near to a major shopping mall. Eventually, it will move to another building, but limited resources have made it impossible to develop the premises. Despite the involvement of the federal government, Ministry of Education, and assessment and employment services, funding for the future remains uncertain. However, it is forging ahead with its plans, and is to have its own watchdog committee, including professionals, employers, government representatives, and members of the community.

As with many other efforts to integrate services, the path forward in Lethbridge has not always been smooth. At the operational level communication problems (heightened by a lack of teacher representation on the pilot committee), fears of disempowerment, and the suspicion that the real motivation behind the initiative is simply cost-cutting, have emerged as difficulties. At the field level, parents in particular have bemoaned the lack of co-operation between local agencies and schools.

The Partners for Youth Project, Edmonton

As the capital of Alberta, Edmonton is a major centre of trade and commerce. It is, in general, a quiet and friendly city. However, youth unemployment as high as 20 per cent in some neighbourhoods, and increasing violence amongst young people, are beginning to threaten the calm.

Edmonton's Partners for Youth Project is focused primarily on schools. Its aim is to develop them as community hubs where families can access a range of services. The project grew out of a congress, called "Safer Cities", held in Montreal in 1989. The following year, the Mayor set up a working party of fifteen members of the public, as well as representatives from the police and employment departments, to discuss ways to prevent crime through social action. In 1991 and 1992, reports drawn up in liaison with local communities pointed to the need for closely targeted initiatives that involved the whole community (thereby fostering ownership). At the same time, the fragmented and specialised nature of Edmonton's human services suggested that benefits could be derived from locating several agencies in one place. Senior officials decided that schools were natural centrepoints, and by the autumn of 1993, two pilot sites had been set up in Wellington Junior High School and Saint Nicholas' Catholic Junior High School.

While the Partners for Youth Project has strong support from senior level officials, it receives no special funding. As in Calgary and Lethbridge, services simply share each others professionals – a relatively inexpensive strategy. The social services department, for instance, has allocated a full-time post to Wellington School, which has a particularly high number of disadvantaged children. It also sends a social worker to St. Nicholas' School for half a day per week to do preventive work. In addition, the police department has freed up half a day per week for a member of staff to liaise with local schools, and the Young Men's Christian Association (YMCA), a voluntary organisation, provides pupils with extra school tuition and literacy training.

The main collaborators in Edmonton's Partners for Youth Project are education, children's, mental health, health and justice services, the city of Edmonton, local schools and the YMCA. Each has allocated staff to the mixed team of professionals which has been set up in each of the two pilot schools. Meeting once each week, these teams share information on cases that come to their attention, and work together to find solutions to children's problems.

The project as a whole is supervised by a steering committee set up several months before the project was launched. Consisting of top officials from government departments and associations, it currently meets once a fortnight, each time at a different project site. Individual members of the committee are assigned responsibility for their own school (mirroring the approach adopted by the provincial working committee towards its five pilot sites). Selected committee members meet with their school teams at least once a month.

The evaluation of the Partners for Youth Project is still being planned, and no firm conclusions on outcomes can be drawn yet. Nevertheless, the early signs are positive: academic achievement and pupils' attitudes have improved; children appear to have a greater sense of security; and the community seems to appreciate the project's efforts to reduce domestic violence. In addition, professionals involved in the project have found that their new work methods have impacted beneficially on other work they do, so much so that the city has received a large number of applications to set up similar programmes. However, red-tape will have to be cut if the system is to become more widespread.

Early teething problems in the scheme still need to be sorted out. The school teams need to develop a common vision and to acquire a better grasp of each other's fields – which may require joint training. They also need to be allocated more time to co-operate so that other work commitments do not impinge on team meetings. At the same time, senior officials from all departments need to adapt to the changes that are happening on the ground, and to find additional ways of supporting professionals' efforts to co-ordinate their activities.

CONCLUSION

The Alberta government has identified five promising local initiatives to integrate services in the province, and has boosted their efforts with its support. As a result of government input, the three pilot sites visited by the OECD share many features in common. Enjoying the special attention of two ministry representatives, each has good links with the upper echelons of government and receives strong political backing. At a slightly lower administrative level, they all receive organisational and planning support from municipal steering committees made up of local representatives. They also have encouraged – and enjoy – a certain amount of community involvement.

While political support has been in plentiful supply, financial backing for the sites has been limited. In other words, they have been required to implement integrated strategies at virtually no extra cost. This has led to widespread "lending" of professionals between agencies, and assignment of individuals to inter-disciplinary teams on a part-time basis. Some agencies have plans to co-locate their activities, but lack of funding has been an obstacle.

Like Saskatchewan, services co-ordination in Alberta has centred on public supported agency involvement, with little input from private agencies. The YMCA in Edmonton is a notable exception. This organisation has adapted well to inter-agency collaboration. Other, public sector agencies have experienced more difficulty, and see multi-disciplinary professional training as an important means to smooth inter-agency relations.

9

ONTARIO, CANADA
Integrating services
in Canada's wealthiest province

by

Philippa Hurrell and Peter Evans

INTRODUCTION AND SUMMARY

Enjoying rich natural resources and close links with America's industrial north east, Ontario is Canada's leading manufacturing province. Historical, climatic and economic factors have also led to relatively widespread settlement in the region. Ontario is currently the home of around one third of Canada's total population.

In spite of its status as a national, economic "heavyweight", it has been fighting recession since the late 1980s, and recently has been hit by competition linked to the North Atlantic Free Trade Area (NAFTA) agreement. In response, as elsewhere in Canada, it has been forced to implement public spending cuts. While, the integration of services may be seen as facilitating this process, efforts to improve co-ordination can be traced back to the early 1970s, and are tightly connected with the notion of improving services.

It seems fair to say that moves to co-ordinate the activities of ministries are at their strongest where specialised projects are concerned. Inter-ministerial collaboration is not yet a general feature of government operations. Fears amongst administrators (which may be valid) that greater collaboration will mean the merging of departments and fewer jobs are doing little to help the cause of integration's supporters.

CHILDREN AT RISK IN ONTARIO

In Ontario, as many as 18 per cent of children aged between 4 and 16 have identifiable conduct disorders, 10 to 15 per cent of school age children have learning difficulties, and 11 per cent drop out of school early (Offord and Boyle, 1987). All of these young people are considered to be at risk of academic or social failure.

The prospects in the province for young people who leave school without qualifications are poor. In 1993, the unemployment rate amongst its youth was 18.7 per cent – around twice the national average for the workforce as a whole.

The Ontario Ministry of Skills Development (1992) has projected that, by the year 2000, 63 per cent of all new jobs in Canada will require an education beyond grade level 12. However, the Economic Council of Canada (Harris, 1992) has reported that during the 1990s, if present drop-out rates continue, around one million young people will join the workforce who are functionally illiterate. Hence, there is a real fear in many provinces – including Ontario – that there will be a mismatch between available and required skill levels.

POLICIES PROMOTING SERVICES INTEGRATION

As early as 1970, the National Commission on Emotional and Learning Disorders in Children identified lack of co-ordination as the "number one problem" facing providers of services to children. Since the late 1970s the Ontario government has sought to reform children's services through integration, the involvement of the community in planning, and the use of comprehensive information systems for evaluation. While the initial drive to co-ordinate services was stimulated by the desire to increase effectiveness, a more recent motivating factor has been the need to implement government spending cuts.

During the 1980s, an impetus to services co-ordination was given by the publication of a report called "Investing in Children" (Ontario Ministry of Community and Social Services, 1988). This document outlined a corporate plan to enable government departments to deal more effectively with children's needs. It strongly emphasised inter-ministerial co-operation; however, in practice, it only stimulated collaboration within ministries.

More recently, further support for integrating services in Ontario has come from two high profile policy reviews. "Children First" (Maloney, 1990), by the Advisory Committee on Children's Services, sets forth an explicit cross-ministry integrated service delivery plan, with the goal of making schools the hub of services provision. "Yours, Mine and Ours: Ontario's Children and Youth" (Offord, 1994), by the Premier's Council on Health, reviews theory and research on major life transitions, and concludes that "cross-ministry collaboration" is needed to facilitate them.

In the last year, the Royal Commission on Learning (1994) has encouraged collaboration at the field level through increased participation by community agencies and parents in local schools.

In the 1980s, one of the main pieces of legislation passed to underpin efforts to integrate services was the Child and Family Services Act (1984). This established a common set of legal requirements for different children's services and made the funding of these services more flexible. Similarly, the Education Act (1989) encouraged collaboration by enabling school boards to run day care centres and by funding the participation of teachers in social and health programmes. Indirect support for collaboration came from the Young Offender's Act (1984) which changed the earliest age of admission to Ontario's "adult" courts from 16 to 18 years. As a result, the Ministries of the Solicitor General and Correctional Services, and Community and Social Services, were required to start working together to support "young" offenders over the age of 16.

More recently, a new impetus to the Child and Family Services Act has been given by the creation of a (new) Children's Services Policy Framework (1994). Developed by the Ministry of Community and Social Services (in liaison with consumers and communities), this framework sets out six broad aims: integration; co-ordinated access to services; enhanced local planning; equity in resource distribution; the establishment of priority groups; and improved accountability. Since its introduction, policy makers from the ministry and other stakeholders have been working together to provide information on the specific changes it requires in the organisation and delivery of services.

One of the outcomes of Ontario's efforts to facilitate integration has been an improvement in the level of co-operation within government ministries. However, co-operation between ministries is still relatively undeveloped: new programmes usually are created and funded separately, and ministries tend to stick to their own designated areas. Fears of job losses amongst bureaucrats, linked to possible amalgamations of departments, are doing little to improve the situation.

In spite of these difficulties, Ontario is still able to boast a number of special projects in which collaboration is key. Some of the best examples are described below.

EXAMPLES OF BEST PRACTICE IN INTEGRATED SERVICES FOR PRE-SCHOOL CHILDREN

The Better Beginnings, Better Futures Project, Sudbury

Set up in 1990, the Better Beginnings, Better Futures Project is a major interministerial initiative involving the Ministries of Health, Education and Training, and Community and Social Services, and the federal department of Indian and Northern Affairs. Its initial five-year funding recently has been extended, and the Ministry of Community and Social Services has made an additional commitment to a 20-year evaluation study. The aim of this research is to track over the long term the emotional and behavioural development of a group of targeted child.

Twelve demonstration sites in economically disadvantaged areas have received support from the initiative so far. To qualify for funding each had to submit a community development plan – incorporating integrated provision and community involvement – to address the social, emotional, behavioural and physical needs of local children between the ages of 0 and 8.

One of the Better Beginnings, Better Futures programmes is in Sudbury. Sudbury is set in an industrial area blackened by emissions from smoke stacks. Only recently has an attempt been made to clean up the environment, and to re-green the barren landscape. Many of Sudbury's most disadvantaged families live in Donovan-Flour Mill, which has French-speaking, English-speaking and aboriginal communities. This area is the focal point of programme activities.

The initiative was conceived in 1989 when a wide array of local organisations got together to discuss how to improve services for local families. The newly formed group included the N'Swakamok Native Centre, the Multicultural Folk Arts Association, the Children's Mental Health Services, the Public Health Unit, Laurentian University, the Sudbury Board of Education, the Sudbury District Housing Authority, SHARE (an association for public housing tenants), and the John Howard Society. With support from the Ministry of Community and Social Services, federal and government agencies, foundations and the community, Better Beginnings was launched in Sudbury in 1991.

The programme places a heavy emphasis on community participation, self-help and leadership. A Better Beginnings, Better Futures Association has been set up, which welcomes the participation of interested community members, and assumed legal and administrative responsibilities for the project in 1995. This is supported by a Community Advisory Committee, which facilitates links between professionals and residents, and is made up of representatives from local organisations. The project also has a paid staff of thirty, of which twenty-six are community people.

Central foci of the programme are community, economic and school development and parent support. Community development activities are strongly supported by members of the Community Advisory Committee, and include leadership building, various kinds of skills training, and re-greening the neighbourhood. Efforts to promote economic development revolve around an organisation called GEODE (Grassroots Economic Opportunity Development and Evaluation), and include the creation of a barter system and skills exchange programme.

Schools have benefited from the programme by the setting up of an aboriginal parents' group, and aboriginal, Afro-Canadian and Latin American cultural programmes. These were developed in direct response to articulated concerns about the cultural gap between schools and the community. Parents, on the other hand, have profited from school child care programmes, social and cultural activities, a "Teen Mom's Drop In" and a Parent Support Centre.

While the longitudinal evaluation of the programme is still being planned, its development, the process of fostering community participation, and early outcomes have been carefully documented. Some noted positive effects have been an increased sense of community identification and belonging, and higher mathematics and reading scores in local schools. These early signs of success can be attributed – at least in part – to one of the programme's leading staff members, who is an experienced and talented community developer, and the willingness of local people to participate in the project.

EXAMPLES OF BEST PRACTICE IN INTEGRATED SERVICES FOR SCHOOL CHILDREN

The Integrated Services for Northern Children Project, Cochrane/Timiskaming

With almost 90 per cent of Ontario's land mass yet only 10 per cent of its population, Northern Ontario presents a formidable challenge to human services providers. Many children live in remote rural areas which are several hours' drive from the nearest town. This means that professionals can easily spend an entire day travelling to and from a single client. As a result, northern children tend not to receive the same level of provision as their contemporaries in the south. The Integrated Services for Northern Children Project was set up to address this inequality.

The project grew out of developments which began in 1978. In the course of the year, the Ministry of Community and Social Services underwent a radical re-organisation in an attempt "to consolidate children's services and improve the co-ordination across programme streams". In order to address the situation in Northern Ontario, the Ministry formed a committee, comprised of its northern regional managers, which was charged to develop long term strategies to improve local services.

The new committee responded by setting up a "Northern Assessment Task Force" including staff from the Ministries of Community and Social Services, Education and Training, and Health. This body was created to improve collaboration between departments, agencies and professionals. One of its first achievements was to develop an inter-ministerial protocol clearly specifying each ministry's responsibilities regarding assessment services. It also lays the groundwork for later developments which recognised the need for co-ordinated provision – including the Integrated Services for Northern Children Project.

This project is a working model of inter-ministerial and inter-agency collaboration. Funded by the Ministries of Community and Social Services, Education and Training, and Health, it aims to provide a comprehensive range of services to isolated rural areas, using multi-disciplinary teams based in six northern cities. This organisational structure is supplemented by satellite offices located in a string of smaller settlements.

The multi-disciplinary teams include a wide spectrum of professionals sponsored by different ministries: psychiatrists, psychologists and psychometrists by Community and Social Services; speech pathologists, physiotherapists and occupational therapists by Health; and speech/language teachers and teacher diagnosticians by Education and Training. These professionals are supported by satellite (case management) workers who perform outreach work and co-ordinate client care. Additional (administrative) backup comes from officials working in the ministries.

The main targets of the multi-disciplinary teams are children in rural areas with multi-dimensional difficulties. While "inner-city" problems are almost non-existent in northern Ontario, isolated community life can lead to important developmental problems amongst children, as well as encouraging incest and other forms of abuse within families.

Each of the six project sites was asked to set up a management information system for case monitoring. This has led to the development of an "electronic web" that links the different programmes together. They also were required to set up an evaluation scheme to keep track of outcomes. Based on assessment criteria, a recent study found that, of all the sites, Cochrane/Timiskaming had the best performance. This achievement appears to have been won through the creation of a harmonious and effective management committee; efforts to target those children with multiple problems who need integrated services most; and success in avoiding competition and duplication in services provision.

The Ontario government has been able to take advantage of the Integrated Services for Northern Project by feeding lessons learned into policy. The Children's Services Policy Framework in particular (see earlier) reflects experiences obtained through the project.

EXAMPLES OF BEST PRACTICE IN INTEGRATED SERVICES FOR YOUTH IN THE TRANSITION TO WORK

The Eastwood Collegiate Institute, Waterloo County

The Eastwood Collegiate Institute is a public high school with a population of 1 398 students ranging in age from 13 to 19 years. Most come from middle or lower-middle socio-economic backgrounds and are by no means the most deprived children in Ontario. However, school drop-out is an important problem, and the current employment situation in the province poses a serious threat to unqualified young people from any social group.

With a mission of encouraging lifelong learning the Eastwood Collegiate Institute, through a Comprehensive Alternative Education Programme, helps students in grades 9 and 10 (15- and 16-year-olds) whose academic performance, attendance or behaviour suggest that they may be in danger of dropping out of school. This aims to find ways of bringing community partners into school to support student learning and to help students make a successful transition to work.

Included in this initiative is the institute's Co-operative Education Programme. This programme is divided into three stages: in the first, students are placed in feeder school classrooms to provide cross-age teaching; in the second, they are given work in a non-profit or community agency; and, in the third, students are allowed to choose their own placement, most obtaining jobs in the commercial sector.

Added to this is a Mentorship Programme in which both senior citizens and company representatives participate. Senior citizens, who have had successful careers, work for the institute on a voluntary basis. They act as advisors to students and help them to develop a sense of community. The inter-generational aspect of the relationship is very much valued by the institute – as is their "neutral" (non-school related) position. However, while there are around 200 applicants on the institute's books, only seven volunteers are active.

The corporate aspect of the Mentorship Programme has been developed in co-operation with the institute's business partner, the Mutual Group. Profiles of company volunteers and students are drawn up to match between 20 and 30 "couples". They meet for one hour a week over a period of six weeks on the school site. Later on students are introduced to their mentor's workplace, and they may also arrange recreational and social skills-based activities together. The mentors see their role as providing "support, guidance and consistency as a role model buddy and friend".

Assessment of the Comprehensive Alternative Education Programme has shown that around 90 per cent of participating students return to the regular system – and a new longitudinal study will reveal their graduation rates.

CONCLUSION

Like Saskatchewan, Ontario is the focal point of an interesting mix of government level and grassroots approaches to integrating services. The Sudbury Better Beginnings programme, for instance, is the product of serious collaborative efforts by a group of state and federal ministries to improve the future prospects of disadvantaged children; and the Northern Children Project benefits from the support and funding of several government ministries. The Sudbury programme is particularly interesting in showing how strategic level and grassroots initiatives can meet "half way". Sudbury's community had already set up a collaborative group before additional support from the ministries became available.

Government backing for integrated approaches has been matched by strong leadership on the ground. Evidence from the Ontario case studies suggests that good leadership can be vital to the success of programmes. In Sudbury, this leadership comes from one key individual with impressive community development skills, while in Northern Ontario it comes from a large but harmonious committee.

Community involvement clearly provides an important boost to both the Sudbury and Eastwood programmes. In Sudbury, Better Beginnings is based almost entirely on local management and decision-making. On the other hand, at the Eastwood Collegiate Institute, while the programme is school-centred, it relies quite heavily on the services of senior citizens and local businesses.

On the basis of the Sudbury and Northern Ontario examples, two different meanings can be attributed to the term "holistic services". Sudbury's Better Beginnings programme provides a range of social, educational, environment and economic services to improve the "health" of the whole community. In contrast, the Northern Children Project is very much geared towards providing a range of human services to improve the "health" of individual children.

As in other parts of Canada, evaluation is given a high priority in Ontario; indeed, no better example of this commitment can be found than in the Ministry of Community and Social Services' support for a 20-year evaluation study of the Better Beginnings Project.

NEW BRUNSWICK, CANADA
Working smarter through integration

by

Peter Evans and Philippa Hurrell

INTRODUCTION AND SUMMARY

New Brunswick is on the eastern seaboard of Canada bordering on Nova Scotia and Quebec. It is Canada's only official bilingual province. It is predominantly rural in nature with three main cities and a population of approximately 730 000. The government structure is centralised and the local taxation system is limited to property taxes only. As with other Canadian provinces federal funding has in recent times been cut.

Growing numbers of children at risk, in the 1980s, led to the realisation that for education to be most effective schools needed support in meeting the extent of the challenges that were presented to them. Successful strategies, to reorganise a wide range of relevant services through their co-ordination at strategic, operational and field levels, which would be responsive to the holistic needs of children and their families, has been the solution developed. The goals have been to improve school readiness, prevent drop-out, raise educational standards and facilitate the transition to work.

In achieving this, an impressive, effective, co-ordinated and comprehensive set of services, responsive to community needs, has developed in the context of generally unfavourable financial circumstances.

CHILDREN AT RISK IN NEW BRUNSWICK

Since 1985 there has been growing concern in New Brunswick (NB) over the increasing numbers of children who live in poverty and who have health related problems inhibiting their readiness for school or who are at risk of failing in school and not obtaining the qualifications necessary to make an effective transition to work.

POLICIES PROMOTING SERVICES INTEGRATION

Since the mid-1980s New Brunswick has recognised the holistic nature of the needs of students at risk and has set about the task of comprehensively reforming its education, health, social services and other support structures in order to meet those needs.

In 1984 an Office of Government Reform working paper noted that:

"The education system cannot depend solely on teachers to provide students with the best possible learning environment. Availability and access to a variety of professional support services is essential to teachers, administrators and parents in order to enhance students' learning process and to ensure a quality learning environment".

To implement the new policy framework demanded by this reform and to address the needs of children and families at risk, the governments of Canada and New Brunswick implemented, between 1988 and 1993, the Youth Strategy and Stay-in-School initiatives. Together these strategies aimed to tackle concerns over education and employment issues for students and youth aged between 12 and 24. More recently an early childhood initiative has been launched which aims to reach the approximately 15 per cent of pre-school aged children believed to be most seriously at risk with the intention of stimulating their readiness for school.

The Student Services Branch of the Department of Education, is responsible to help co-ordinate programmes for all exceptional students which are intended to help them be successful in school, such as stay-in-school programmes, counselling programmes, curriculum development, transition to work. But their delivery requires collaboration and consultation among several provincial government departments including Health and Community Services, Human Resources Development (NB), Recreation and Sport, Advanced Education and Labour, Solicitor-General, Justice, Supply and Services and Federal agencies, such as Health and Welfare, Human Resources, Canada and Indian Affairs.

In 1986, a mandate was agreed to explore the means to implement support services to education which would be managed by Health and Community Services. This in turn led to a new model of provision which provided for a limited array of needed support services provided by both the Department of Education and Health and Community Services. The services were developed through joint planning to avoid, for example, clashes in services delivery philosophy inherent in educational and clinical approaches and to avoid services from different areas being delivered to any single child or family.

The arrangements were guided by the principle that resource allocation and service provision could most efficiently and effectively be provided to school aged children by the Department which delivered such services to the population as a whole. The arrangements were seen as providing the improved co-ordination of services, the avoidance of duplication, the development of provincial standards for professional services, and ensuring the effective use of staff including the reduction of unnecessary competition between systems for scarce professionals.

The arrangements operate under the Schools Act and the Family Services Act and cover services provided by education, public health and community services, mental health, income assistance, alcohol and drug dependency, housing and recreation and the Atlantic Provinces Special Education Authority. Eleven principles guide the provision of the services. They should be community based, delivered to the school and the home, accessible, flexible, bilingual, consult parents and involve them in decision-making, support students to enhance their learning with minimal disruption, reduce dependency, promote as normal a lifestyle as possible, avoid fragmentation and duplication and be accountable through the determination of clear authority and responsibility lines.

The responsibility for the implementation of support services to education lies centrally with the Omnibus Committee for Children and Youth which comprises members of the Departments of Health and Community Services, Education, the Mental Health Commission and Human Resources Development (NB). This committee reports to the Assistant Deputy Minister of the Family and Community Services Division and serves as a link between departments in planning services for children and youth and their families and deals with the establishment of protocols between departments, setting of priorities, funding and problem-solving.

The detailed implementation of these arrangements is overseen by a Regional Omnibus Committee whose function and structure mirrors its central equivalent. Services are delivered by a professional resource pool which responds to referrals. Professionals who deliver the services are required to develop and maintain an implementation plan for clients which must identify clear goals and how they are to be achieved. Among other things, the plan must show evidence of collaboration with the family and/or the child and the school, as well as with other relevant professionals. Furthermore a monitoring and evaluation procedure is required which notes objectives achieved and progress made.

EXAMPLES OF BEST PRACTICE IN INTEGRATED SERVICES FOR PRE-SCHOOL CHILDREN

Early childhood initiatives

The Early Childhood Initiatives for Priority Children and their Families commenced in 1992 following recommendations from the report on excellence in education. The Early Childhood Initiatives (ECI) is an integrated and co-ordinated service delivery system for childhood services that target priority pre-school children aged from 0 to 4. The ECI brings together the collaborative efforts of public health and medical services division and the family and community services division. They have been planned to bring young children to school who are as healthy and ready as possible to achieve their potential. There are seven major components. These provide enhanced pre-natal screening and intervention in order to increase healthy pregnancy outcomes; enhanced post-natal screening and intervention in order to enhance factors and conditions known to foster healthy growth and development; the re-targeting of pre-school clinics to 3.5 years of age in order to support the healthy growth and development of pre-school children; home-based early intervention services aimed at improving childhood outcomes and enhancing family self-sufficiency; integrated day care services whose goals are the full participation of the high priority child in developmentally appropriate child care services, and improved childhood outcomes among high priority children; social work prevention services whose goal is the secondary prevention of the abuse and neglect of children, through the strengthened parenting competences of high priority parents; and home economics services whose goal is to have priority families develop skills in the areas of resource management and family development with the intention of stimulating greater self-reliance.

The services are co-ordinated across the entire province via a single entry point system through the public health nurse. Regional public health ECI co-ordinators register priority families, conduct an assessment and refer the families to a range of existing government and community based services including the school districts. At 3.5 years a student health profile form is completed on each child and is passed to the school before entry into kindergarten.

The Carelton Victoria Child Development Services Incorporated Early Intervention Programme is an example of a non-statutory, community based service which stresses child development from a family-centred perspective. It is an external agency for the Department of Health and Community Services and is funded by them at the rate of C$3 000 per family. It works through home visits, need assessment and the formulation in conjunction with the family and other service providers of an individual family service plan. Regular home visits provide the support necessary to encourage the development of the appropriate family dynamics and competences for successful living.

The professionals noted that the benefits of the co-ordination of services that have so far been seen, include earlier identification and referral and thus improved prevention, improved communication and sharing among professionals and a better database. Improved social, health and education outcomes are anticipated. On the downside, they reported an increased workload.

EXAMPLES OF BEST PRACTICE IN INTEGRATED SERVICES FOR SCHOOL CHILDREN

General

School district 12 – Woodstock – has a school population of some 5 000 students and, as judged by the numbers of students supported by student services, falls in the mid-range of the other school districts of NB. A survey completed in 1991 showed that the kinds of problems that schools faced included drop-out, lack of attendance, academic difficulty, lack of interest shown by educators and parents in students with difficulties. A second survey completed in 1992 discovered that the kinds of problems associated with teaching children at risk included problems of co-ordinating provision and communication with other agencies. Thus the need for the integration of services and a holistic approach was recognised and following pressure from parents, supported by local administrators, the goal became the provision of better services for students and their families intended to reduce the load on parents through developing the "one-stop-shop", by sharing information and increasing efficiency. The key partners are parents, students, health and community services, early intervention services, local associations for community living, teachers, public health, administrators, probation officers, mental health, police, and the community suicide committee.

Students at risk as well as those with disabilities are serviced in Woodstock by a student services team of 14 (plus a Director) comprising teachers (with specialisms in job placement, classroom management, pedagogy and community involvement), school psychometrist, specialists of the hearing and visually impaired, social workers, speech and language pathologists and an occupational therapist. Professionals from education and from family and community services work together and are co-located. This group also co-ordinates with many other services offered to children and families within the Department of Health and Community Services, as well as with services offered by Public Health, Mental Health, Early Intervention (private, non-profit), the Department of Income Assistance and the Federal Department of Human Resources Development.

As noted above the support services to education staff are co-located with educational personnel. They work in schools to help the classroom teacher to address the needs of all children and are seen as a key part of the success of this model. There has been more effective targeting of resources, case planning and intervention. In particular, they work in the areas of developing general parenting skills, specific behaviour management, suicide intervention, skills in developing conflict resolution, native education issues, community tutoring and family counselling, teacher education and awareness, liaison with other community agencies and resources, school planning for at risk students (both social and academic) and direct services counselling with students and their families. The services are delivered in the home, the school or other community settings.

Social workers have been working with educators in this way since 1988 when the new carefully planned delivery model was implemented. This co-operative model was agreed to ensure that school social workers did not operate traditionally by providing direct services to clients. The approach has been accepted and provides a better preventive-reactive balance of service provision.

All of the professionals in the student services team work with the schools through collaboration and teamwork and use a problem-solving method involving a constant review and development of the process. The interactive style with the client is forward looking and holistic. Client involvement in decision-making is an important objective. The community too, plays a significant role in the overall success of the strategy.

Woodstock Junior High

The team approach described above works with the school via methods and resources teachers (M&R). These teachers have the responsibility of planning the day to day details of the school-work and other relevant aspects of school life for the student in the light of consultations with the student services team. This team encourages the M&R teachers to be creative and to adopt a problem-solving approach. In addition this teacher will co-ordinate with other supports which may be in place such as a teacher assistant, a counsellor, a co-op education coordinator, a school mentor, and a work site supervisor (the last two of whom provide friendship and support for the student).

In reviewing the outcomes of this integrated approach few if any negative comments can be identified. All parties agreed that there were benefits for at risk students in terms of social behaviour, progress in learning and self-esteem. Parents and teachers also reported that they felt better supported and understood more about the way services worked. Communication improved between professionals as did efficiency. A more exciting working environment and "esprit de corps" were also noted. The service provision was simply better and more efficient.

EXAMPLES OF BEST PRACTICE IN INTEGRATED SERVICES FOR YOUTH IN THE TRANSITION TO WORK

Between 1989 and 1995 support given to those students at risk seeking work were provided through small community based Access Centres in the three major cities of NB, funded by the joint Federal and Provincial Youth Strategy. Since 1995 the services have been provided through either Federal or Provincial Human Resources Development Offices, following the replacement of the Youth Strategy with the Youth Services Partnership. This latter initiative builds on the experience gained in the Access Centres and retains the goal of maintaining collaborative efforts to provide youth with support to facilitate their transition to the labour market. It reinforces the role of case managers who help youngsters access federal and provincial programmes and services.

These new arrangements were not in place at the time of the OECD visit to New Brunswick (in 1994). However, since the method of working in the new structure has built on the work of the Access Centres the following observations based on information obtained from the Woodstock Access Centre remain valid.

This Access Centre provided personal employment/career counselling in the context of a basis of a wide range of assessment services. The clients aged between 15 and 24 were either unemployed, underemployed or out of school. Those at risk tended to have poor family support often with drug and alcohol problems and the centre functioned as a friend and ally focusing on educational and personal needs and an alternative to school when necessary. Clients could attend either through appointment or on a drop-in basis. Key partners in the service have been Canada Employment and Immigration, Human Resources Development (Canada), the NB Department of Advanced Education and Labour. Other partners also include the NB Department of Education, the NB Department of Income Assistance (Human Resources Development, NB), and the NB Department of the Solicitor-General. In this collaboration the labour force needs identified by the lead departments were recognised. The objective was to provide an enhanced service to youth, who were out of school and work, by providing education and training opportunities and work experience, viewed as necessary for labour market entry.

Counsellors in the centre worked for instance with other agencies to secure the resources needed to assist in the implementation of case plans and had for example places in Community Colleges especially purchased for Access Centre clients. In addition the counsellors operated the STAR initiative (Services Targeted for Adolescents at Risk) which was planned to co-ordinate existing services for its at risk clients. Steered by Human Resource Development, Education, Advanced Education and Labour and the Department of Health and Community services, the STAR programme addressed problems faced by young people at risk aged 16-18 with the intention of maintaining them in, or returning them to school, or maintaining them in or returning them to employment or securing employment.

Independent evaluations of the STAR programme demonstrated the need for the service and its effectiveness. These integrated services approaches were seen by the workers in this centre as successful with few negative outcomes. Client needs were perceived to be becoming better known with increased educational support. The responsibilities of the different departments were being clarified and better understood and some new approaches had been developed. However, it was noted that the process of inter-agency collaboration did not reach the level intended in the Youth Strategy Agreement, reportedly due mainly to an imbalance in the funding arrangements and to different management styles and turf disputes. In addition, a greater need for the involvement of the community and the youth private sector was seen as essential, and while they were reported to be sympathetic the need for more financial support from them was noted.

Over the first five years of the Access Centre's work, a change in the demands on the service, from the upgrading of education and training levels to a greater need for employment services, had been observed. However, employment outcomes were reported to be not as good as would be liked; an outcome attributed to the general lack of employment assistance services in Woodstock.

CONCLUSION

The Canadian province of New Brunswick has since the late 1980s implemented a co-ordinated services policy for children at risk based on the recognition of the holistic needs of children and families which recognises that schools and teachers can only provide "the best possible learning environment" when adequately supported by other professionals and services. The innovations have been essentially a "top-down" process which have rationalised the contributions made by a large number of both Federal and Provincial government departments, with the effect of improving the co-ordination of community based services, avoiding duplication, developing provincial standards for professional services, ensuring the effective use of staff and reducing unnecessary competition for scarce professionals.

Services for children and youth aged 0 to 24, are co-ordinated by "omnibus committees" at both central and regional levels. In the district visited there is strong local vision and leadership and a real and continuing commitment can be seen to co-operation and to the development of better support structures for schools, teachers, children and their families and for the professionals themselves. The fact that transition to work services have found that the balance of service needs of their clientele have changed over the past few years from education to employment may perhaps be taken to indicate the success of these reforms.

The advantages of the co-ordinated approach is seen throughout all levels of the system, from policy makers to professionals (in all services studied) to parents and students. This attests to the comprehensiveness and effectiveness of these new arrangements in tackling the difficulties some children and families have in coping with the problems of current day living. The gilt on the gingerbread would perhaps be a greater involvement of the community and employees in the process, in order to strengthen the demand side of labour market policy.

VICTORIA, AUSTRALIA
Working towards co-ordination of services at the local level

by

Peter Evans and Philippa Hurrell

INTRODUCTION AND SUMMARY

Up until 1945, the majority of immigrants to Australia came from Britain and Ireland; afterwards, increasing numbers came from other parts of Europe, and in the last ten years many immigrants have come from the Asia Pacific region. The aboriginal population now stands at just 2 per cent of the total population. Australia's traditional dependency on agriculture and the extraction of natural resources continues, but the services sector – particularly finance, tourism and government – is growing in importance.

Federal and state government involvement in programmes to support disadvantaged children and youth in Victoria is strong. Programmes which allow flexibility at the local level, such as the Students at Risk initiative, appear to be well supported and effective and complemented by Victorian education policy to give management responsibility to schools. This approach will serve to improve co-ordination with other initiatives at the local level, such as the Youth Access Scheme.

A broad range of welfare staff can be found in Victoria's schools. Significantly, teachers play an important role in welfare provision which is viewed as an integral component of the teaching process. A growing number of staff are being trained in welfare in recognition of the importance of this part of the teacher's work.

CHILDREN AT RISK IN VICTORIA

Inbuilt into the Students at Risk (STAR) component of the federal National Equity Programme for Schools (NEPS) is a broad definition of pupils at risk which has been used by the Victoria government for service planning. They are defined as children up to the age of 19 who intend to leave school or have already left, and whose level of educational achievement is affected by problems such as family breakdown, parental violence, transience, homelessness, substance abuse and truancy. Special attention is given by the STAR initiative to Aborigines and Torres Strait Islanders, children with non-English speaking backgrounds, students from low income families, young offenders, and young people who do not enter into tertiary education.

POLICIES PROMOTING SERVICES INTEGRATION

The federal and state governments share responsibility for designing educational programmes for Aborigines, migrants and disadvantaged students – with the state government taking responsibility for policy development, programme delivery and accountability.

One major federal initiative, the National Equity Programme for Schools (NEPS), brings together eleven formerly separate programmes. Implemented in 1994, it continues to develop federal and state policies on equity and access and to create equal opportunities in schools for disadvantaged and disabled children. The Students at Risk (STAR) component of the programme – which was first implemented prior to NEPS in 1990 – addresses the particular needs of children who are in danger of dropping out of school. STAR funded projects have to be school-based, but the involvement of outside agencies is encouraged. In Victoria, 10 per cent of secondary colleges receive STAR money. This is used mainly to provide welfare support and to develop the curriculum.

Senior managers from government and non-government school systems, reported that co-ordination at the local level has a range of advantages, including improving the cost-effectiveness of public services. Good communication links exist between community agencies which provide for children at risk although there is scope for additional bridges to be built with schools.

The State's Extra Edge Programme aims to achieve greater collaboration in this area. Involving the Department of Education, the Department of Health and Community Services, the Office of Youth Affairs, the Municipal Association of Victoria, and Non-government Organisations, the programme provides special funding to employ additional teachers as service co-ordinators. A total of 18 Extra Edge projects currently exist in Victoria.

The federal government also takes primary responsibility for improving the employment opportunities of young adults at risk. In 1985, federal government policy led to the setting up of Youth Access Centres (YACs) across Australia. Linked to Commonwealth Employment Services, these are places where young people can obtain information and advice on education, training and employment, income support, health, accommodation and legal issues. Following the release of a report entitled "Towards A Fairer Australia: Social Justice Strategy in 1991-92", which noted the fragmentation of local youth services, Youth Access Centres were given the responsibility for facilitating co-ordination amongst them. With the goal of meeting the needs of four specific groups – young homeless people in cities, young offenders, Aboriginal and Torres Strait Islander youth, and young people from non-English speaking backgrounds – the YACs have been charged with the following co-ordinating functions:

- developing local youth profiles, including information on young people and service providers;

- circulating and using this information through local inter-agency networks;

- identifying gaps and duplication in services provision, and assisting in the development of inter-agency strategies to overcome them;

- developing linkages with other youth service providers;

- participating in co-ordinated planning, including (where possible) the development of outcome measures for inter-agency activities; and

- assisting in the development of inter-agency strategies, including some one-off projects with other youth services.

Rather than taking a leading role in services co-ordination at the local level, YACs are to support existing co-ordination networks through activities such as providing venues for meetings, secretarial back-up, youth profile information and details on the services they offer. Where a co-ordination network for youth services does not exist, YACs can initiate and adopt a leading role in co-ordination at the local level.

At the state level, Youth Co-ordination Committees have been set up to ensure that local, state and federal governments work together to facilitate joint service delivery at the community level.

An evaluation of YACs, published in 1992, discovered that there was "confusion and uncertainty at the local level surrounding the YACs' role in co-ordination" (Waller, 1992, p.13). Some local agencies were suspicious that the government wanted to use co-ordination as a means to cut costs; others were resentful that the (federally controlled) YACs were trying to "take over" local co-ordinating structures which were already in place. However, on a positive note, some agencies found the inter-agency meetings and information sharing activities organised by YACs very useful, and wanted to extend them to joint project planning and implementation.

A later evaluation, published in 1994, reported a high level of satisfaction among young people with YAC services (Department of Employment, Education and Training, 1994). Most received assistance with employment or education. However, over 40 per cent of clients were given advice on government benefits or allowances, health, accommodation or personal matters – showing that YACs were performing a multi-purpose function. Schools appeared to be satisfied with the services provided by YACs – which consisted mainly of providing information on job or study-related topics. Other types of youth service had less contact with YACs, with only 64 per cent reporting dealings with them in the last six months. Nationally, 57 per cent of youth agencies were satisfied or very satisfied with the co-ordinating efforts of YACs, although "co-ordination activities were identified by youth service providers and schools as the main areas for improvement" (Department of Employment, Education and Training, 1994).

Senior managers responsible for Victoria's Commonwealth Employment Services and Youth Access Centres believe that there is a lack of communication between federal, state and local government officials. At the local level, problems have been created by the introduction of a case management approach which focuses on the most needy. Since, as part of the government's drive to bring down costs, private agencies can compete for case management work. Staff in YACs expressed concern about their future role, since YAC priority functions such as the schools programme, co-ordination and outreach would be changed as a result of the introduction of case management. State cuts in education and welfare have reduced the number of services with which YACs potentially can co-operate. Even so, senior managers believe that co-operation is greater at the local level than at higher levels in the services hierarchy.

EXAMPLES OF BEST PRACTICE IN INTEGRATED SERVICES FOR SCHOOL CHILDREN

The Bendigo senior secondary college, Bendigo

Bendigo is located 156 kilometres north of Melbourne and is the largest city in the area. While its original wealth was derived from gold mining, agriculture and manufacturing are now important. Its population is predominantly Anglo-Saxon, but it also has a well established Chinese community.

Through Victoria's Schools of the Future scheme, Bendigo Senior Secondary College, like other schools, has been given greater responsibility for its own management. As a result, efforts to co-ordinate school-linked services are to a large extent determined by the college itself.

The needs of students with difficulties in the school are met by a student management and welfare team made up of two student welfare co-ordinators, two careers advisers, and nine-year level co-ordinators. Form teachers are seen as having primary responsibility for identifying children's problems, and for reporting them to team members. The student welfare co-ordinators play a leading role in supporting children at risk – addressing family, financial, and housing difficulties. Children who are homeless are referred by them to St. Luke's hostel which has strong links with the school.

The college also boasts a Resource Centre in which a youth activities services worker and a youth development worker are located. The youth development worker's role is to build bridges between the school and the community, although this role reportedly has needed to be clarified. In addition to offices for non-teaching staff, the Resource Centre also houses a "coffee corner", a meeting room, and an information shop. Collaboration in the college is stimulated further by its participation in the State's Extra Edge initiative for children at risk. One of the goals of the initiative is to encourage the co-location and co-ordination of resources and personnel. To this effect, the school is planning to locate all of its school support staff in a single office. Extra Edge money has also been used to set up a traineeship programme in hospitality for older students in danger of unemployment. This has involved input from the Central Victorian Training Company and the federal Department of Employment, Education and Training. The programme is overseen by an Extra Edge co-ordinator who works in the school.

A recent survey carried out in the school showed that 97 per cent of students and 97 per cent of parents were satisfied with the services it provided; and students interviewed during the site visit said that support staff had helped them to settle into school and to solve personal problems. However, reportedly, there is still room for improvement in the co-ordination of school services.

The Sunshine Deanery Students at Risk Project, Melbourne

The Sunshine Deanery is made up of a group of Catholic secondary schools, parish primary schools and community services, which are located in a traditional manufacturing area in the west of Melbourne which has suffered from industrial restructuring. The area is made up of a diverse ethnic mix due to earlier migration waves from southern Europe and recent waves from Indo-China and Africa. Average family incomes are lower than in other parts of Melbourne and unemployment is relatively high.

The Deanery model aids clusters of schools in identifying and assisting target groups of students. This model emphasises the links between the secondary school, the home, parish communities and church, municipal and other agencies. The main systems to which young people belong are recognised and encouraged to interact co-operatively in promoting their growth.

The integration of services at the school level is an evolving process within the Sunshine Deanery. It has developed from key learnings that have arisen during the course of the STAR Project. Within the Sunshine Deanery there has been an increasing use of approaches which involve the integration of services at the school level. The STAR Project has enabled a range of programmes and strategies to be explored, attempting to build upon the ways in which schools work with young people at risk.

The integration of services at the school level is aimed at meeting the needs of young people through an holistic approach being applied. This involves staff from community agencies and services and working with school staff, young people and their families, using the school as a base. This approach also positions the school as a central focus in the life of the youth person.

Responsibility for the on-going management and co-ordination of the programme lies with the STAR Deanery Reference Group, which is composed of school principals, STAR contact teachers, the STAR project officer, and a representative from the Catholic Education Office and Priest's Deanery. It has planned a range of initiatives, many of which require collaboration. These include:

- *Community linkage*: within this approach the particular learning and social needs of a young person are addressed through developing a "curriculum related" placement in the community *e.g.* at a florist, peer tutoring in a primary school. Such programmes focus upon students' competencies as well as developing self-esteem and confidence. They allow learning to be meaningful and integrated.

- *Case management model*: the case planning approach involves personnel who are directly responsible for the student at risk, including school and community agency staff. Meetings concentrate upon identifying issues of concern in the life of the young person with all parties developing a realistic shared response involving input from the various sectors. In this way the student receives a broad range of support at the school level. Families, too, can be involved in the process, receiving support through the school based framework. Possible outcomes of Case Planning may include:

  - Financial and Material Aid.

  - Curriculum – greater flexibility and/or modification.

  - Agency Support – Counselling, Mentor Programme.

  - Programmes, for example Vietnamese Girls' Group and School Support Group.

A Directory of Resources and Services to support young people in the west, which provides information on a wide variety of local agencies, has been published.

The STAR Programme in the Sunshine Deanery has a strong evaluation component and has contributed to a national STAR evaluation. At a more anecdotal level, students reported that they had found the specific programmes useful. For example, girls providing peer tutoring in one of the Deanery's primary schools said that their confidence had increased, and others who had been on "job placements" felt that it had given them the chance to confront the "real world".

EXAMPLES OF BEST PRACTICE IN INTEGRATED SERVICES FOR YOUTH IN THE TRANSITION TO WORK

YACs in Melbourne

A total of four YACs were visited in Melbourne, namely, Footscray, Brunswick, Preston Koori and Melbourne City Centre. All are located in socio-economically deprived areas, with high populations of poorly educated, low income, unemployed, and transient migrant people. As a consequence, many of their clients have multiple problems, including mental and physical health difficulties, family problems, and homelessness. This has made co-operation and networking with other local agencies essential.

According to staff, government youth policy is very much "top-down", with poor linkages between the federal government, state government and the local level. Recently, the federal government has attempted to implement two initiatives which have received minimal local support: one concerns family mediation (which service providers do not regard as a priority); and the other, case management (which local workers are reluctant to implement). The case management model implemented by the Department is highly structured, operating as it does within a legislative framework. It has specific entry and exit points, a requirement for detailed record keeping and particular contact points along the way. The case management model and possibly the manner of its implementation in YACs, may have caused some nostalgia for the generally less bureaucratic, informal case management style adopted by YAC staff in the past. However, the concept of case management per se is not problematic for YAC staff.

Two of the YACs visited were designed to meet specific local needs. The Preston Koori YAC was set up to cater for aboriginal young people, and is enmeshed in the local aboriginal community. Young Koori people continue to be highly disadvantaged in education and in the labour market. Many have multiple problems or issues that preclude them from participating fully in employment, education and training, and so a welfare-oriented YAC service culture has evolved. Additionally, Koori YAC staff themselves have possibly not adequately represented the complete range of Departmental services, systems, resources and general infrastructure that would have enabled the provision of a more proactive approach to labour market interventions for their clients.

Initial plans for the Koori YAC were to co-locate the service physically within another agency, which itself was highly visible in the Koori community, and which had an existing mandate to co-ordinate services to the Victorian Aboriginal community. Various tensions regarding funding arrangements and physical resource allocations in the end stymied prolonged attempts to co-ordinate and co-locate these services. Nevertheless, it makes strong efforts to link up young people with programmes which have an aboriginal focus, such as ABSTUDY, through which they can get education grants, and LEAP, through which they can obtain experience in environmental work.

The Melbourne City Centre YAC, on the other hand, is geared towards the needs of homeless young people. It is co-located with the Young People's Health Service and the Youth Information Centre. As a result, young people are able to access at one site the services of a broad range of professionals, including employment and social security staff, social workers, doctors, nurses and psychologists. Joint protocols have been established between the three services, and an informal agreement exists for resource sharing (such as the photocopier and fax). However, they have experienced some initial teething problems, such as target group definitions, concerns about confidentiality, and staff difficulties in adapting to a multi-disciplinary environment.

CONCLUSION

Funding for programmes for students at risk is provided by federal and state governments, however decisions about what kind of services should be offered often are made at the local level. The Deanery's secondary schools in Melbourne, for example, have instituted a broad array of programmes for children at risk which have been designed by staff and others in the community. This ties in with new state government policy to devolve management responsibility to schools.

Teachers in Victoria play an important role in addressing the holistic needs of all strudents including those at risk. They may be responsible for identifying children with problems (Bendigo College), involved in multi-disciplinary welfare teams (Bendigo College and the Sunshine Deanery), and may also act as welfare co-ordinators (the Sunshine Deanery). Thus it seems clear that teachers are prepared to involve themselves in supporting students' needs in a general way, whether they are of either a mainly welfare or educational nature.

Concerns expressed both at national, state and local levels have led to the setting up of some innovative programmes for students at risk of not completing their education. The emphasis is placed on supporting students before they drop out, as well as providing opportunities for re-entry.

At the local level, the commitment of staff and their willingness to work collaboratively was most impressive. Teachers and other workers were willing to look and change structures and programmes to meet the needs of students more flexibly. It was notable that this was one of the key aspects which students valued highly.

Aspects of the projects which supported collaboration appeared to be:

– good communication between staff;

– joint training of staff;

– cultural sensitivity;
– the presence of a co-ordinator;
– clear goals;
– thorough evaluation leading to adaptation of programmes;
– keeping the needs of the child as a central focus; and
– the availability of funding.

12

SOUTH AUSTRALIA
A leader in building effective structures for services integration

by

Philippa Hurrell and Peter Evans

INTRODUCTION AND SUMMARY

South Australia has a reputation for being "the harshest, driest State in the most arid of the earth's populated continents" (Fodor's, 1994). Because of the inhospitability of the land, almost 99 per cent of the population live in close proximity to the more fertile coastline.

Since 1991, the South Australian economy has been in the throes of a severe recession – one that has forced as many as 30 per cent of teenage school-leavers into unemployment. During the relatively "good" years in South Australia, between 1989 and 1991, the government pumped significant amounts of money into the establishment of an Interagency Referral Process. However, recent financial restraints are threatening the progress that has been made in this area. The efforts of school based staff and Regional Services of the Department for Education and Children's services (DECS) to co-ordinate different services for children at risk continue to be quite healthy – and teachers have emerged as willing players in the collaboration process.

CHILDREN AT RISK IN SOUTH AUSTRALIA

As in many OECD countries, children at risk in South Australia are often those who come from impoverished families or belong to ethnic minority groups. In 1995, unemployment stood at around 10 per cent, forcing many families to live on minimal incomes. Poor qualifications, and difficulties in juggling child care with work, have also resulted in many single parents staying at home – indeed their unemployment rate (18 per cent) is almost double that of the population as a whole. However, the worst affected by the limited job supply is the State's aboriginal people, whose unemployment rate is around three times that of the general population.

A report by Stratmann (1988) calculated that around 5 per cent of school children have serious social and behavioural problems which require integrated services. Later, a "working definition" of these children referred to individuals whose chances of successfully completing school, and making a successful transition to work and adult life, were endangered by: severe withdrawal or emotional disturbance; serious disruptive, violent and illegal acts; or absence from school because of truancy, family mobility, and suchlike.

POLICIES PROMOTING SERVICES INTEGRATION

The year 1987 marked the beginning of a comprehensive drive to promote the co-ordination of health, education and social welfare services in South Australia for the "5 per cent" of school children considered to be most at risk. The Ministries of Education, Health and Community Welfare (now Family and Community Services) for the first time set up a high level team of senior directors and planners to explore the feasibility of a multidisciplinary approach to the care of these children. This team came up with 32 recommendations for improving interagency co-ordination – which were approved for implementation in the years 1989 to 1991 (Stratmann, 1988). Responsibility for this operation was handed to the Human Services Committee, a group of senior government ministers with portfolios in health, education, welfare, housing, local government and related services. However, the management of activities was delegated to a State Interagency Committee (SIC), made up of department directors, which itself presided (and indeed still presides) over several state and regional interagency committees. An evaluation component was built into the three-year initiative to assess its impact.

Discussions with direct service personnel led the State Interagency Committee to endorse a (voluntary) Interagency Referral Process (IRP) which has been in operation since 1991. The philosophy behind this initiative is that there should be a single contact point in each geographic area through which all health, education and welfare services (offered outside schools) can be accessed. The IRP concept embraces the following features:

- an integrated and holistic approach to case assessment, management and review;
- contact points to give health and welfare sectors improved education services for their clients;
- link people appointed in the health and welfare sectors to facilitate access to their services;
- a number of different pathways to cater for individual needs;
- quality control to prevent duplication and over-servicing, as well as to ensure that students are not removed unnecessarily from mainstream school;

- sensitivity to the ethnicity or the disability of the individual; and
- an interagency protocol for information exchange about clients.

IRP referral points are located in each of the six regional offices of the Department for Education and Children's Services. Referrals can be made by a variety of sources, including school based personnel, middle management personnel from the health and welfare sectors, non-government agencies, and private practitioners. Each office has an Interagency Referral Manager who co-ordinates agency involvement with a group of field managers from health, welfare and education offices in the area (or other professionals on the ground in sparsely populated regions).

Interagency Referral Managers are given the freedom to adapt their working methods to local situations and to adopt their own personal working styles. In general, they have teaching and counselling backgrounds, behaviour support teams and learning centre staff.

The Department for Education and Children's Services also places a strong emphasis on making schools important focal points for social welfare and health provision for students. DECS' School Discipline Policy states that teachers and the wider school community are best placed to address these problems and, in connection with this, provides a programme of behaviour management support to school personnel. Teachers inter-agency referral managers are frequently slotted into the role of co-ordinating services for children at risk and, while they are reportedly highly sympathetic to the notion of collaboration as participants in the education system they are often more concerned with the here and now than in taking a longer, holistic view. Counselling and vocational advice is often limited by a lack of knowledge of the needs and requirements of the labour market.

EXAMPLES OF BEST PRACTICE IN INTEGRATED SERVICES FOR PRE-SCHOOL CHILDREN

The Far West Aboriginal Progress Association and the Murat Bay District Council, Ceduna

In March 1990, the federal government created the Aboriginal and Torres Strait Islander Commission (ATSIC) which for the first time gave indigenous Australians the right to make decisions affecting their communities. It has 35 Regional Councils which are located throughout Australia and are elected by aboriginal people. The Regional Council serving Ceduna provides funding for local services through the Far West Aboriginal Progress Association (FWAPA).

The FWAPA, and other aboriginal associations in the area, work in close association with the Murat Bay District Council, which also serves Ceduna. Since they both receive money from different sources to provide local services, they have chosen to develop a shared economic plan to avoid potential duplication in expenditure (and effort) to support similar projects. As part of this strategy, they have adopted joint financial planning and management approaches.

This partnership was originally initiated by the District Council. Early difficulties in building a relationship with the aboriginal community disappeared as personal relationships developed. It is now considered nationally as an exemplary collaborative arrangement which other local governments would do well to adopt.

Provision for pre-school children in Ceduna reflects the collaborative philosophy which predominates in the area – with either the District Council or aboriginal groups funding different projects, or sometimes pooling their resources to provide a single service.

In the case of Ceduna's aboriginal pre-kindergarten, the Far West Aboriginal Progress Association has taken responsibility for funding support. This pre-kindergarten, which was initiated 20 years ago by indigenous parents, is run by an aboriginal lady who is qualified as a primary school teacher. It provides places for around 20 aboriginal children between the ages of 3 and 4. Its main goals are to socialise children in an environment sensitive to aboriginal culture and language, and to prepare them for regular kindergarten.

One of the local kindergartens – whose intake is 50 per cent aboriginal – is the Murat Bay Children's Centre. This is government funded, receiving extra support as a "high needs" institution. However, funding is insufficient for operational needs and has to be supplemented by money raised by the Local Management Committee and parental contributions. The centre provides both health and dental services, and also benefits from transport services provided by the Far West Aboriginal Progress Association (in conjunction with the pre-kindergarten) and the education department (school buses). Ceduna's isolated location makes it particularly vital that local resources are shared.

Kindergarten staff regularly attend an interagency in-service training group with professionals from other institutions. Topics covered by outside experts include racism, social development and child abuse. They also frequently liaise with staff from other agencies concerning children served in common. For example, they meet with professionals from the local child care and family day care centres to plan approaches to behaviour management, and from local primary schools to facilitate children's transition from kindergarten to school.

Thus collaboration between the District Council and the Far West Aboriginal Progress Association for pre-school provision in Ceduna is supplemented by co-operation between local services.

EXAMPLES OF BEST PRACTICE IN INTEGRATED SERVICES FOR SCHOOL CHILDREN

Interagency Referral Managers, Adelaide

The role of South Australia's Interagency Referral Managers (IRMs) was described by two such professionals – both with counselling and family therapy backgrounds – working in the Adelaide metropolitan area.

Interagency Referral Managers are supported at the strategic level by an Inter-agency Consultancy Group of senior managers with whom they convene periodically to discuss resource commitments, case management decisions, referrals and future needs. Occupying the middle layer of management, they in turn provide support to professionals in local agencies who identify, and refer, children with multiple needs.

Initial referrals may be informal and, as such, do not need to be mentioned to the children and parents concerned. They are used to discuss the presenting issues without revealing the identity of the client and convene a meeting of an agency representative and the parent and student. If a formal referral is decided upon, the Interagency Referral Manager finds out which agencies have been involved with the client in the past and convenes a meeting of agency representatives. The aim of this gathering is to develop a clear picture of the following:

– what assessments have been conducted already;

– what kind of professional opinions have already been formed;

– what approaches to care have "worked" with the child;

– what aspects of the child's behaviour may still require evaluation or intervention; and

– what steps can be taken to prevent duplication and over-assessment (Department for Education and Children's Services, 1990).

Together they develop a management strategy, and decide who should be responsible for contacting the client's parents.

The voluntary co-operation of both client and parents is vital if an interagency case management process is to proceed. The Interagency Referral Manager is responsible for ensuring that both the client and his or her parents sign an Involvement and Information Release Form. This enables them to obtain information from agencies outside of the Department for Education. Clients are involved as fully as possible in the whole process – commensurate with their age and cognitive ability. Students who are 13 years of age or older must be fully involved in all aspects of the referral process, and are allowed to nominate a support person to assist them when participating in case meetings.

In most instances a case manager is nominated from one of the participating agencies on the basis of the child's most pressing needs, although the choice may be influenced by the involvement of a statutory authority, such as the juvenile courts. Once this leadership is decided upon, another meeting is convened (with the IRM, case manager, and direct services personnel) to devise a case management plan. As part of this, the roles and responsibilities of each member of the group are agreed upon.

With the aim of providing a flexible response to individual needs, case planning and management tend to centre around one of four different strategies: an in-school programme supervised by school personnel; an out-of-school programme involving education department professionals; a programme involving student support personnel from the health or welfare departments; and an interagency programme involving joint services. Case review meetings are held on a regular basis to discuss client progress following programme implementation. If the programme is unsuccessful, other strategies will be tried and, if they fail, an Alternative Placement will be arranged. This may be in an alternative school (either mainstream or specialist) or an appropriate withdrawal facility or programme. Alternatively, the child may be referred to an Open Access Schooling programme (in which a professional supervises school work and provides support and counselling). Equally, the children may be given the option of on-the-job training, or other tailored activities – such as "wilderness trekking" – which aim to instigate behaviour change. These activities are provided in conjunction with other services.

The success of the South Australian government in establishing and sustaining the Interagency Referral Process can be attributed to the leadership of top and middle management, and their commitment to improving it through experience. In addition, the Stratmann Report and the provision of additional resources to implement its recommendations established a climate that was receptive to co-ordination throughout the three major child serving agencies. The creation of a State Interagency Committee and regional policy and planning groups, as well as wide consultation to learn about existing and successful service networks, also helped. Equally, the initiative was boosted by the development of local interagency committees to identify emerging barriers to the IRP, and the production of training materials designed for professionals from the education, health and welfare sectors.

However, these facilitating factors have been counter-balanced by certain barriers to integration. Specifically, IRP activities are promoted amongst state agencies, and not amongst federal and local agencies who may also be involved with clients; different agencies may be responsible for geographic areas which are not contiguous making it hard to collaborate for all cases. Continual staff changes in non-DECS agencies make training about the IRP difficult. What is more, the IRP approach is not mentioned in all job descriptions, meaning that it may not receive the attention it warrants. Finally – and perhaps most seriously of all – recent economic problems and fiscal restraints have put serious pressure on funding for it.

In 1995, around 3 700 or 2 per cent of state school pupils benefited from the IRP. It is widely felt that this approach helps different services to learn more about each other, to identify duplication in effort, and to eliminate barriers to co-ordination. Indeed, its perceived success has led other government sectors – such as juvenile justice – to consider applying the process in their own domains. However, while there is unanimous agreement that the IRP results in improved support for children and their families, and better educational outcomes, many feel that a more systematic way of documenting the fruits of this approach is needed.

EXAMPLES OF BEST PRACTICE IN INTEGRATED SERVICES FOR YOUTH IN THE TRANSITION TO WORK

The Ceduna Youth Network

In addition to developing collaborative links with local aboriginal associations, the Murat Bay District Council has also recognised the importance of generating partnerships between its local youth organisations. Once again, this is seen as an effective way to avoid duplication in effort and to provide more efficient services. Following a Youth Workers and Agency Workshop organised by the District Council in 1994, a Ceduna Youth Network was set up. This network is used as a forum through which agencies can share information about their mandates, goals, resources and gaps in services, and through which they can combine efforts and resources, avoid duplication, and develop additional services for youth. While the Ceduna Area School authorities were initially reluctant to be associated with this degree of openness and sharing, they are now participating in the network more fully. Indeed, a Youth Information Room recently has been established by the network in the school.

One of the institutions involved in the network is the Spencer Institute of the Technical and Further Education (TAFE) College. In addition to several "standard" courses, it also offers a Special Initiative Vocational Training Programme, designed for youth who drop out of the Ceduna Area School. This programme is funded in cash or in kind by the federal Department of Employment, Education, Training and Youth Affairs (DEETYA), the local Crime Prevention Committee, the Ceduna Area School, the Rural Access Programme, Kickstart (a state initiative for unemployed people), the TAFE College itself, and others in the local community. However, new funding is now needed to continue the programme beyond its first year.

The programme's Management Committee is made up of five people with one DEETYA/CES (Commonwealth Employment Services) representative, the local Crime Prevention Committee, the Ceduna Area School, the TAFE College, the Family and Children's Service, and one co-ordinator/lecturer. The co-ordinator plays a leading role in providing counselling and support to students, as well as monitoring their progress. The curriculum for students who participate in the programme focuses on basic reading and writing skills, practical work-related activities, interview skills, résumé writing, and job searches. Students are treated like adults, and as a result tend to behave more responsibly than they did in the Ceduna Area School, from whence they came.

Since its inception in May 1994, the Special Initiative Vocational Training Programme has catered for 27 young people. Six of these have secured employment, six have chosen to work towards their Certificate of Education, twelve are still in the programme, and three have uncertain futures. The overall success of the programme has been put down to the direction, commitment and problem-solving abilities of the Management Committee; the personal qualities and leadership of the co-ordinator; and the college's links with the Ceduna Youth Network. However, reportedly it has been won in spite of – rather than with the help of – administrative support. Those involved in the programme believe that government red-tape and inflexible funding have tended to hamper efforts to provide holistic services to individuals.

CONCLUSION

In setting up a State Interagency Committee (SIC), South Australia has created an important working structure to promote the integration of its human services. While, strictly speaking, the committee is a strategic level enterprise, the government has also taken care to consult field level workers in many aspects of interagency planning. The Interagency Referral Process which has been endorsed by SIC provides a clear, state-wide mechanism through which holistic support for children can be delivered – although the fact that it is not mandatory, and only applies to agencies run by the State, has weakened its impact somewhat.

While the Interagency Referral Process provides an important means through which services outside of the educational system can co-operate, this does not prevent extensive efforts to provide holistic services within schools. As well as being able to access the services of (external) Interagency Referral Managers, schools are able to make use of their own extensive resources to address children's needs – resources which have been boosted by the government's commitment to social justice and equity. What is interesting about South Australia is that, in marked contrast to many OECD countries, education personnel generally are very positive towards collaboration and are highly implicated in it.

As can be seen in Ceduna, the establishment of partnerships and networks in the State provides a means through which services for young people can be provided in a more efficient and non-duplicative manner. Equally, the development of joint economic planning with aboriginal groups has helped to make more effective use of general funding from the State on the one hand, and federal funding for aboriginal use on the other.

13

NEW SOUTH WALES, AUSTRALIA
How integrated services can be used to address broad ranging problems, from unacceptable behaviour to violent crime

by

Philippa Hurrell and Peter Evans

INTRODUCTION AND SUMMARY

New South Wales, which boasts Sydney as its capital, is the richest and most populous State in Australia. Of Australia's 17.6 million inhabitants (1993), close to 5 million live there. Most of the population is concentrated along the coastline. New South Wales has been hit hard by a recession that has kept unemployment at unprecedented levels since 1990.

Most interesting in the New South Wales case studies was the attention given to co-ordinated initiatives involving criminal justice and police services, as well as those for education, health and social welfare. While evidence suggested that criminal justice and youth workers, and the police and schools, are able to form effective partnerships, it also pointed to a certain amount of friction between education and criminal services, and youth workers and the police. This appears to relate to the different models according to which they operate.

Determined leadership and an entrepreneurial approach emerged as important facilitators of integration in New South Wales. In contrast, the inflexibility and rigidity of some government services, as well as a lack of funding for grassroots initiatives emerged as inhibiting factors.

CHILDREN AT RISK IN NEW SOUTH WALES

With its substantial population, New South Wales is home to a large proportion of the children and youth at risk in Australia. In addition to drug use and homelessness, suicide is a major problem in the State. Australia as a whole has one of the highest youth suicide rates in the world (around 2 000 each year), with more young people dying by their own hands than in road accidents. As in the rest of the country, unemployment among young people in the State is a major problem, standing at around 25 per cent. And when jobs are found they are often poorly paid, low skilled, and insecure.

Sydney, which acts as a magnet to young people, has many of the problems associated with other major cities. Prostitution and crime are part of the landscape. Many young people reportedly feel alienated and in deep despair.

POLICIES PROMOTING SERVICES INTEGRATION

New South Wales has been operating a Staying On programme since 1988. Its goal is to encourage young people to remain in school up to and beyond compulsory age. The initiative has six broad objectives of which one relates to integration. This concerns parent and community involvement. It is:

> "To increase the involvement of parents in their children's schooling by fostering positive attitudes towards education; involving parents in school planning; assisting parents to help their children study at home; and encouraging links between the school and its community [Department of Employment, Education and Training (1992)]".

Schools which participate in the Staying On programme are those with the lowest retention rates in the State. They are grouped into clusters. A Deputy Principal is appointed to a base school in each cluster as the co-ordinator of their activities. At the regional level, community liaison and consultants have been appointed to provide services to all "Staying On" schools. Reportedly, their co-ordinating efforts have been very important to the success of the whole programme.

In spite of communalities in the nature of Staying On programmes across and between clusters of schools, individual clusters and schools also have the freedom to adapt them to meet local needs. Thus they have organised a myriad of different educational, social welfare, community development and community liaison activities.

Interestingly, federal STAR funding originally was used to support the New South Wales Staying On initiative. However, more recently the money has been used to set up a discrete programme which targets those students who are most at risk of dropping out of school.

The case study visits in New South Wales focused on services for school children and youth in the transition to work only. No information was collected on services for pre-school children.

EXAMPLES OF BEST PRACTICE IN INTEGRATED SERVICES FOR SCHOOL CHILDREN

Cranebrook High School, Penrith, Western Sydney

Cranebrook High School serves Penrith, which is a new and growing housing area in Western Sydney. Families in the neighbourhood are generally from the middle and lower income groups, and the school population reflects this social mix. Problems in the local community include unemployment, family dysfunction, family violence, and youth crime.

Staff from the school work closely with the Barnardo's Penrith Children's Centre, which is located opposite Cranebrook. Barnardo's is a charity (originally British) which focuses its activities on family support and preservation during periods of family crisis. In co-operation with Cranebrook School and the nearby Jamison High School, the centre operates a STAR funded Radical Adolescent Programme. This is targeted at children who are in danger of not completing their education due to reasons such as homelessness, family dysfunction and peer relationship problems. As part of the programme, weekly hour long classes, focusing on communication skills, self-esteem building, information provision, and social care and support, are provided. An additional, and reportedly essential aspect of this programme is a two-day camp.

The staff also run another programme called Project Links, in collaboration with Penrith Police Citizens Youth Club. The youth club is a (charitable) branch of the local police department, and is part of a nationwide effort to help youth between the ages of 8 and 21. Like other clubs of its kind, it provides crime prevention programmes which are tailored to meet local community needs. Project Links, which is run out of the youth club, aims to facilitate the return of students to school after suspension, by providing academic and social skills lessons, and leisure activities.

Students at risk who are of school leaving age either are encouraged to stay on at school to gain additional qualifications, or are helped to look for work. Through a Worklink Programme, Cranebrook is connected into a network of local community agencies and companies which offer educational opportunities through structured work placements.

Evaluations of the various programmes in which Cranebrook High School is involved have been positive. The school attendance of participants has improved, their behaviour has ameliorated, and they have developed a more positive attitude towards school and family life.

EXAMPLES OF BEST PRACTICE IN INTEGRATED SERVICES FOR YOUTH IN THE TRANSITION TO WORK

South Sydney Youth Services

South Sydney is a working class neighbourhood made up of a diverse range of ethnic groups, including a large number of "urban" aboriginal people. Unemployment is three times the national average but, in spite of this, the community is active and dynamic.

South Sydney Youth Services is, essentially, the product of a grassroots initiative. Community people wanted an outreach service for young people; the local Interagency (made up of 25 youth service providers) responded by supporting the creation of a new agency. South Sydney Youth Services is funded by a wide range of federal, state and local bodies representing education, employment, community services and juvenile justice. However, the amount of ongoing funding that it receives is relatively small, and it has to rely on additional one-off grants from other sources. The lack of long term funding for South Sydney Youth Services makes planning ahead quite difficult, and the Services' co-ordinator continually has to search for new sources of support. Being unusually dedicated, imaginative and determined, he is often successful.

South Sydney Youth Services has an extraordinarily broad range of partners with whom it co-operates. These include the federal Department of Education and Employment, the Department of Social Security Youth Services Unit, the Department of Community Services, Youth Access Centres, the Central Sydney Community Health Centre, the New South Wales Police, local magistrates, housing services, non-government organisations and members of the local community. It also works closely with Upstart Graphics, a design company, which it created itself to provide jobs for local young people, and which is now independent and profit-making.

In general, the co-ordinator of South Sydney Youth Services takes the initiative in forging new relationships with other agencies. These often start off in an informal way, and later evolve into something more formal. For example, the co-ordinator asked a nurse from the Central Sydney Community Health Centre if she would do some unofficial work for him, and eventually the arrangement developed into a commitment by the centre to make one of their staff available to the South Sydney Youth Services on a permanent basis. The agency has a particularly good relationship with the local juvenile justice services which reportedly are very flexible, but a poor one with the Department of Community Services which, according to the co-ordinator, can be rigid in the way it works. Many of the agencies with which South Sydney Youth Services has successful relationships are willing to visit the Services' centre to provide support and advice on site. As a result it is able to provide a wide array of services: social security, employment, health, counselling, social welfare, education and leisure.

The co-ordinator is very pro-active, and is willing to "cold call" agencies (or companies) to obtain the services (or jobs) his clients need. His flexible approach contrasts with that of many government services which reportedly can be too bureaucratic and unapproachable for young people at the margins of society. By creating an informal and friendly environment for young people and agency workers alike (coffee is always on hand), the co-ordinator has developed an apparently very successful youth service.

The Annexe, Worimi School, Broadmeadow

The annexe was an initiative of the Worimi School to deal with and support students who have come into contact with the Juvenile Justice system. Worimi School is located within the Worimi Juvenile Justice Centre at Broadmeadow (Newcastle). The annexe is located away from the centre at the Police Citizens Youth Club, Broadmeadow. This location was specifically chosen because of the need to form a positive relationship with the police and also their willingness to be involved. The Worimi Juvenile Justice Centre caters for clients aged from 10-20 but mainly deals with students in the age range 14-16. Most clients in the centre have committed a range of minor and major offences. The centre has a different "culture" in that its main responsibility is safety and security whilst the culture of the school and the annexe are that of "risk taker". Whilst these may appear to be at different ends of the continuum the (growing) relationship between the school and the centre is both positive and constructive.

The annexe was set up to offer the court system a community-based alternative to incarceration/custody. One of the annexe's main aims is that of "diversion from crime". It also operates as a halfway house for students being released from custody who are wanting to return to school/further education or are looking for work placement. The annexe works extensively with other service providers and government departments in order to ensure the most positive outcomes for students.

The school has also established Worimi School's Framing Service which gives opportunities for its students to gain work experience. The school, the centre and the annexe have all used this service for placement of students. Other schools have also used this service to place at risk students. The service employs three full-time staff and operates as a commercial small business.

Worimi School is part of the New South Wales Department of School Education (state government funded). The annexe is funded by the Department of Employment, Education, Training and Youth Affairs (federal government funded through a pilot project under the 1995 Education Counselling for Young People Programme). The school has ongoing funding but the annexe has to continually seek annual funding. Worimi Juvenile Justice Centre is funded by the Department of Juvenile Justice (state government).

Worimi School is essentially an example of how services can be co-ordinated for a particularly difficult group of clients. It offers educational activities to all eligible children with the goal of providing a substitute for normal schooling. Individual Education Plans are developed for students attending both the annexe and Worimi School. These plans include academic, social and life skills. Daily teaching continuity within the school is difficult to the large number of services who need to contact and work with the students (e.g. solicitors, visitors, medical services, etc.).

The school develops, in conjunction with the Case Manager (Juvenile Justice Centre) an exit plan which may include placement back into mainstream school. If this is the most appropriate placement then the school refers those students (via the annexe) to the Hunter Adolescent Support Unit at Jesmond High School. If placement back in schools is outside the Newcastle area then the process will be done on a case by case basis with direct contact with the school. Other exit plans may include further education/training at the local Youth Access Centre.

CONCLUSION

As in other Australian States, federally funded STAR programmes is New South Wales are designed to meet local needs. Cranebrook School has formed a triumvirate with another school, Jamison High, and the charity, Barnardo's, to provide special classes for children at risk. Thus, STAR money is being used to fund a "mixed" programmes involving both the public and private sectors.

Efforts are being made in New South Wales to involve both the police and juvenile justice services in integrated activities – with varying success. Children who are suspended from Cranebrook School attend the Penrith Police Citizens Youth Club which provides an informal and friendly atmosphere in which they can learn, as well as developing more positive relationships with the police. South Sydney Youth Services has built up friendly relationships with juvenile justice workers, and has improved its relationship with the police. Reportedly, youth workers and the police normally "do not get on", perhaps because of their contrasting approaches to addressing youth problems. Worimi School has implemented a programme of police visitation whereby clients leaving the centre after serving their committal are given advice on how to successfully deal with police in their local area.

In contrast to the many federally funded programmes for children and youth at risk in New South Wales, some grassroots initiatives can also be found. A particularly good example is South Sydney Youth Services. Set up in response to community needs, this agency combines flexibility, accessibility and entrepreneurial leadership to provide a very wide range of services to young people with serious problems. Rather than expecting young people to get to grips with formal and sometimes intimidating government bureaucracy, South Sydney Youth Services meets them half way in their own cultural milieu. However, lack of financial support from the government has limited its ability to make long term plans.

Section 2

CASE STUDY ABSTRACTS CARRIED OUT BY COUNTRIES

14

FINLAND
Experimental efforts to integrate human services

by

Philippa Hurrell and Peter Evans

INTRODUCTION AND SUMMARY

While the cases studies carried out in Finland by OECD experts focused on nationwide or fairly established types of integrated services provision, those commissioned by the Finnish government were devoted to new, experimental programmes departing from traditional patterns. These programmes are of particular interest because in many ways they reflect new directions in Finnish service provision.

Like their counterparts in "mainstream" services, the staff of experimental programmes view integration as an effective way to improve services while at the same time reducing costs. However, with limited funding to implement change, many of them are experiencing increased workloads.

CHILDREN AT RISK IN FINLAND

Please refer to the case studies carried out by OECD experts for this information.

POLICIES PROMOTING SERVICES INTEGRATION

Please also refer to the case studies carried out by OECD experts.

EXAMPLES OF BEST PRACTICE IN INTEGRATED SERVICES
FOR PRE-SCHOOL CHILDREN

In line with government policy which stresses "quality teamwork" in pre-school education, a number of local, experimental initiatives have sprung up throughout Finland which aim to achieve more profound levels of integration. One of the central goals of integration in pre-school education is the early prevention of children's problems (traditionally efforts have focused on school aged children). The need for new initiatives to support young children and their families has been made more urgent by high levels of unemployment and significant cuts in other public services.

Co-ordinated by the National Research and Development Centre for Welfare and Health, the Somersault Ride for Early Childhood Programme supports local efforts to develop child-centred initiatives. As part of the programme, several development centres have been set up. These serve as the focal points of networks which are made up of various pre-school institutions. Each centre focuses on a specific theme with the goal of improving childhood learning. To this end, some have chosen collaboration as a strategy. The Kirkkonummi Centre, for example, has attempted to harmonise pre-school and primary education by introducing co-operative education in both. The Mikkeli, Uusikaupunki and Pyhäsalmi centres, on the other hand, each provide multi-disciplinary professional training with the goal of improving co-operation and communication between workers and increasing general skill levels.

At the Ristikivi and Lahti-Mustikkamäki day nurseries, experimental projects have been set up for families who require help with child-rearing. These have involved multi-disciplinary teams who provide family support. Families also benefit from mutual assistance in group meetings. The goal of these projects is to prevent children's problems by helping families to meet their needs at home. Aiming to carry out "family-oriented work in co-operation with other partners", the Pieksämäki Development Centre has a similar orientation although its goals are broader. Its main objectives are to eliminate duplication in services, to increase communication between agency partners, to intensify support for child upbringing, and to instil in the local community a sense of joint responsibility. A recent initiative has involved developing pre-school curricula in collaboration with local schools. The idea of improving links between pre-school institutions and schools has also been taken up by the Active Lippuniemi Residents' Association in Iisalmi which has set up a project to transform a nursery into a centre offering day care, the first year of school education, and afternoon care.

Many of these experimental projects were initiated at the grassroots and operate with little or no additional funding. In general, they enjoy a high level of support from field workers, although some do not appreciate the extra work that collaboration involves. Several claim that they have improved the quality of the services they provide as well as reducing costs; however, these claims are not backed up by empirical evidence. In some cases, support from individuals at higher levels in the services hierarchy has been poor, suggesting a reluctance by them to back grassroots initiatives.

EXAMPLES OF BEST PRACTICE IN INTEGRATED SERVICES FOR CHILDREN AND YOUTH

The Latokartano Health and Social Services Centre, Helsinki

For the purposes of health and social services provision, Helsinki is divided up into seven districts, which themselves are split into many smaller districts. One of these is Latokartano, which is a particularly disadvantaged part of the North East District. On the initiative of the Deputy Mayor for social affairs and public health, Latokartano was chosen in 1990 as the site for a new experiment in integrated services provision.

Initial planning for the experiment was carried out by a project team made up of representatives from all of the different professions who would be involved in it. The team was briefed on other similar projects in Finland and was provided with relevant training. At the same time, a client survey was carried out in the district to determine how great the need for integrated services was. Information was collected on the various social welfare and health services used by local people with the goal of identifying areas of overlap. It was discovered that while only a fraction of the population used multiple services, those who did were important consumers of agency resources. Therefore, it was concluded that improvements in the co-ordination of services would be valuable.

A consultant was brought in to help the project team to develop a new "joint operating model". The planning of the model took into account the results of another survey which identified the problems experienced by social welfare and health personnel in their (traditionally specialised) jobs. It was concluded that professionals should be given broader job responsibilities, that they should work in multi-disciplinary teams, and that they should serve the whole population in a defined area. Other agreed aims were to build stronger co-operative links with the community, to develop an integrated client information system, and to strengthen the relationship between resources and needs.

During the planning period, a specially designed building to house the project was constructed. Christened the Latokartano Health and Social Services Centre, it was officially opened in 1994.

The project is now in its implementation stage. Ongoing funding for the centre is provided by the North East Social Services Centre and the North East Health Centre. In spite of its experimental status, the centre has received no extra funding beyond normal levels, and is expected to implement change without extra staff. On the positive side, however, it does benefit from an unusual degree of autonomy, with control over its own joint budget, and with an independent management team.

The centre currently houses the Pihlajisto Health Centre, the Pihlajamäki Maternity and Child Health Centre, the Pihlajamäki Dental Unit, and community care, intoxicant abuse, and social security services. Staff from these services are divided into four teams serving four different areas in Latokartano. Each team consists of one (or two) doctor(s), public health nurses, social workers, office clerks and community care personnel.

An evaluation of the outcomes of the centre's "team approach" to client care has yet to be undertaken. However, factors which have facilitated or inhibited the implementation of this approach have been documented. According to the Development Manager of the North East Social Services Centre, the planning of the project was expedited in an important way by the support of the outside consultant who helped to develop the new approach. Integration has also been facilitated by the location of team members in adjacent offices, and by the high level of commitment of both social welfare and health managers. Continuing vocational education to widen the knowledge and abilities of staff is regarded by the Development Manager as desirable, if not yet widely available.

Integration has been impeded, on the other hand, by the unwillingness of some staff to alter old habits, difficulties amongst staff in finding a common language, and the strain of extra work connected with change. The constant need to reconcile different working procedures and the frequent need to adjust to new team members have also been problematic. Faced with these problems, staff have had little time to co-operate with other agencies in the locality.

The Korso-Rekola Social Welfare and Health Centre and Peijas Child Psychiatry Clinic, Vantaa

In 1991, the Korso-Rekola Social Welfare and Health Centre launched a five-year project to improve the functioning of child welfare and psychiatric services in Vantaa, as a response to the perceived failure of social services to provide assistance to the most needy. This initiative was also stimulated by economic recession, cuts in public spending, and increasing socio-economic pressures on the local population. These factors contributed to making the job of social workers one of crisis management rather than prevention.

Subject to pressures associated with increasingly complex cases, staff at the Peijas Child Psychiatry Clinic were also keen to revise their approach. And, like staff at the Social Welfare and Health Centre, they were concerned that those who most needed help were not getting it.

The five-year project in which both institutions are involved has (in relation to services integration) the following key objectives:

- to develop a procedure for integrating social work and child psychiatry;
- to prevent the need for children to go into care by intervening earlier and more effectively;

- to develop the ability of social workers who are working with adults to identify and address the needs of their families too;

- to arrange joint primary health care and social welfare training events in order to build links with other services in the area; and

- to support parents, with the help of a family worker, in running their homes and caring for their children.

The Social Welfare and Health Centre is staffed by twelve social workers. In line with new decentralisation policies, they operate according to a "patchwork approach" in which they are responsible for a small geographic area in which they performed multiple functions. The Psychiatric Clinic, on the other hand, offers the services of two child psychiatrists, a specialist nurse, a social worker, two psychologists and a psychology trainee – who serve the same geographic area.

Key to the whole project is its family worker (trained as a childminder). She is responsible for making the first visit to families' homes and building up good relationships with them. Her role is to find out what practical help families need and to provide assistance. On later home visits, she may take along one of the social workers who, in turn, may arrange a visit with one of the psychiatric workers. The family worker is also "plugged" into a wide network of other agencies on whose services she can call. In this way, she acts as an important "bridge" between families and the services they need.

Joint home visits by Social Welfare and Health Centre and Psychiatric Clinic staff are supplemented by regular joint meetings. Initially they concentrated on planning new approaches to service delivery, but now they focus on individual client cases. Believing in the principle of client autonomy, families are always involved by them in important decision-making processes.

Collaboration between staff from the two institutions has led to the development of mutual respect and a willingness to draw on each other's expertise. Most of the staff are eager to develop and modify their working patterns in the direction of increased co-operation. A doubling of the number of child welfare cases in the area between 1990 and 1993 suggests improved efficiency in identifying families with problems (although economic factors may also be significant in this respect). At the same time a number of difficulties have been encountered. It has become harder for staff to comprehend what their specific role should be. The demands of work have become greater as individuals have had to adapt to new working procedures. And, as team members have changed, staff have had to constantly build new working relationships.

Children and families have benefited from access to the expertise of two or more professionals simultaneously, often in their own homes. Furthermore, evidence suggests that particularly disadvantaged families are receiving more support services. In this respect the project appears to have achieved its central goal.

CONCLUSION

Recent "experiments" in Finland reveal a common wish among service providers to expand their collaborative activities. They also reflect a growing interest in providing support to the families of children at risk – as well as to the children themselves. Furthermore, they suggest an increased sensitivity to client needs and staff perspectives, and an enhanced desire to involve community people in programme activities. Most of the initiatives emanate from the grassroots level, with minimal intervention from the higher echelons of government. And, in many ways, they differ from traditional Finnish approaches to services provision which tend to be centralised, client-centred, and closed to community influences.

Many of the projects have been bolstered by the enthusiasm of the professionals involved. Joint training schemes, through which professionals have been able to benefit from each other's knowledge and experience, have also proved helpful. However, the development of some projects has been impeded both by a lack of financial support from the government, and by the weight of extra work connected with co-ordinated activities.

NETHERLANDS
The quest for economy, efficiency and effectiveness

by

Guido Walraven and Peter Evans

INTRODUCTION AND SUMMARY

Although geographically small, the Netherlands is one of the wealthier Members of the OECD. The socio-economic climate in the Netherlands in recent years has been characterised by cuts in government budgets and the rethinking of its core roles. As a consequence, in some respects the welfare state has come under pressure. Against this background, the concerns for economy, efficiency and effectiveness has strengthened interest in services for children and youth at risk. To achieve these goals the government has stimulated cohesion in the supply of services and co-operation between the agencies involved, and has encouraged better responses to the demands of clients. The decentralisation of welfare policies and, more recently, some parts of educational policy has led to increased cohesion and integration especially at the local level.

CHILDREN AND YOUTH AT RISK IN THE NETHERLANDS

The main "at risk" groups concerning educational, social, and vocational failure are children and youth from families with a low socio-economic status. This group is relatively large among ethnic minorities, such as Turks and Moroccans, primarily because these groups were recruited as unskilled labourers. Until recently, the groups at risk of educational failure were determined in primary education by looking at the level of education, occupational status and ethnicity of the family. The present criteria focus on the educational level of both parents. The aim is to arrive at a group of 20-25 per cent of all pupils who are most in need of extra support. However, this is still more than the welfare policy sector regards as "at risk". In the Netherlands 15 per cent of all young people experience problems or disorders in their development requiring special attention. For 10 per cent of these, it is necessary to take special preventive action, to provide mild forms of assistance and to offer extra attention, while the remaining 5 per cent need a more intensive type of assistance to solve their problems.

To achieve these changes, policy is focusing on decentralisation and the involvement of client groups at the local level, while at the same time decreasing the emphasis on "compartmentalisation" – the pooling of social forces along political and denominational lines.

EXAMPLE OF BEST PRACTICE IN INTEGRATED SERVICES FOR PRE-SCHOOL CHILDREN

The case study was carried out in the municipality of Emmen, which is situated in the province of Drenthe in the north-east of the Netherlands. During the last few years work has been in progress in Emmen on a model for the development of policy and activities in the field of pre-school education. The Dutch abbreviation of the model's name is MOVE. The final model is explicitly intended to facilitate the movement towards more integration of services in the pre-school phase in other municipalities.

The problems caused by educational deprivation call for a broad range of solutions. Children and their parents should be positively stimulated by various means in order to improve their chances and this requires co-operation between education and welfare (health care, help services, welfare work and child care). This co-operation must result in a clear and well tuned supply of facilities for parents and children. On the one hand family-oriented programmes are needed and, on the other, an accessible infrastructure of services, which calls on parents to play an active role in the stimulation and guidance of the development of their children.

The principal innovative element in the project plan is the figure of a "go-between" mother. She sees to building up a relationship with the family in the home and links their demands to the existing supply. In other words, an investment in relations and trust is the basis for change and a more demand-oriented way of working.

At the same time it is a stepping stone towards the realisation of integrated policy. The intended target group is defined as: the 10 per cent of children aged between 0 and 6 years, who are vulnerable in their development as a result of socio-economic and cultural circumstances, and with parents in need of support and help in accessing available services.

At the strategic level the project management engaged the programme directors and guided them in their work. The management involved the field level, for example in the co-ordination and acquisition of supplementary funds. Contact was made with the Averroës Foundation which helped in the development of the methodology and the training of staff.

An important event at the operational level was the appointment of the pro-gramme leader in December 1994. She received training at the beginning of 1995 and did preliminary work for the implementation of the project, for example by making contacts at neighbourhood level and drawing up a basic package of facilities.

At the field level there are three pilot sites within the municipality of Emmen. A plan of action was drawn up for each site. The training of the selected contact mothers took place in September/October 1995, and it is intended that the activities in the neighbourhoods should start in November.

MOVE is a development project which has already been running for several years, but is not yet fully implemented. Thus only provisional or interim results can be reported on here. These results will be viewed on the three levels which have been distinguished. Since the process has mainly been top-down, it is not very surprising that up to now most change has been achieved at the strategic level and the least at the field level. There seems to be a broad consensus on MOVE's success at all levels. The method comprises amongst other things: making plans which are well underpinned substantively; clear and realistic objectives; clear phasing; well-defined division of tasks; and concrete activities with the expectation of results.

The not insignificant results which have been achieved at the strategic level concern a covenant between the actors most involved and a basis of support with a broader political-administrative reach. Amongst the things this has led to are a concentration of the flow of funds and the co-operation of the covenant partners in MOVE senior management consultations. A project management team has also been installed, which meets monthly and both directs the progress of the project as well as creating the conditions for implementation. If necessary the project manage-ment initiates consultations with the senior management of the covenant partners.

EXAMPLE OF BEST PRACTICE IN INTEGRATED SERVICES FOR SCHOOL CHILDREN

The case study was carried out in the city of Rotterdam, the second city of the Netherlands and the world's biggest port.

In Rotterdam the main co-operation is between the municipality and education and welfare in the municipal Fund for the Reduction of Educational Disadvantages (FAO). The FAO is a platform for educational priority policy in greater Rotterdam and is responsible for the preparation and determination of policy for the reduction of educational disadvantage. For content and funding, the forces of the municipal-ity, the Rotterdam schools and welfare institutions, which are involved in educa-tional priority policy, are combined in the FAO. The FAO works both preventively and remedially, but emphasises prevention.

At the strategic level the FAO board develops policy and exercises control. Municipal council members, members of school governing bodies and members of the board of a welfare institution sit on the FAO board. The operational level consists of representatives from education and welfare. School management (members of school management teams) and the senior management of the welfare institution, and project leaders, put the policy into practice and create the conditions for the field to negotiate the details of the co-operation between the various sectors.

The main objective of the FAO is "the improvement of educational performance in the basic skills and school careers of pupils at risk". To achieve this a four-track policy has been mapped out consisting of: facilitation of schools; exchange of good practices; evaluation; and projects. The next section focuses on the last track only – the projects.

In order to achieve its objectives, the FAO finances and supports projects on a systematic policy basis; some already exist but others are new projects. Normally, there is co-operation between the school, welfare institutions and immigrant organisations. The central objective of a project is always to try to find practical answers. The projects are grouped around five themes:

– pre-school period;

– Dutch as a second language and multi-lingualism;

– effective learning time;

– co-operation with parents; and

– reduction of early school leaving rates.

The projects with an integrated approach including welfare and education are shown in Table 4 below.

The co-operation between education and welfare within the FAO has had good results. At the administrative level, there has been better use of resources and at the field level, clients have benefited.

Through the experience which has been gained with joint projects, but also on account of the social problems of pupils with which schools are confronted, the willingness and the need to tackle them jointly have become ever greater. People at all levels (strategic, operational and field) are convinced of the necessity of cutting across the boundaries of their own sector and are rapidly learning how this should be done.

Table 4. **Projects with an integrated approach from education or welfare**

Theme	Project	Schools	Welfare
Care for newly arrived immigrant school entrants	• BOA: out of school care for non-Dutch speakers	3	10
	• GIDS: care for non-Dutch speaking new-comers	4	1
Effective learning time	• Extended school day	9	10
Effective relationship with parents	• Model project school social work	10	5
	• Project on migrant organisations	n.a.	n.a.
School careers and times of particular risk	• Learning outcomes and health (*Binnenboord*)	5	6
	• Help in reading books on list for public examination	3	1
	• Library in the class	5	6

EXAMPLES OF BEST PRACTICE IN INTEGRATED SERVICES FOR YOUTH IN THE TRANSITION TO WORK

For those young people who are failing in the mainstream educational system, special projects have been set up as part of an "integral approach" (Veenman *et al.*, 1995). An example is the successful Rotterdam Compact that was started up to stimulate potential school-leavers to rekindle an interest in education through "hands-on" work experience. The national Unqualified School-leavers Project (POS) is an example of another successful project directed at young people who have dropped out of school. It is not theory but practical experience which is the basis on which the pupils can obtain qualifications, and they find out in practice what knowledge is needed to be able to function properly on the labour market. The LTO (Junior Secondary Technical Education) Project in Amsterdam is oriented to a slightly later phase, when young people are in the last class of VBO (pre-vocational education). Since it is those pupils with a certificate at A or B level, who find it most difficult to get work, they are steered towards the labour market by means of intensive and short courses to help identify the right job and develop the necessary work and social skills. Finally the Inside Out Project has been successfully initiated to put young offenders onto the right track. Through actively preparing prisoners for participation in the labour market after their discharge, they are better equipped for reintegration in society. In this summary we will concentrate on one of the examples of best practice for youth in transition to work in the Netherlands: the programme of POS.

The Projects for Unqualified School-leavers form one of the three types of projects in the Netherlands which are financed in the framework of social priority policy. This takes place via various ministries. The main objective of the POS is to improve the alignment between education and the labour market for young people who have left Junior General Secondary Education of Pre-vocational Education without a vocational qualification. The POS started in 1986 and has gained good results. The number of pupils who left the projects and went into a job amounted to 70 per cent for the first two years. In the following years those leaving and going into a job dropped to 65 per cent in 1989 and 1990 to 63 per cent in 1991 and 54 per cent in 1993. For 1994 the number leaving for a job or a trainee post increased again to 70 per cent. In most of the cases where the participants have got a "real" job after the project, it is in the enterprise in which they did their practical work.

The fact that the POS are attuned to the characteristics of the target group, contributes to their success in steering youth at risk into a full-time job, a trainee job or to re-entry into mainstream education. Also the assiduous cultivation of contacts is one of the conditions for success as far as the other parties involved in the project are concerned: intensive co-operation with a variety of institutions such as the employment office, the school, the social services, trade and industry, the community and, if need be, the probation and after-care service. Apart from that, intensive supervision of the young people helps them to transfer smoothly from education to the labour market. This transfer, as well as the contacts with various institutions, raises considerable barriers for the POS target group. The POS supervisors in particular are the people who seem able to help promote a smooth transfer. One of the reasons they can achieve this is that the possibilities for the operation of the POS are almost unlimited. Here we see the importance of a flexible educational package, which is put together outside traditional and rigid rules and regulations. In this connection the basic principle of the project co-ordinators is of importance, namely that the lines must be kept as short as possible, both for the contacts between the pupil and the supervisors, and also for the contacts between the organisations involved. For the success of the projects the world of trade and industry is one of the most important parties involved. The number of work experience places is after all dependent on the willingness of the employers. It is made quite clear to the enterprises that it is a question of a work experience place for problem pupils. From a sense of social responsibility and also from economic considerations (the worker is free and completely "malleable" for the employer) many employers are prepared to offer a work experience place. These places are sought as far as possible in smaller enterprises, with a staff of 2 to 10 people, as the POS participants need personal guidance. In larger enterprises such supervision is often much more difficult.

There are concrete policy intentions to create facilities within mainstream education which would make projects such as POS unnecessary (the Inside Out project has its own objectives and target group). The main policy objective remains unchanged: to allow every pupil to acquire at least a basic qualification, at least to the level of a beginning employee (the international SEDOC-2 level**). Since it is realised that this is not attainable for every pupil, the Ministry of Education has put a proposal before parliament to develop within mainstream education a nationally recognised basic qualification for the level of an assistant employee (the international SEDOC-1 level). The quality assurance system which is usual in mainstream education, will in that case also be applicable to training at this level. A proposal has also been made for the benefit of those who cannot attain even this level, to develop courses at the level of specific job qualifications. It is true that these would not receive national recognition, but as part of mainstream education they would be subject to quality control. Moreover, there is a provision for the development of a support structure for mainstream education. Extra resources will be made available for supervision and guidance. The municipalities will be given a superintending function, which means amongst other things that they are responsible for the mobilisation and co-ordination of bodies from the field of education, the labour market and youth services. In this way a structure for integrated services could be created.

It seems to us that this is an important step in the right direction, given the fact that 15 to 20 per cent of pupils are unable to reach the SEDOC-2 level, and that for some of them the SEDOC-1 level is also beyond their reach. Fitting the relevant courses into the framework of mainstream education gives such courses a firm financial basis, and thus also a clearer, structural position, while it also contributes to better quality control. On the other hand there is a danger of loss of flexibility. If the results of this study are taken seriously, in which case the conditions for success will also receive attention, then it is to be hoped that this point will be met. Youth at risk, who form the central theme in this study, will then be able to count on education which is specially oriented to them, of a flexible nature, with a significant practical component and little (superfluous) theory, and with intensive supervision and guidance.

CONCLUSION

Recent developments in the Netherlands reveal attempts at all age levels to reform and develop services emphasising clear objectives and meeting clients' needs. Co-ordination has developed between ministries as well as with foundations

---

* SEDOC is an international classification system (five levels) of secondary vocational training.

and others working at the grass-roots level with the main purpose of involving families in helping children at risk to adapt more fully to Dutch society, to prevent school failure, and to help older pupils successfully enter the labour market.

The projects, although at an early stage of development, show good results and have convinced professionals at all levels of the need to work more co-operatively.

Part III

LEGISLATION AND POLICY: COUNTRY DETAILS

by

Janet Friedman

BELGIUM – FLEMISH COMMUNITY

In recent years, anti-poverty policy in the Flemish Community in Belgium has been evolving in several ways including: greater attention to the population at risk within existing legal constructs and policies as well as the promulgation of measures designed to diminish exclusion of these groups, development of special programmes for those at risk, decentralisation and implementation of anti-poverty policy at the regional and local levels, and development of anti-poverty policy not merely as a separate entity but as an inclusive aspect of other policies including education, employment, and welfare. While as yet, no one clear definition of poverty has been adopted in Flanders by the various departments and government institutions, the recognised need for co-ordination of diverse measures and programmes has resulted in the establishment of several new institutions.

To co-ordinate and evaluate anti-poverty policy, the Flemish Intersectorial Commission for the Struggle Against Poverty was established. In addition to reporting annually to the Flemish government and the Flemish Council on the progress to combat poverty, the commission is charged with co-ordination of initiatives including: local policy affecting more vulnerable population groups, the Special Fund for Social Welfare, special employment programmes, and projects financed by the European Social Fund. In addition, a decree of the Flemish Council on 31 July, 1990 established the Flemish Fund for the Integration of the Underprivileged. The fund was initiated to support in a purposeful and efficient way, local policies on "opportunity privation" and the integration of migrants. Also, the King Boudewijn Foundation operates in close interaction with government anti-poverty policy by supporting a number of pilot projects.

A measure established in 1984 to promote services integration for young children and their families is Child and Family, subsidised by the Flemish government to oversee the welfare and healthy development of young children in Flanders. Through house visits, health centres, counselling, surveillance of child care, and by means of serving as the central recipient of applications from young families for financial relief and mediation by the Queen, the institution provides a preventive orientation to the support and care for expectant parents and families with children up to 3 years old. Child and Family seeks to promote co-operation amongst programmes and organisations at all levels including the Flemish community, the provincial, and the regional-local levels. Among other measures, the institution has promoted an agreement of collaboration with the School Medical Inspection to communicate relevant information.

Much of day care for children under 2.5 years old and aimed at working parents is provided by primary schools. Day care subsidised by Child and Family is also available to working parents and to parents with children in problematic situations who are in need of temporary placement. Early childhood education for children 2.5 to 6 is provided free of charge and is integrated with primary education with a large proportion of Flemish children attending. However, 85 per cent of school repeaters in the first school year are children of underprivileged families, and for this reason, in 1993-94 and again in 1994-95, primary schools were granted supplementary staff to provide additional assistance to children with educational disadvantage. To address problems as early as possible and to help prevent school failure, this supplemental measure was extended in 1994-95 to 4- and 5-year-old children as well. In educational priority areas, special programmes have been developed for migrants, refugees and itinerant populations including instruction in the migrants' language. In addition, in primary education, children with learning problems and those considered at risk may receive services from Psycho-Medico-Social centres (PMS centres) which operate independently but in close collaboration with the schools and families. Among other activities, the centres trace, diagnose and seek to resolve problems resulting from students' socio-cultural backgrounds. Centres employ a multi-disciplinary approach with teams of psychologists, educators, social workers, physicians and paramedics working to address the problems and needs of children from pre-school through the end of secondary education. Counselling services are provided with significant attention focused on the transition from pre-school to primary school. For older students and their parents, the centres provide vocational guidance and information regarding the educational system.

In April 1991, as a result of legislation regarding the policy related to immigrant children in the Flemish educational system, the Home-school Liaison programme was created. The programme, largely funded by the Flemish Fund for the Integration of the Underprivileged, targets Gypsies, travellers and other immigrants with an underprivileged background and operates in schools and local or regional agencies in areas with high concentrations of groups at risk. The programme seeks to strengthen ties between home and school and foster positive educational outcomes. Co-ordination with other community services is encouraged and generally organised through contractual collaboration.

At the secondary school level, in urban areas, integrative projects focusing on the prevention of truancy and other troublesome behaviours have been piloted. For youth in transition to work, integrative programmes include various forms of alternation training. Alternation training involves a combination of "part-time work and training in a private company and supplementary part-time vocational and general training in the school or another training institution". Alternation training encompasses a number of programmes including trader's apprenticeship for 15-16 year-olds still subject to compulsory education, and gives students practical training in trades or business along with a supplementary course in general and professional-technical training at a recognised institute or training centre. In another programme of part-time vocational secondary education, students from the age of 15 after completing two years of full time secondary education may attend classes two days a week, and for the remainder, enter a part-time labour or apprenticeship contract to gain hands on experience. As an inducement to employers to participate, a special fund was set up which provides premiums to those offering part-time employment to the students. The industrial apprenticeship system, sponsored by the Federal Ministry of Employment and Labour, provides youth up to age 21 with experience in a manual labour profession along with two days of additional training from the Centres for Part-time Education. In another initiative, work-training agreements are contracted for unemployed youth ages 18 through 25. Youth are actually employed at least half-time for pay under a part-time permanent labour contract and the remainder of the time is devoted to training associated with the profession with youth working from one to three years within the system. Employers are rewarded for their participation through a temporary reduction of the employer's contribution to social security. An additional incentive to youth is their eligibility to receive a partial unemployment benefit to supplement their part-time wages if they were not previously entitled to this benefit.

The Flemish Service for Labour Mediation plays a co-ordinating role regarding anti-poverty policy and social action in relation to employment. On the one hand, the service is charged with addressing the vacancy needs or demand side as well as the supply side of the employment picture, while on the other hand, it needs to assess and project the long term demands of the labour market and address the training needs of the long term unemployed. One of the major goals is to create additional employment for unemployed people at risk. The Flemish employment scheme seeks to improve the transition from education to the labour market, to provide counselling of youth aged 18 to 25 who are seeking employment, and to provide immediate employment through the "Youth Work Guarantee Plan". The plan seeks to provide one year of labour experience to those youth considered most at risk who have low qualifications, are younger than 25, and have been unemployed for at least two years, while drastically lowering the costs to employers for such labour. Additional measures include a counselling plan for those under the age of 46 as well as a new system of "grow in" jobs to provide enhanced opportunities for first employment to youth under 30. Sub-regional co-ordination and decentralisation are key themes of the Flemish employment policy. However, in practice, additional co-ordination is required amongst non-profit organisations, community action programmes, training centres and schools, all of which seek to promote new projects. In March 1994, agreements on local co-operation regarding training and employment of those at risk were delivered to the Flemish Minister of Employment. The Federal Minister of Social Integration is also involved in promoting measures to foster co-operation amongst services for the integration of at risk groups. The King Boudewijn Foundation as well as the Flemish Self-Employment Institute have supported various initiatives and pilot projects to combat unemployment of those at risk.

Integration of services and assistance provided under the General Welfare Work represents one of the Flemish government's central objectives. A 1991 Decree seeks to unify a number of functions including information and advice, reception, counselling and treatment, prevention, sensitisation and structural problem approach to social and psycho-social problems for various problem groups with plans that they be offered by one central organisation. Recognising the importance of integration and collaboration as well as the need for efficient and effective services, the Decree includes provision for compulsory collaboration and consultation between the various Centres for General Welfare Work, and between the centres and the other public and private welfare and social organisations. "The theme 'integration-co-ordination-co-operation in care' is a major subject of talks and an important topic of discussion between the government administration and the federations, umbrella organisations and advisory bodies of the General Welfare Work."

For families of children and youth at risk within the Flemish Community, a number of recent initiatives have been launched. The 1990 Act for Basic Adult Education specifies rules for basic education centres to combat illiteracy and address the training and educational needs of adults with little or no schooling. The policy is co-ordinated by the Basic Education Council including representatives of the education, culture, employment, and welfare policy sectors. A variety of preventive services as well as relief and curative aid is available to families and particularly those at risk, through the Public Centre for Social Welfare, including financial support, housing, advice, cleaning and meals on wheels. The Public Centres for Social Welfare Law permits the centres to function as independent administrative agencies with the ability to decide autonomously on co-ordination.

Provisions for family and elderly support are covered by a 1990 Decree of the Flemish Executive and are part of the home care under the Administration for Health Care. Co-operation related to elderly care is somewhat restrained by the various regulations of different administrations and ministries and the conflict of interests between the medically-oriented and the housekeeping-oriented support. In the area of housing, experimental programmes involving co-ordination between the public and private sectors are being tried. For example, one project launched in 1993, seeks to make private rental sector housing available to groups experiencing difficulties, with the Flemish government intervening in the rent. With regard to health care, formal co-operation and integration exist between the teams for School Medical Inspection, the Psycho-Medical-Social centres, the schools and the school networks. Preventive health care is provided, and all children enrolled in school from the age of 3 are served until the level of higher non-university education.

In the area of youth work, from 1995-98, the focus will be on youth work with the socially underprivileged, and in 1995, municipalities became eligible for subsidies for municipal youth work policy plans. As noted above with regard to alternation training, Youth Welfare Work subsidises both training programmes for working youth aged 15 to 25 and the Part-time Education programmes for youth aged 15 through 18. The Youth Welfare Work is directed at all youngsters in or thought to be at risk of being in problematic education situations. Collaboration is largely the result of local initiatives, and the Special Juvenile Assistance Administration charged with monitoring the services to minors and their families in problematic education situations, strongly emphasises activities of a preventive nature.

The Flemish government, with the Flemish Fund for the Integration of the Underprivileged, subsidises additional projects within the framework of a general municipal policy plan for the struggle against "opportunity privation", with municipalities having high concentrations of disadvantaged. On the basis of a number of risk indicators, 15 municipalities were selected. Therefore, the municipality in which individuals live influences their eligibility for services. By linking funding for projects to their inclusion in a general municipal policy plan regarding opportunity privation, the Flemish government promotes services integration at the local level.

2

CANADA

ALBERTA

Two major government initiatives which foster services integration for children and youth in Alberta are the Co-ordination of Services for Children and the Commissioner of Services for Children. Under the former, a committee comprised of the Assistant Deputy Ministers of the Departments of Family and Social Services, Health, Education and Justice as well as a Working Committee made up of officials of the departments, are charged with improving services for children and families while eliminating duplication and seeking to identify and fill existing needs. Local input is valued, and partnerships have been formed with five communities selected as pilot sites to seek solutions to improving services. The Commissioner of Services for Children is charged with reviewing services for children and families provided by the departments of Health, Education, Justice and Family and Social Services and recommending a plan for reform. Integration of the services of provincial departments and integration and co-ordination of efforts at the community level are among the goals for the reorganised approach.

A collaborative effort between the government of Canada and the provincial government to benefit pre-schoolers at risk and their families is the Community Action Programme for Children in Alberta. The programme places a premium on prevention and early intervention to reduce risks of social, emotional, health, development and learning problems. "Integration of health, mental health, social and educational services for children and their families will be an important feature in the design of community programmes." Additionally, early childhood education providers who enrol a high proportion of students considered at risk, are eligible for Programme Enhancement Projects grants from Alberta Education to provide additional instructional time and compensatory programming with emphasis on easing the transition from early childhood programmes to grade one. Grant recipients are expected to co-ordinate with community-based government and private agencies, local schools and families.

For school aged children, the Enhanced Opportunity Grant programme is directed to schools in Edmonton and Calgary which enrol high proportions of children at risk. Headstart services for pre-schoolers may also be funded under this programme in sites demonstrating need. A federal Stay-In-School Initiative has been launched including the START programme which targets at risk students aged 12-18 and recent drop-outs. Programmes are developed with schools, youth groups, community agencies, Indian bands, aboriginal social service organisations, and others.

A number of laws including the School Act, the Apprenticeship and Training Act, the Employment Standards Code, and the Worker's Compensation Act mandate programmes for youth in transition to work. Some of these programmes involve off-campus education activities supported by school-community partnerships. Alberta youths who are 18 or older, out of secondary school at least one year, and unemployed are eligible for assistance, with the goal of helping them to achieve financial independence, under the 1994 Skills Development Programme, if they enrol in approved full-time skills training programmes. The programme is administered by Alberta Advanced Education and Career Development and represents a consolidation of assistance programmes previously administered by three separate departments. "The objective of the recent consolidation was to ensure a fair, equitable students assistance system with unified policies, consistent eligibility criteria, need assessment methodology and benefit levels and streamlined administration." The Department of Family and Social Services along with the Department of Justice co-operate under the Young Offenders Protocol which outlines procedures for staff of both departments to work together to ensure co-ordinated service delivery for youths. The Child Abuse Reporting and Investigation Protocol, developed jointly by the Departments of Education, Family and Social Services, Health, and Justice, created an integrated approach to reporting and investigating child abuse and neglect and provides guidelines for development and implementation of local protocols.

To support policies which encourage the healthy functioning of families, the Premier's Council in Support of Alberta's Families was established. Additionally, the Family and Community Support Services (FCSS) programme is a municipal/provincial partnership which co-ordinates with other community organisations to develop community solutions to family and community problems. The programme, mandated by the Family and Community Support Services Act, is preventive in nature and makes considerable use of volunteers in planning, managing and implementing programmes.

To date, services integration is proceeding in Alberta largely as a result of policy both at the provincial and community levels. The government supports services integration as a primary means of accomplishing the goals of its three-year business plans across departments: to provide services more efficiently and effectively and at the same time, to reduce the deficit.

MANITOBA

In June, 1990, the Minister of Education and Training released a document, "Answering the Challenge: Strategies for Success in Manitoba High Schools", stating that the Department would develop an action plan by 1992 which would identify the conditions that place students at risk and cause them to drop out. The plan's goals included identification of necessary programmes and services to address needs and improve outcomes for at risk students. In 1991, a panel was appointed by the government to hold public hearings on possible education legislation to provide recommendations. Their "Report of the Panel on Education Legislation Reform" is under review by the government, and identifies partnerships and co-ordination of services as effective elements in meeting the needs of students. The report urges those involved in service delivery for children to abandon jurisdictional turf and act in the best interests of the children.

As a means of supporting and encouraging the development of comprehensive services for at risk students, in 1992, the Department established the Student Support Grants Programme which allocated $10.5 million annually to school-based intervention and prevention programmes expected to have a long term impact on students' school success. Among its other goals, the programme seeks to support development of appropriate student assessment and instructional practices for at risk students. Professional development programmes are seen as a necessary element to bringing about effective change to classroom practice, and alliances and partnerships among schools, families and community organisations are encouraged. Co-ordination with other government departments, educational institutions and community agencies and organisations is mandated. The grants are reserved for schools (grades K-12) with high concentrations of at-risk students, and eligibility is based on a number of factors including socio-economic characteristics (poverty and single parent families), low academic performance and other special school factors (for example, English as a second language populations). Programme proposals must include plans for development of all of the following six key areas thought to be essential to improving the educational outcomes for at risk students: curriculum adaptation and development, instructional and assessment practices, positive and supportive learning environments, parental involvement, staff development, and community participation.

In 1993, the Department published a draft document, "An Education of Value for At Risk Students: Possibilities for Practice", which identified community involvement along with improvements to schooling and parental involvement as important elements in improving the chances for successful outcomes for at risk students. In regard to services integration, the document states, "Community collaboration and the integration of services have the potential to offer a more comprehensive range of services, a more effective use of personnel, and the elimination of programme duplication". As part of its draft educational policy for at risk students, the department included community participation along with the other five areas listed above under the Student Support Grants Programme as essential to addressing the needs of at risk students. Included under community participation, services integration is seen "as an effective initiative in assisting at risk students to overcome personal, social, and economic barriers to learning and achieve success in school".

The Manitoba Department of Education and Training has launched a number of policy initiatives in support of services integration and funded a number of programmes that integrate services as an effective means to address the needs of children and youth at risk. Efforts continue to promote partnerships and encourage those involved in service delivery to work together to meet children's needs.

ONTARIO

The government in Ontario is seeking to integrate services "in order to provide a more effective and comprehensive system based on equity". Services for children and youth currently fall under the jurisdiction of several ministries including the Ministries of Education and Training (MET), Community and Social Services (MCSS), and Health, as well as hundreds of local authorities with over a thousand agencies delivering services. Changes are being pursued within disciplines and across ministries with ministries working together through the Inter-ministry Committee on Services for Children and Youth. For example, the MCSS has designed a policy framework regarding specialised children's services funded under the Child and Family Services Act (CFSA). The act, enacted in 1984, brought "a wide range of children's services under a flexible funding envelope and one set of legal requirements". The law covers child development services, child treatment services, child and family intervention services, child welfare services, young offender services, and community support services. The framework regarding specialised children's services encompasses six broad policy directions, including the development of a cohesive, integrated service system, improvements to the accessibility of services, increased local community participation in the planning process, resources tied to specified priority groups (including children at risk), equitable distribution of resources, and accountability. Local area offices will work with local communities towards achieving the objectives. Parents, service providers, labour, and others are being encouraged to form partnerships for the planning of co-ordinated services. Programmes for children at risk include toy lending libraries, family resource centres, and community development in low income neighbourhoods. At the same time, change is being pursued towards broader long term reforms through the Inter-ministry Committee. The committee is charged with identifying barriers to services integration and recommending corrective measures. The government has also established a Royal Commission on Learning to provide recommendations regarding a variety of issues including those affecting children and youth at risk and their families.

One example of an inter-ministerial activity is the 1988 MCSS policy document, "New Directions in Child Care", which includes a joint MCSS/MET policy encouraging school boards to actively collaborate with child care providers to develop co-ordinated services for young children. Funding responsibility is shared with MET providing construction money and MCSS contributing operating funds. Services are for school-aged children from 3 years 8 months to 12 years, but may be extended to pre-schoolers with community needs assessments determining programme elements. Presently, one-third of child care centres are located in schools. The Education Act and the Day Nurseries Act allow school boards to establish, operate and maintain child care centres. While the act does not dictate that school boards collaborate with community, social and health services, in practice, many seek to do so.

Other agreements include the General Legislative Grants under which MET funds teachers and supplies for services to students in care, or in correction or treatment facilities. The programmes are administered under the auspices of MCSS. In another agreement between MET and the Ministry of Health, the Ministry of Health provides school health services for students with special medical and physical needs.

Ontario funds a number of integrated services projects including the Better Beginnings, Better Futures Project. The project is jointly sponsored by the Ministries of Health, Education and Training, Community and Social Services, and the Department of Indian and Northern Affairs. As a condition for funding, communities must "demonstrate an integrated model of service planning and delivery and incorporate a major community development focus". The programme supports research to prevent emotional and behavioural problems in children within economically disadvantaged communities. Another programme, the Integrated Services for Northern Children project, seeks to integrate services for children with special needs in Ontario's vast and sparsely populated rural and remote areas, where geographic and demographic conditions would be considered barriers to services integration.

For youth in transition to work, in 1985, the government consolidated six youth employment programmes (Youth Works, Youth Corps, Ontario Career Action Programme, Youth Tourism, Youth Start and Residential Centres) into the FUTURES programme which served approximately 30 000 young people in 1992/93. The programme, under the Ontario Training and Adjustment Board (OTAB), seeks, "in participation with communities, [to] prepare employment disadvantaged youth 15-24 years of age, for success in education, training and the labour market". One of the programme features is a full minimum wage subsidy for work placement experiences for up to 52 weeks. Within the youth area of OTAB, service integration is a requirement of community delivery agencies receiving provincial funds for employment preparation and work placement programmes [FUTURES and Youth Employment Counselling Centres (YECCS)]. The YECC programme provides a wide range of job counselling and training related services to youths with little experience and education and also acts as a referral point to other community social services. To increase school retention of native students in particular, in 1990 MET in partnership with three local school boards sponsored the Alternative Secondary School Demonstration Pilot Projects for Native Students. Additional initiatives include the Co-operative Education Programme which serves 25 per cent of grade 11 and 12 students by providing work experience as a credit for graduation, and the Secondary School Workplace Apprenticeship Programme, a school-to-work transition programme for students in grade 11 or higher who spend two to three years gaining academic and apprenticeship credits towards a Certificate of Qualification in addition to an Ontario Secondary School Diploma.

By making services integration a requirement for government funding of various programmes, the Ontario government is stimulating local involvement in integrated planning and service delivery. At the same time, by creating the Interministry Committee on Services for Children and Youth, Ontario has affirmed its commitment towards broad long term reforms.

QUEBEC

The organisational framework for services integration involving health, social services and education are incorporated in a 1993 Quebec government publication entitled *Health and Social Services in Schools: Guide to Ensure Concerted Action between CLSCs (Local Community Service Centres) and School Boards*. The guide is a joint effort developed through the collaboration of the Ministry of Health and Social Services and the Ministry of Education and delineates the health and social services which should be provided to students in schools. These services include: health education, diet and nutrition, dental care, screening and monitoring, routine nursing services, routine psycho-social services, mental health, use of psychotropic substances, sexuality, verification of immunisation/vaccination, hygiene and safety, first aid, screening and monitoring of young victims of abuse or neglect, and care for young people suffering from a deficiency, allergy, temporary or chronic illness requiring occasional or regular treatment.

The guide is intended to aid community schools and local organisations in their efforts to develop priorities and formulate a joint action plan tailored to the specific needs of the locale. Examples of specific types of integrated services likely to be incorporated in local joint action plans include preventive programmes for students in danger of dropping out, and for those encountering difficulties relating to drug abuse, sexual abuse, and AIDS. Other activities may include screening and monitoring programmes, development of curriculum learning objectives, support to parents caring for children with illnesses, supplying of school meals, and provision of hygiene and safety services. Parents are encouraged to play a major role in the development of action plans. Parental education programmes are also suggested joint activities.

The legislative basis for co-operation between the education and health and social services networks is found in both the "Act Respecting Health Services and Social Services" and the "Education Act". The "Rules for Pre-school and Primary Education and the Rules for Secondary Education" contain the regulations for implementing the Education Act, and include the provision that health and social services shall be included as "complementary services" in the schools. Article 224 of the "Education Act" supports agreements for the purpose of delivering health and social services, therefore encouraging services integration between the schools and local organisations. The guidelines recognise the need for harmonisation among all community groups and public service organisations with activities planned jointly by the schools and local community services centres. The guidelines include provisions for organising and periodically reviewing services according to the financial resources of both the education network and the health and social services network. Guidelines include the need to provide "preventive, curative, readjustive and reintegrative services" and recognise the primary responsibility of parents regarding the health and education of their children. The important partnership which must exist between the parents, the schools, and the health and social services network is recognised in Quebec.

SASKATCHEWAN

Government departments and human service providers face many challenges as they work together to more effectively meet the diverse needs of Saskatchewan people. Traditional methods of planning, problem-solving, and delivering services were not achieving the desired outcomes. Financial pressures also contributed to the need to make the most efficient and effective use of limited resources. However, the more compelling reason was found in the problems facing many Saskatchewan children and their families. It is estimated that 40 per cent of Saskatchewan children are considered to be at risk. As a result, the government has developed a number of supports which facilitate the integration of services for children at risk and their families.

In 1993, eight provincial government departments and secretariats announced details of a comprehensive Child Action Plan designed to mobilise communities, organisations and individuals to join government in community-based action plans to improve the lives of children. This policy framework was entitled Children First: An Invitation to Work Together. Over 1 200 organisations were invited to share their ideas and proposals towards the goal that Saskatchewan children grow in an environment that supports their well-being and enables them to reach their potential. The Progress Report: Saskatchewan's Action Plan for Children – One Year Later was released in 1994. It contains profiles of provincial and local community actions which began under the Action Plan as well as a summary of budget initiatives.

The Saskatchewan Action Plan for Children represents a commitment to address and respond to the needs and well-being of all children through co-ordinated work by government and communities. Co-ordinating community-based ideas and solutions means improved co-ordination of new and existing pro-grammes, new partnerships, new service delivery models, and an improved co-ordination of existing legislation, policies, programmes and services.

Under the Saskatchewan Action Plan for Children, Integrated School-Linked Services was identified as a priority. The Integrated School-Linked Services Pro-gramme was initiated to identify and facilitate new collaborative approaches in the delivery of school-linked services to at risk children and youth. Education partners produced two documents in 1994-95: "Working Together to Address Barriers to Learning, Policy Framework", and "Integrated School-Linked Services for Children and Youth at Risk, Implementation Guide". These documents outline frameworks for partnerships among school division, schools, communities and human services agencies to provide integrated services based on community-identified needs. A video entitled "Working Together" was created to support the policy framework and the implementation guide.

A Minister's Working Committee on Integrated School-Linked Services was formed in 1992 to identify and remove barriers to interagency collaboration and service approaches. A priority action of the committee was to conduct an analysis of legislation and recommend protocols concerning confidentiality and information sharing. The report of the Legislative Review proposed that legislation should facilitate information sharing and collaboration among human service providers.

While changes to the legislation are being implemented, the Integrated School-Linked Services agenda will continue to be supported through several key tasks, for instance the development of a series of stand alone booklets which, when taken together, will comprise a "Handbook for Human Service Providers".

The Associate/Assistant Deputy Minister's Forum began in the Autumn of 1994. Its focus is on central policy and programme development and regional service integration. Eleven regional interdepartmental committees have been formed to co-ordinate local planning, services and the key initiatives.

Since 1994, grant funding has been allocated under Saskatchewan's Action Plan for Children to assist community groups in developing projects and services that prevent problems and provide support for children, youth and families. Funds for these Prevention and Support Grants are pooled by four different departments to provide one point of access for community groups. These departments include Education, Health, Justice, and Social Services. Priorities for grant funding are made by local interagency committees to support local service planning. A provincial committee finalises the selection of projects to receive funding. Examples of projects include parent education programmes, violence education and abuse prevention programmes, social workers in schools and social skills and behaviour programmes.

Recent specific integrative programmes which combine efforts of government and community agencies include the Pre-school Support Pilot Projects located in prince Albert and La Loche. Central and regional offices of the departments of Education, Health, and Social Services, as well as community organisations which have contributed donations, renovations, supplies, and extensive volunteer time, assist centres in providing co-ordinated education, health and social services for pre-school children and their families. The pre-schools were opened in 1993 in response to increases in the number of children experiencing "lack of school readiness and dropping out of school, abuse, neglect, and lack of positive parenting: accidents and preventable diseases; family violence and breakdown; and poverty". Evaluations completed for the first two years demonstrated positive results in the areas of high attendance, positive changes in children's listening and social skills and increased integration between government and community.

Through collaborative efforts among departments and with community, the government of Saskatchewan is committed to provide more responsive, integrated and comprehensive services while maintaining a cost effective and caring system of delivery.

3

FINLAND

"In Finland, the role of the society especially the municipalities as providers of services is widely accepted and established", with the government funding a wide array of services not only for those at risk, but for the population as a whole. Frequent co-operation within the provincial offices is reported between departments of different sectors including the Department of Education and the Department of Social Affairs and Health. Recent legislation adopted in Finland has moved in the direction of decentralisation and localisation with services planned and implemented for people living in a particular geographical area. The 1994-97 welfare plan includes development of community-based services with provision of health and social services in a unified, co-operative, and integrative way taking into account prevention. "The principles of welfare and health legislation can be stated in short as follows: aim to serve citizens, aim to normality, freedom of choice, confidentiality and prevention." Current economic realities are requiring attention to efficiency while striving to maintain high quality in meeting needs and promoting the social security of the population. The emphasis on prevention is seen as being economical by comparison to the provision of remedial services. "The scope of remedial services is largely explained by the scope of preventive services – when the scope of remedial services is small, the scope of preventive services has to be relatively large, and vice versa."

Municipalities have increasingly been uniting previously separate health and social service agencies. Recent legislation, the Planning and State Subsidies for Welfare Act of 1992, united in the same law the provisions for funding and planning both social welfare and health care. The new law contains fewer regulations and universal requirements and grants municipalities more leeway to plan their operations according to local needs. In this regard it is considered a boost to services integration at the local level where integrated services are implemented. The law also specifically calls for communication and co-operation with regard to health and social services, although in practice, civil servants continue to seek more concrete communication between ministries and offices. The system of financial accountability is seen as having a contradictory effect to integration, although evaluation over time is necessary since these reforms are relatively new. Under the new law, municipalities receive a fixed sum based on population density, rate of employment and other factors, thus encouraging fiscal responsibility since over-spending must be paid by the municipality.

Statutes related to social care do explicitly mention co-operation with various authorities and point to the importance of integrated services. Among these are the Mental Health Care Act of 1990, the Social Welfare Act of 1982, the Child Welfare Act of 1983 and Social Welfare for the Disabled Act of 1987. Problems remain, however, at an institutional and administrative level, resulting directly from separate but related pieces of legislation. For example, the Mental Health Care Act of 1990, the Specialised Health Care Act of 1989 and the Child Welfare Act of 1983 are implemented by separate organisations creating problems in the comparability of statistics, the allocation of staff resources, and the division of labour and collaboration between service providers.

Finland's health policy is based on the World Health Organisation's programme of "Health for All By the Year 2000" which stresses the need for intersectoral co-operation. One example of a successful integrated programme is the maternity benefit which combines health inspections with social benefit. Essentially, pregnant women who avail themselves of physical examinations, no later than the end of the fourth month of pregnancy, receive maternity benefit either in cash or in kind in the form of useful items for the care of an infant. Today, Finland reports more than 95 per cent of mothers receive maternity care throughout their pregnancies. Within Maternity and Child Health Care Centres which are generally located in close proximity to young families, professionals collaborate with social workers and social welfare authorities as needed. In an effort to foster healthy family development, typically, child guidance and family counselling centres in Finland integrate medical, psychological and social work approaches in their services. A new service offered is conciliation for families provided by social workers, psychologists, and others to encourage discussion between family members in crisis or conflict. Notably, in 1993, 25 to 70 per cent of most municipal welfare expenditure was subsidised by the State with many services provided free of charge, including social work, child guidance, and family counselling. "The aim in Finland is to develop community and structural social work in parallel with individual and family social work. The purpose of structural social work is to influence planning in other sectors so as to prevent social problems from arising."

In the area of day care, efforts are increasing to integrate day care with the schools. In general, municipalities either provide or subsidise day care centres. A few private day care homes also supply care, and home care allowances are available for parents who choose to care for their children themselves or who elect to place them with a child-minder. Approximately 58 per cent of 6-year-olds participate in voluntary pre-school education under the Finnish day care system. Additional pre-school education programmes are provided in comprehensive schools and are administered by the Ministry of Education and the National Board of

Education. Presently common curricula exist for the two types of pre-school education.[1] Compulsory education in Finland is a 9-year programme from age 7 though 16. Education at the national level is the responsibility of the Ministry of Education, which prepares legislation and drafts government resolutions, and the National Board of Education, which develops objectives and curriculum. Provincial departments play an administrative role in general and vocational education, but local administration and responsibility for educational provision are delegated to the municipalities.

Post-compulsory education is available in upper secondary schools and vocational schools and colleges with approximately 90 per cent of comprehensive and upper secondary school leavers continuing their education in vocational institutes or universities.[2] In addition, for young people requiring long-term guidance and intensive support, authorities have developed orientation training which involves courses spanning from two weeks to six months with the objective of providing general skills and knowledge necessary to working and everyday life. Plans are to increase opportunities for orientation training to extend the same opportunities to all immigrants. Finland also has laws which recognise minorities' rights to receive education in their native language. Within schools, student welfare groups represent an integrative unit generally comprised of the headmaster or the assistant headmaster, the student counsellor, the school social worker, and the public health nurse, and where applicable, a special education teacher, and a school psychologist. These groups provide a close, co-operative support network both for the individual student and for the positive development of the school community.

In recent years, the government has initiated reforms related to education to improve services and to make them more cost-effective. A number of laws and policies favour services integration including, for example, the Apprenticeship Training Act of 1992 which provides for co-operation between vocational institutions, labour authorities and businesses.

Another measure, the Labour Force Services Act of 1993, gives schools more responsibility for vocational guidance and assisting students towards making a smooth transition to the work force. There is a long tradition of co-operation, based on the Vocational Guidance Act, which requires co-operation between the youth employment services in employment offices under the Ministry of Labour and the vocational guidance programmes in the schools. The Vocational Education Act of 1987 sets objectives for vocational education including provisions for co-operation with other educational service providers to ensure a student's total rehabilitation. More recently in 1991, the Act on Co-operative Client Services in Rehabilitation calls for co-operation at the local, regional and national levels among the social and health authorities, the labour and education authorities, and the National Pensions Agency in co-ordinating rehabilitation measures. Co-operation between authorities and other service systems is also promoted.

Two measures, the Primary Health Care Act of 1972 and the Child Welfare Act of 1983, require the municipalities to provide pupils with school health care as well as support and guidance to help students to overcome any social or mental difficulties associated with schooling. School psychologists and school social workers may be employed by the municipality. Both the Child Welfare Act of 1983 and the Comprehensive School Act of 1983 call for building co-operation between the school and home. Research conducted on teacher training specifically related to building co-operation with parents suggests that such training needs to be increased. Additional attention has been given to the co-operation of schools and social and health services in special education and indeed, in 1985, the three separate National Boards of Education, Social Affairs, and Health, distributed identical instructions regarding the treatment, rehabilitation and education of students in difficulties including plans for how these were to interface. In another health related matter, the Act on Restrictive Measures Against Smoking of 1976, prohibits smoking in schools except in restricted areas and encourages co-operation among various national boards, research centres, voluntary organisations and municipalities with an annual plan being required to show how State financed activities mesh with public health services, social services, and health education.

In addition, the Act on Municipal Educational Administration of 1992 obliges staff of public health services and educational services to exchange information between them and to provide information to municipal authorities as necessary to fulfilling their responsibilities. Similarly, the law authorises an exchange of information, including statistics, between state and municipal authorities for the purpose of planning and organising educational services. The law helps to address the matter of confidentiality, which when applied too literally, becomes a barrier to services integration.

With regard to funding, reform of the state subsidy system for education and culture was introduced at the same time as the reform of subsidies for social and health services. Under the reform, increased decision-making and authority are designated to the municipalities and the other providers of educational and cultural services for the use of state funds. Initially funds are being allocated at the same level as prior to the reform and will be revised, annually based on the standard of costs, and every four years, according to actual expenditures realised. The purpose of the reform of educational administration is "to cut bureaucracy, transfer power to the municipalities, and cut costs". Recently, legislation has also been amended to transfer more powers to the municipalities with regard to curriculum to better utilise local knowledge of needs and wishes.

Individual ministries in Finland are charged with preparing legislation and policy statements within their sectors, but there is co-operation amongst civil servants of various ministries in matters of common interest. Close co-operation is realised between the national boards and the research and development centres in

Helsinki. Within provincial offices there is frequent co-operation amongst the various departments including the Department of Education and the Department of Social Affairs and Health. In the face of societal changes, economic recession and higher unemployment rates, the number of children and youth at risk is growing at the same time that supportive resources are experiencing cutbacks. Areas requiring special attention include preventive efforts as well as encouraging families with young children at risk to use the services of child guidance clinics or day care. For youth, it is recognised that efforts must be made to involve labour authorities more actively in assisting youth during the critical phase of transition to work. In Finland, co-operation between social and health services and education has been increasing. With the reform of the state subsidy system, and as municipalities assume greater responsibility for planning, it is expected that services integration and co-operation will be implemented on a larger scale.

NOTES

1. According to the approved plan for developing education the aim when organising preschool teaching is to achieve a situation where the entire age-group participates in preschool education for the duration of one year prior to entering comprehensive school.

2. The number of openings is dimensioned in a way that the whole finishing year of comprehensive school is offered an opening at some secondary level educational institution.

4

FRANCE

In France, integration of public services represents one of the goals of the inter-ministerial urban policy in which the Education Ministry is a partner. Urban policy seeks to create an environment which favours social cohesion within the broader context of promoting national solidarity. The Education Ministry participates in various inter-ministerial committees which meet several times a year. These include the Inter-ministerial Committee for Urban Affairs and Urban Social Development (CIV), the Inter-ministerial Committee for National Development (CIAT), and the Inter-ministerial Committee for Rural Development (CIDAR).

To help ensure equal educational opportunity for all children and youth, in 1982, the Education Ministry initiated a policy of *Zones d'éducation prioritaires* (ZEP) or "educational priority areas". The creation of ZEPs marked a major shift in policy towards improving equal opportunity through positive discrimination. Approximately 10 per cent of all suburbs in France and 2 million pupils are involved in ZEPs. Within these areas, schools and educational establishments receive additional resources "with the aim of obtaining a significant improvement in educational achievement", particularly for those students with social, economic, and cultural handicaps. Partnership with other community resources and those involved in social affairs is an important aspect of this policy, since it is recognised that the school alone cannot address all of the problems affecting children at risk and their families. Specifically ZEP policy calls for co-ordinated support not only of teachers but also of various specialists (psychologists, socio-cultural makers, medical and paramedical professions) and often public services such as the courts and police who together may be called upon to take concerted action on behalf of the child, the family and the school. Parents are also involved in planning and monitoring ZEP projects. The Circular of 28 February 1981 on ZEPs calls upon schools to create links with the broader social, economic, and cultural environment. The Education Ministry has urged that community efforts be mobilised around the school, with area boards "set up to formulate, monitor, and assess projects of a contractual nature with partners". To tackle issues such as drug abuse and high risk behaviour, social environment committees, chaired by school heads and including representatives of various sectors including government services, regional and local authorities, associations, businesses, and tradespeople, have been organised.

ZEPs receive additional teaching posts as well as operational resources. During the first cycle of the programme, an additional 2 470 posts and operating grants totalling FF 163.93 millions were awarded. During the second cycle, 3 976 additional hours/year and specific grants totalling FF 36.3 millions were allocated with the total cost of additional staff estimated at FF 531 millions. Approximately 13 per cent of primary school pupils and 15 per cent of lower secondary school and 10 per cent of upper secondary school pupils attend ZEP schools. In addition policies that favour the extension downwards of pre-school education to include 2-year-olds, already operating in ZEPs, are being considered more generally.

Other preventive services co-ordinated with education include the school health services which provide: medical examinations at key transition points in the child's schooling including transition from nursery school to primary school, entry into lower secondary education, and completion of lower secondary education. School health services conduct examinations at the request of parents, professionals, or the student and monitor students considered to be at risk. School doctors and their teams provide health education services and work to combat such problems as child abuse.

Other measures include educational support initiatives, designed to assist students who are experiencing difficulties. Services are provided free of charge with support for these initiatives from the voluntary sector working in liaison with teachers. Financial assistance is obtained from the government and local authorities. During the summer months, also in co-operation with the voluntary sector, some colleges and lycees are open to offer students educational, sporting, cultural and leisure activities. Finally, a special form of national service, makes "conscripts (...) available to schools in at risk areas for supervision, assistance, educational activities and education support. This measure, increasing the presence of adults in schools, has been highly successful".

Promoting educational success is seen as a major element in fostering social cohesion. Integrated services are viewed as an important part of the formula to ensure that children and youth experience equality of opportunity to achieve their potential.

5

GERMANY

German unification has presented both a challenge and an impetus for policy development in Germany and went together with major changes in legislation which originally were intended to become effective only in the old West Germany. Positive outcomes in eastern Germany have included the transformation to a market economy, the reorganisation of public administration, and efforts to repair environmental damage. High levels of unemployment, however, coupled with economic changes, characterised by the use of new technologies, have led to a concomitant need to retrain and restructure the work force. Social changes in eastern Germany, such as falls in family size and birth rate and a big reduction in availability of child care facilities associated with financial constraints, have followed similar trends in western Germany, with the effect of increasing the pressures on services for those at risk. However, in response to the demand for services, partly due to the large number of working mothers, new legislation does require communities to guarantee child care until 1988, for all pre-school children, whose parents want it.

Clear divisions and boundaries exist in Germany as to the responsibilities of departments regarding welfare, health, youth, education, and training, with "the educational and training authorities [having] only limited formal responsibilities regarding the welfare of young people", unlike the situation which existed in East Germany prior to reunification where the educational authorities played a central role in youth welfare. Historically, in West Germany, the principle of subsidiarity was adhered to meaning that the smallest private unit closest to the individual should intervene with care and aid (e.g. the family, the neighbourhood or the church), prior to public sector intervention. However it should be noted that these social services, although delivered by private agencies, were almost totally subsidised by public money. After reunification, this principle was transferred to the east as well, and over 300 new laws and regulations were passed in 1990 resulting in significant changes in the east including "a differentiated social insurance system; manpower services; accident insurance; local welfare offices, etc.".

A significant piece of recent legislation affecting children and youth at risk is the Children and Youth Services Act (KHJG), 1990. It came into force in eastern Germany in July 1990 and in western Germany in January 1991. It seeks to develop a new concept of youth aid focusing on prevention with youth offices taking responsibility for a variety of tasks including among others, family and parent counselling and support for families in difficulty. Specifically, the law requires local authorities to develop a local youth aid plan which includes: "the establishment of an inventory of existing institutions and a needs analysis; the obligation for public services to involve voluntary service providers in the planning procedure; and the co-ordination and concentration of all relevant local provision". The law is consistent with local and regional efforts towards "clearer target group orientation (*i.e.* schemes are provided on a clearer analysis and an inventory of young people's characteristics and needs) and local/regional (or even neighbourhood) approach".

The law also calls for co-operation of youth welfare agencies with schools, training institutions and public health services. The government must present a national Youth Report to Parliament every four years which includes an analysis and inventory of schemes and policy directives. Every third of these reports must give a general overview of the situation of children and youth and the status of child and youth welfare. The two in between may focus on special subjects regarding children and youth in Germany. While the law makes reference to co-operation and integration of services, however, it stops short of requiring integration through qualifiers such as "oughts" or "shoulds", thus leading critics to fear that agencies faced with limited funds will not implement co-operative initiatives that are not required by law.

Other factors identified as barriers to services integration include competition between those primarily concerned with prevention of problems and those concerned with remediation and response to the effects of the problem. With regard to funding, competition is also created between service providers who vie for limited funds. Another inhibitor cited is professionalisation characterised by "different methods and different ideas and definitions of goals, different professional standards, different criteria of success and only a vague knowledge of the other professions' mode of operation", therefore indicating a need for broader understanding of the standards of other professions through training. Additional factors include fragmentation and discontinuity of service provision created by different organisations being responsible for varying aspects of a problem and at different stages of a person's life. Concerted effort by professionals is needed over longer periods of time, and at the key transition points of kindergarten to school, school to vocational training and vocational training to work.

The Children and Youth Services Act together with the legislation, such as that referred to earlier concerning child care, also affirms that all children in need of day care should be provided with day care services, and in 1991, an official declaration asserted the government's desire to establish a legal right for day care. Despite this fact, service provision remains insufficient and is in practice generally extended to high priority groups such as children of single-mothers or those with working parents. The provision of services varies considerably based on geographical location and particularly the eastern and the western parts. In the seventies, consideration was given to developing an integrated education course for 5- and 6-year-olds; however, the fact that separate institutions are responsible for these age groups, namely the *Länder* Ministries of Social Affairs responsible for kindergartens and the Education Ministries responsible for the school system, served to inhibit progress towards this goal. Afternoon care for school children needs to be expanded to meet need, and currently since it is still (but rapidly improving) less socially accepted than kindergarten, it tends to attract more children from disadvantaged backgrounds. With regard to services for children with particular deficits, "new attempts have been made towards community-oriented networks and integrated services". Efforts have also been made to integrate child guidance services with both a "preventive and supportive" function in kindergarten and day care centres. While "until now school based social work has not yet been established as a regular service in Germany, the activities of the German Youth Institute to support such developments by counselling, organising conferences and giving publicity to existing initiatives in this field and individual projects such as the *Dietrich-Bonhoeffer Schule (Mult Schule)* in Weinheim, have attempted to develop co-operative relationships between social workers and teachers leading to the realisation that "sharing of basic concepts in both areas – education and social services – is a prerequisite for any successful co-operation between school and social workers". Schemes have also been supported for working with families, particularly in light of increased divorce rates and separation. Programmes include counselling and guidance, family centres, children centres, mobile play facilities, and neighbourhood based street work.

Each of the *Länder* in Germany is responsible for its own education system including curriculum and employment of teachers, with the local municipalities generally providing the buildings, equipment and administrative staff. The independence and division of youth welfare services from schools was codified in 1924. In the 1980s, with changes in family structure including more single-parent families and more families with two parents working, the need for co-operation of schools and youth services received increased attention. Services working with youth at risk co-operated with regard to pre-vocational education and integrating youth into vocational training. Recently, problems of violence and political extremism have led to a realisation that co-operative efforts between teachers, school social work, and youth services are needed, giving rise to a number of schemes incorporating sports and school clubs and those designed to address the problems of youth gangs.

The population of young people considered most at risk in Germany includes those who leave school without completing a diploma or vocational training, those who are socially disadvantaged, and those who are members of an ethnic minority. Approximately 14 per cent of young people aged 20 to 25 (an estimated

500 000 persons) in western Germany and probably as many in eastern Germany have not completed formal vocational training despite the fact that Germany offers a "dual system" of vocational education providing a formal vocational training diploma with apprenticeships involving both schools and companies. The Vocational Training Act provides for the in-company provision of "dual system" training. While vocational training courses offered in schools falls under the jurisdiction of the educational authorities of the *Länder*, the training offered on site in companies is regulated by the Federal Ministry of Education, Science, Research and Technology. At the local, especially in regions with discrepancies between supply and demand for apprenticeships, often multi-partite level committees including employers unions and representatives of public authorities seek to co-ordinate efforts. "Despite the tripartite structure of these committees, a lack of co-operation between schools and enterprises as well as lacking co-ordination between school-based and on-the-job training have been frequently criticised by experts and the social partners". The law eliminates the "semi-skilled" qualifications for all but disabled persons and requires qualification at the skilled worker level for formal certification.

Prior to reunification, training through "dual system" apprenticeships had been available in both the East and West Germany although it should be noted that the detailed structures were not the same. In East Germany vocational training had been concentrated mostly in larger industrial companies, in factory owned vocational schools and practical training facilities. After reunification, however, many companies collapsed and the schools became the property of the municipalities. The practical training facilities were often lost together with the companies, thus creating a strain on the system and a decreased number of available training places. As a result, state manpower services training schemes, originally conceived for the "disadvantaged" in the former West Germany, replaced many of the regular "dual system" apprenticeships, with private companies, youth aid institutions, voluntary associations, churches, trade unions, chambers and other employers' organisations involved. The manpower services schemes of the *Bundesanstalt für Arbeit* [Federal Institute of Labour (BA)] are regulated under the Employment Promotion Act of 1969 with governance by a tripartite board at the federal level. The BA provides the funding for schemes, but provision is delegated to commercial or non-profit organisations. Largely, BA schemes are for previously employed workers who have contributed to unemployment insurance, but the BA is also charged with vocational guidance responsibilities including dissemination of printed and audio-visual information as well as individual counselling, and some training of youth at risk through financial aid to apprentices or participants in training schemes not run by employers.

Strategies have been developed in a number of German towns to provide co-ordinated help for youth in transition from school to training and work including:

providing vocational guidance, promoting co-operation between general education and vocational teachers, including all relevant local partners in co-ordinated training conferences and involving them in planning, creating a local agency to co-ordinate relevant activities, establishing regional agencies for young migrants and their families, developing mentoring and social work schemes during training facilitating contact with all relevant agencies. Often, joint actions of several organisations and the efforts of voluntary associations play a major role in youth training support, although the Children and Youth Services Act calls for public agencies to assist untrained and unemployed youth. Another law promoting co-operation and co-ordination is the law regarding Youth Courts. This law regulates the role of youth offices and calls for their co-operation with youth courts for young people under 18 and "growing up" youth aged 18-21.

With recent legislation and particularly, the Children and Youth Services Act, the government has provided an impetus towards services integration for those at risk in recognising the need for joint planning and co-operative effort over time by professionals from various disciplines. Despite the challenges created by unification and economic pressures including high levels of unemployment, integrative efforts, particularly between the social work sector and education and youth aid are advancing in Germany.

6

ITALY

Recent legislation in Italy has laid the fundamental groundwork necessary to effective services integration for children and youth at risk and their families. Specifically, two laws, Law No. 142 (June 8, 1990) and Law No. 241 (August 7, 1990) regulate service agreements between official organisations. The latter states, "public administrations may at all times enter into agreements with one another in order to regulate activities of common interest in a context of collaboration".

With legislation enacted in 1990 and 1993, the Department of Social Affairs in conjunction with the Ministry of Education, is engaged in developing programmes for the prevention and treatment of drug abuse and educational handicaps. Legislation enacted in 1990 designated the Ministry of Education to co-ordinate health education initiatives with an emphasis on prevention. The legislation calls for teacher training programmes encompassing coursework as well as experiences acquired by allowing teachers to be seconded to host communities. Additionally, the laws provide for family and student involvement in school board initiatives, the establishment of information and counselling centres not limited solely to issues of drug abuse, efforts to identify new methodologies, the rationalisation of data, as well as funding for the evaluation and monitoring of projects implemented. Other examples of recent legislation emphasising the need for agreements concerning programmes include a law enacted in 1991 directed at youth at risk of involvement in criminal activity and the 1992 "Framework law on assistance, social integration and the rights of handicapped citizens".

A number of laws passed in 1993 focused on the urgency of combating educational dysfunction with the Education Minister being designated to develop a three-year action programme for the entire country. Legislation provided that regions and cities with high numbers of students at risk be assigned an additional 250 primary and lower secondary teachers to "ensure the more highly qualified and rational performance of teaching and educational activities for the prevention of, and fight against, educational dysfunction". Pilot schemes are developed according to local needs to target the most at risk pupils and their families and "take a broad and inclusive approach, involving teachers, pupils and parents in primary schools and lower and higher secondary schools". While the school plays a central role, co-ordination of community psychological, social and health care services is fostered. The schemes have been implemented in 135 districts, in 34 provinces and in 10 regions and involve 182 nursery schools, 176 primary schools, and 213 lower secondary schools. Funding has been augmented by contributions from the regional rectorates and the local authorities.

"The main obstacle to genuine services integration lies in the difficulties of approaching the problem. In order to tackle the problem effectively, operating methods based on results (which are therefore "project-specific") need to be implemented." Administrative structures entrenched in emphasising compliance with procedures have sometimes hampered efforts to achieve genuine services integration. The importance of training is recognised and programmes for a variety of service providers at district, regional and provincial levels have been sponsored, in the hopes of laying the foundation for increased integrated efforts in the future.

7

NETHERLANDS

The Netherlands' policy related to children and youth at risk and their families is evolving towards a less "compartmentalised" and a more decentralised system. Compartmentalisation refers to the Dutch phenomenon of "the pooling of social forces along political and denominational lines". Essentially, in the Netherlands, since the late nineteenth century, various social groups including liberals, social-democrats, Catholics and Protestants founded their own institutions including political parties, sports associations, welfare groups, and schools. Compartmentalisation has enabled groups to develop regional power bases and to gain access to national decision-making centres. Despite the 1960s trend towards greater independence from religious and ideological groups, today, compartmentalisation is a factor in services integration since "compartmentalised organisations still dominate certain sectors of society, particularly (...) education and voluntary social work, and, to a lesser extent, welfare work and health care". Administrative compartmentalisation, characterised by a tradition of autonomy amongst ministries as well as directorates and individual departments within ministries, is a factor which must be addressed in seeking a more collaborative approach to policy making and services integration.

During the 1980s, decentralisation policies were implemented in the Netherlands, with the effect of transferring to the local authorities greater autonomy in policy making as well as financial support for local policy implementation. As a result of decentralisation initiatives, the tasks associated with welfare policies in particular were divided amongst the national, regional, and local administrative levels. The national level is responsible for the general policy framework and national priorities as well as output financing; monitoring; research; and experimentation, dissemination, and implementation of innovations. The regional level plays a support and guidance role and is responsible for some development of activities while the local level is charged with local policy making and implementation, local activity development and integration of services. In education, while local school boards have been relatively independent, compartmentalisation has remained a counter force to further decentralisation efforts.

Compartmentalisation has led to two categories of schools in the Netherlands, the state schools and private-authority schools, with each having equal rights to state funding. Though education remains rather centralised and strictly regulated, consensus exists at the national level that municipalities should enjoy greater autonomy within the national policy framework with regard to education of the disadvantaged. At the same time, it is recognised that the government has a role in protecting disadvantaged groups. This dichotomy has led to the government exercising "a selective type of control by encouraging the establishment of partnerships and local or regional networks, involving links between schools, local governments (especially in the areas of social renewal and educational policies), youth care organisations, as well as intensive co-operation between ordinary and special schools".

To address the needs of children and youth at risk, in 1986, the Dutch government initiated the Educational Priority Policy (OVB) programme which allocates additional resources to schools in areas with high proportions of students considered educationally disadvantaged due to socio-economic or ethnic factors. Networks of primary and secondary schools in disadvantaged areas may also qualify for funding for joint activities organised by the schools or by others, including school advisory services and welfare institutions. The policy promotes co-operation amongst schools and between schools and other organisations in seeking to address the complex problems associated with educational disadvantage. The programme was incorporated into law in 1993 as part of the Primary Education Act and the Secondary Education Act with the endorsement of the Minister of Welfare, Health and Cultural Affairs. The law requires the government to develop a "national priority policy framework" every four years to provide direction for local and regional level activities. The plan established for 1993-97 includes, among others, objectives such as "improving achievement in language and mathematics; (...) ensuring a more balanced distribution of pupils from differing backgrounds across the secondary education system; [and] reducing the incidence of absenteeism and early school leaving"; as well as themes including "promoting the development of pre-school children; (...) smoothing the transfer from primary to secondary school; organising parental involvement; [and] providing vocational guidance ".

Social renewal legislation currently being drafted seeks to improve co-operation amongst schools, local authorities and other organisations. The bill permits schools and local authorities to deviate from existing legislation that would impede efforts to combat disadvantage, thus allowing such measures as an extended school day and the allocation of resources to benefit pre-schoolers. It also authorises the establishment of a local fund through which local partners including schools as well as other institutions and organisations may pool resources to meet local needs in the fight against disadvantage. "A major aspect of social renewal philosophy is to delegate powers from central to lower-level authorities. Evaluation studies have revealed that this has indeed helped to reduce fragmentation of provisions at the local level. Furthermore, government ministries are co-operating more closely to support local renewal policies."

A bill concerning municipal policies towards disadvantaged groups is currently being drafted. The aim of this bill is to decentralise tasks and competencies from central government to local government as of August 1997. The rationale behind this is that the wide differences exist between municipalities with regard to problems related to disadvantage. That is why municipal governments are considered to be in a better position to make and manage local policies aimed at combatting disadvantage.

For youth in transition to work, including those at risk, government policies have sought to ease the transition in two major ways: *i)* by attempting to ensure that all youths possess at least a basic vocational qualification upon leaving school; and *ii)* by creating and providing temporary jobs. Since it is recognised that, in fact, many students at risk fail to achieve a regular basic vocational qualification, one avenue currently being pursued by the government is development of courses at junior level or below the basic level while seeking the co-operation and full recognition of both employers and trade unions. Other objectives include improving course offerings leading to recognised qualifications, increasing student awareness of the value of a qualification, and increasing "transparency" in course supply and government as well as industry recognition of the courses offered. Government measures to boost employment and reduce the numbers receiving social benefit involve an interface of the Ministry of Education and Science, the Ministry of Social Affairs, and the Ministry of Economic Affairs, with the Ministry of Agriculture, Nature Management, and Fisheries contributing to agricultural education matters.

The government is promoting "inter-sector integration" by actively seeking to expand the role of industry and employers in providing jobs and training in co-operation with the education sector to foster a more gradual transition to work. The government has established agreements with employers and trade unions at the national level, while also encouraging regional partnerships and joint activities. Additionally, government subsidies are available for companies supervising trainees, with bonuses provided for training members of target groups. The government stimulates services integration and the development of networks by offering additional funding on condition that co-operation is established at the local level among schools as well as between schools and other institutions. Regional networking is also encouraged. For example, additional funding is provided to network participants for regional action programmes detailing agreements and targets as well as activity and achievement reports regarding policies ensuring "a basic vocational qualification for all" including a comprehensive registration system of all early school leavers. "Intra-sector integration" is occurring at the regional level with vocational education and adult education offered in Regional Training

Centres. In 1994, a bill was presented to Parliament to create one Adult and Vocational Education Act to replace a number of separate laws. Efforts are being made to develop a "national qualification structure" to foster greater coherence and co-ordination of curricula. The government has also sought to expand enrolment in the "dual" apprenticeship training courses by 20 000, particularly targeting drop-outs from lower secondary school.

In the area of youth services, the Ministry of Welfare, Health and Cultural Affairs has primarily been responsible for youth care and youth welfare policies, while the Ministry of Justice has been charged with youth protection and juvenile delinquency policies. Co-operation between the two is common, however, particularly through collaboration on pilot projects, and recently, in July 1989, the two ministries were awarded joint responsibility for implementation of the Youth Care Act including planning and funding. The Act combines provisions for voluntary youth care, judicial youth protection, and juvenile criminal law and, among other principles, is based on the tenets that co-operation between institutions should be encouraged and voluntary organisations are preferred over public bodies for the implementation of services. The system has evolved from a supply-oriented system to a demand-oriented system with an emphasis on activating the careseekers' own resources. The promotion of economies of scale by provinces and metropolitan areas is resulting in the formation of multi-functional organisations in the field of youth care, and it is expected that by 1996, the number of youth care institutions will decrease from 400 in 1992 to maximally 120.

Youth protection policies in the Netherlands aim towards restoring the relationship between parent and child with the court deciding when intervention is warranted for the child's well-being. The Youth Care Act contains provisions applying to guardianship, partial responsibility known as "family guardianship", as well as judicial child protection institutions. The government has recently started the "Innovation" project to ensure that departments within the Ministry of Justice are equipped "to prepare the way for an effective youth protection system based on children's right to an upbringing". Both the Ministry of Welfare, Health, and Cultural Affairs and the Ministry of Justice see "a need for greater harmonisation with the fields of youth health care, education and other relevant sectors. The ministries are consulting with other levels of government to reach agreement about improving coherence between the various sectors". A government policy paper, entitled "Inter-sector youth policy" released in November 1993, outlines a policy aimed at co-operation amongst the sectors involved in youth affairs with the "aims to improve young people's opportunities and to reduce and prevent "drop-out". Drop-out is defined broadly to include "dropping out from the family, from school, or from work".

The 1994 Welfare Act calls for joint management, sharing responsibilities, and fostering collaboration. Decentralisation is encouraged along with collaboration among government agencies, with voluntary organisations, and with youth welfare professionals to work towards prevention of marginalisation and resultant dependence on social welfare. The same ideas of mobilising people's own resources and preferably utilising voluntary organisations as those promoted in the youth care system, are espoused.

Government policies with regard to juvenile delinquency favour an integrated approach to prevention with the Ministry of Justice seeking to involve all sectors in supporting preventive initiatives. The government also seeks to reduce the numbers of delinquents and to help youth to return to education or work. An integrated report on the security of Dutch citizens has recently been prepared with the co-operation of several ministries at the request of the Ministry of the Interior and will be used in developing integrated security policies. The Ministry, in recognition of the interrelationship of juvenile delinquency, school drop-out and unemployment is supporting a number of projects aimed at prevention of all of these.

Another act which promotes services integration is the Guaranteed Youth Employment Act, adopted in 1992. The Act established the Guaranteed Youth Employment Scheme which targets school-leavers aged 16 through 27 who have left school without a qualification and who have been unemployed for at least six months. The Scheme provides work experience, vocational training, and guidance, and participants receive a minimum wage for 32 hours a week of either work or training. "(...) the municipal authorities draw up plans outlining, among other things, the co-operation between industry, schools, job centres, youth welfare organisations and youth care institutions." In practice, it is difficult to find sufficient vacancies to guarantee a work experience for all, and consequently, initiatives are being launched to encourage private companies to participate.

In the field of health care, administered by the Ministry of Welfare, Health, and Cultural Affairs, policies and programmes aim for prevention and alleviating differences caused by low socio-economic position which is believed to be associated with poorer health conditions and lower life expectancies. A variety of services exist including home nursing services, home care organisations, baby clinics and municipal health services, and projects including the World Health Organisation's "Healthy Cities" programme seek to reduce the effects of poverty on health. The Ministry also sponsors literacy projects with some for the entire population and others specifically for children at risk. The HIPPY (Home Instruction Programme for Pre-school Youngsters) programme, also called "Opstap", concentrates on development of general abilities, and "Overstap" focuses on initial reading instruction and long-term parent involvement.

The need for co-operation between the sectors in responding to the needs of children at risk is well recognised and understood in the Netherlands. It became clear in the 1980s that simply extending public spending did not automatically produce the desired results: "problems were not clearly solved, citizens became more dependent, and professionals seemed busier creating work for themselves than giving satisfactory response to the questions and problems they were asked to address". As a result of increasing decentralisation, policies towards youth at risk are expanding the responsibility of local authorities. "Increasing appeals are made to local governments and private organisations to bridge differences between sectors of policy and to pool resources." A variety of models are used in the Netherlands to encourage integration which generally involve participation by a co-ordinator. This includes, among others, the following situations: where the co-ordinator is responsible for "pulling down the walls" between local political and administrative departments; setting up projects with private organisations requiring separate administrative departments to consult and co-operate with each other; and utilising a special budget to involve the active participation of young people, parents and local residents. Other approaches include: establishment of formal co-operation agreements drawn up between participating schools and institutions; establishment of a foundation to create new policies, by participating schools and institutions, who give up part of their autonomy and powers; and the creation of a "covenant" in which the participants announce their intention to pursue specific common goals, specifying the resources they are prepared to invest.

Finally, Dutch policy is placing greater emphasis on the involvement of the target groups themselves. This trend can be seen in the growth of home-based projects, increasingly individualised approaches to target groups and a growing emphasis on the active participation of youths and parents. Despite a history of compartmentalisation, however, a variety of innovative approaches and recent legislation represent significant efforts to foster both "inter-sector" and "intra-sector" co-ordination and collaboration with regard to meeting the needs of children and youth at risk.

PORTUGAL

Public policy and recent laws in Portugal include provision for intervention and services integration to assist children and youth at risk. The Basic Law of the educational outlines the fundamental structure and characteristics of education in Portugal. It includes articles which seek to ensure that the educational system will be responsive to students' individual needs including support for students' psychological growth and development as well as counselling from professionals engaged in regional educational centres. School social work activities and aid are intended to help to compensate for economic, social and cultural disadvantages. The law calls for co-operation with special services from the community health centres to work with the schools to provide for the healthy development of students. Pre-school education is optional in Portugal and is intended for children aged 3 through 6 at which time they begin 9 years of compulsory education with an additional 3 years of secondary education offered. The law also provides for continuing and adult education to eliminate illiteracy and to afford those who have dropped out early or who have not had the benefit of education at the normal developmental age an opportunity to pursue education and achieve qualification.

In the area of social action, a number of policy objectives are articulated which include measures promoting services integration for children and youth at risk: developing preventive measures and modes of promoting social integration and solidarity; promoting better use of existing services in terms of targeting the client group and adapting the responses to current social needs; and intensifying co-ordination among services and institutions of social security, employment, professional training and other sectors towards preventing marginalisation of economically disadvantaged groups. Additional goals include: assuring the successful implementation at the national level, in conjunction with other sectors, of the Project of Aid to Families and Children, created in 1992, and comprised of representatives of the sectors of justice, social action, and health to identify situations involving child abuse or improper treatment and develop programmes to aid these children and families; and activating preventive measures and measures to combat poverty through inter-sectoral co-ordination of efforts by maximal utilisation of international co-operation in this domain, especially of European Union programmes, and by active participation of the population.

With regard to education, policy objectives centre particularly on the fight against students' school failure and seek to improve the quality of education by extending compulsory and free education to 12 years. In addition, efforts include augmenting pre-school education in the public, private and co-operative sectors; implementing a new curriculum with provision for individualised instruction; creating educational counselling and psychological services; developing aid and complementary educational activities; encouraging forms of integrated special education. Further objectives include modernising the management of the system through administrative and pedagogic decentralisation and promoting school autonomy and community involvement in management of the school; and adapting the educational system to the world of work by promoting technical-professional teaching, professional training in the arts as well as adult and continuing education.

In the 1980s and 90s, a substantial number of laws and amendments were passed which favour services integration. These include, for example, amendment No. 3/85 – DR No. 104, II Series (1985) which establishes priorities of action in the pursuit of specific objectives agreed by the Ministry of Education and Social Security to establish co-operative studies and actions. Another important measure, amendment 119/ME/88 – DR No. 162, II Series (1988) defines schools for special intervention situated in zones or localities where isolation is an obstacle to retaining teachers, and which contain a significant number of children with learning difficulties and disabilities and where students' school failure is a significant problem. More recently, amendment 3-1/SEEBS/SERE/93 regulates the annual definition of schools for priority intervention.

In addition, Law No. 43/89 – DR No. 29, I Series (1989) creates compensatory educational activities included in the Educational Project of the School, as an appropriate instrument to promote educational success and permit individualisation of instruction. Another measure, Law No. 383/91 defines a general course of pre-training created by common agreement of the Ministry of Employment, Social Security, and Education for young people aged 15 to 21 who have not completed compulsory education. Amendment No. 75/92, DR No. 116, I Series B (1992) establishes norms governing the co-operative accords between the regional Social Security centres, the private social solidarity centres and other non-profit organisations sharing similar goals. The Council of Ministers resolution No. 30/92 – DR No. 189, I Series B (1992) reinforces the pedagogic activity to be exercised towards the family in developing an aid programme, the Project of Aid to the Families and Children, designed to improve interpersonal relationships within the family and to address problems of child abuse and maltreatment. The amendments 116/SERE/SEEBS/93 – DR No. 162, I Series A (1990) regulates aid and educational supplement in the area of school social work. Finally, two integrative measures dedicated to improving the conditions of immigrants to Portugal are: the Council of Minister resolution No. 38/93 – DR No. 113, I Series B (1993) which approves aid to immigrants and ethnic minorities towards achieving their total social and professional integration, and the joint amendment of the Ministries of Interior, Education, Public Works, Transport and Communication, and Health Employment and Social Security – DR No. 239, II Series (1993), which creates an Interdepartmental Commission for the Integration of Immigrants and Ethnic Minorities.

Despite substantial recent legislation and progress being made, barriers remain to services integration for children and youth at risk. It is up to the regional and local levels to operationalise the legislative acts passed at the national level which tend to reflect sectoral biases. For example, in the area of pre-school education, a 1979 law sought to develop a diverse group of methods and solutions and norms related to pre-school education. Ten years later, however, norms and rules clearly delineating the roles and modes of intervention of each of the sectors concerned are still not established. Rapid societal changes represent a constant challenge as well, including increases in divorce and single family households, requiring periodic assessments and timely responses adjusted accordingly. To address current needs, changes in the legislation regarding activity centres for youth, in addition to extending the duration of compulsory education are being proposed to address current needs.

The need for preventive programmes and plans of action to aid children and youth at risk is recognised, and a number of such programmes have been established recently in Portugal. These include the Educational Programme for All in the Year 2000 which is an inter-ministerial programme targeted to prevent school dropout and facilitate professional training and qualification. The Project of Intercultural Education was created to co-ordinate and support programmes building tolerance and social solidarity among people of different cultures and is targeted to priority zones with concentrations of ethnic minorities and high rates of school failure. To integrate health education in the curriculum, the Programme of Promotion of Health Education was recently created and particularly promotes activities related to prevention of drug addiction and AIDS and supports a co-ordination of activities across all state services in these areas.

In the justice sector, the General Directorship of Guardianship Service to Minors (DGSTM) seeks to study, co-ordinate and oversee the implementation of measures decreed by the juveniles courts and institutions to promote preventive measures and the rehabilitation of minors, and it seeks to foster co-operation between public and private entities. The courts, which deal with young people aged 12-16 who are at risk, benefit from the professional input of teams of social workers and psychologists from the DGSTM who also assist with co-ordination with community services for children and youth at risk. Two additional institutions, the Centres of Observation and Social Action and the Commissions of Protection of Minors were created recently, to seek to protect the interests of minors. The Commissions of Protection of Minors function at the community level particularly dealing with those who are victims of maltreatment and targeting preventive services which seek to avoid the further escalation of problems and possible uprooting of minors. Each commission is a multi-sectoral, inter-disciplinary group composed of a psychologist and representatives of the public ministry, of the municipality, of the regional Centre of Social Security, of local services of the Department of Education, of the Institute of Youth, of the Minister of Health, of the private institutions of social solidarity, of the forces of security and of associations of parents. It should be noted, however, that despite the existence of these innovative services, the large numbers of children at risk pose a great challenge and place a variety of strains on the system. Another interdepartmental unit, the Interdepartmental Commission for the Integration of Immigrants and Ethnic Minorities, set up by common agreement of the Ministers of Internal Administration, of Education, of Public Works, of Transport, of Communication, of Health, and of Social Security, seeks to plan, co-ordinate, and evaluate activities to improve the outlook for these groups.

In another integrative effort, a work group comprised of representatives of the sectors of social action, the family and justice, has been set up to co-ordinate intervention of various institutions in matters relating to adoption. In addition, to evaluate the need to create kindergartens and to plan for effective operation and funding, a work group comprised of the representatives of the Secretaries of State for Educational Reform and Social Security was established in 1991. In the field of employment and professional training, it is recognised that integrated programmes uniting services in education, professional training, and employment with a host of other resources are necessary to assist youth to successfully transition to the world of work. Notably, Programme Horizon, created by the Commission of European Communities, as well as the Institute for Employment and Professional Training seek to promote integrated programmes which benefit disadvantaged youth to enter successfully into employment.

Recent years have seen significant efforts to integrate services and support preventive efforts regarding children and youth at risk in Portugal. The creation of interdepartmental multi-disciplinary groups for purposes both of co-ordinating planning and implementing programmes is improving communication between the sectors. Presently, the educational system is undergoing reform and is becoming more decentralised at the regional level with the expectation of increased responsiveness to local needs and further integration of services to children and youth at risk.

9

SLOVENIA

The educational system in Slovenia is currently undergoing significant changes. While legislation regarding services integration for children and youth at risk was not reported, it was noted that education researchers in Slovenia are devoting time to the study of at risk children and youth. Current efforts are directed at defining who is at risk and which measures will most appropriately and effectively address the needs of this group. One project, conducted at the Educational Research Institute of the University of Ljubljana, focused on "school newcomers" in the belief that the period of transition into school is a critical one and a time when, for some children, the change from a play-oriented environment to a more organised educational process is a difficult one. The researchers identified the following subgroups of children at risk: emotionally unstable (immature) children, socially deprived children, children with immature personalities, and "suspected risk children", and according to this definition, estimated that about 30 to 40 per cent of school newcomers are at risk. The researchers recommend intervention and various forms of assistance early in the educational process including some integrative measures: preventing the influence of risk-connected elements, caring for and maintaining the child's health, informing the family of the educational work done with the child, strengthening the co-operation between parents and school, attracting volunteers from various fields to work with the children at risk, and supervising as many of the tasks as possible throughout the interaction between the environment and the child at risk.

In Slovenia, health care institutions keep track of the locomotive development of new-borns thought to be at risk. Potentially retarded children are monitored on a regular basis during the first year of life, and medical experts as well as experts in sociology, education, and workers from humanitarian organisations are included in a team approach to the diagnosis and treatment of these children. Up to the age of 3, individual treatment is generally administered; group therapy generally is provided after the age of 3. Systematic tests are employed for 3-year-olds, and later, upon enrolment in school, to identify children at risk who may not have been recognised earlier.

Another Educational Research Institute project includes an analysis of communication competence as a contributor to the at risk status of children. Preliminary results suggest a correlation between lack of communication competence and poor school achievement. "Pragmatic competence" which includes the student's involvement in the "micro-social organisation of the educational process" and "a way of expressing attitudes and points of view in relation to the content of the curriculum" correlates with socio-cultural status of pupils and is considered a factor in at risk status.

Another study focuses on the self-image and psychological issues of 17-18 year olds who are experiencing the transition from middle to late adolescence and who represent the first group of students to be included in the new educational programme. It is expected that the research will encourage efforts to improve both preventive and curative programmes of psychological help.

At the Institute for Ethnic Studies, research is being conducted focusing on Romanies as a risk group. The Romany children speak a language different from that of the majority population and many live in minimal living conditions in isolated settlements located on the fringes of urban areas. The Romany social and cultural environment differs from that of the majority population. Many Romany children remain in primary school only at the first level mostly in the first and second years. Many Romany adults are unemployed or work at jobs reflecting their low level of education. Often Romanies attend schools with specially adapted programmes geared for the mentally retarded, thus raising questions as to why they are included in such programmes, whether their needs are being met, and for how long their development should be monitored. Staff turnover for those involved with Romany children is very high, and the Education Institute for the Republic of Slovenia is providing a variety of training experiences to help better prepare teachers for their work with Romany children. A number of preventive and integrative measures are being proposed including re-evaluating criteria for classifying Romany school children and increasing compulsory school preparation to two years. Efforts to improve conditions for the entire family include improving employment possibilities for Romanies and offering adult education classes for youth and adults who have dropped out of primary schooling.

Research projects such as those described above, particularly in an era in which the educational system is undergoing significant changes, hold promise towards identifying risk-related elements and influencing policies aimed at integrative measures for children and youth at risk in Slovenia. Research which demonstrates the positive effects of preventive efforts as well as the advantages of early intervention and the strengthening of co-operation between parents and school has the potential to influence implementation of new measures and reforms of existing programmes to achieve these goals.

10

SWEDEN

The school system in Sweden has been moving towards decentralisation with increased responsibilities delegated to the municipalities. In 1973, larger municipalities were created by merging, thus creating opportunities for developing alternative solutions to meeting educational needs, child care needs and the needs of the elderly. At the same time schools in Sweden have moved from a largely rule-based system towards a goal-oriented one with the State setting the national goals. The National Agency for Education is charged with evaluating municipalities' efforts. Recently, a bill suggesting new national curricula was introduced to Parliament for decision this year. The suggested national curriculum calls for students in need of special help to receive support from all school employees and emphasises the co-operative role of the school and home in fostering the child's learning and development.

For students with special needs, a 1978 grant emphasised the school's responsibility in the treatment of this group, and dictated that they should receive special consideration before the remaining resources were distributed. Today, a single municipal grant combining all state grants including those originally earmarked for education is awarded to the municipality which is charged with setting priorities and determining the distribution of funds. The national curriculum contains provision for flexibility in meeting students' needs and building on their strong points with an emphasis on co-operation among school, students and parents. Alternative measures include student participation in special, small educational groups for the receipt of additional pedagogic help, adjusted curriculum options with the possibility of combining academic subjects with practical professional experiences under school supervision, and "special day school." The special day school provides longer days and a larger staff to meet the needs of students from a variety of social environments and backgrounds who are having difficulty adjusting to a regular school setting. The services of child and youth psychiatrists are offered in close co-operation with the schools.

July 1992 saw the creation of "the 17th programme", which increases the responsibility of the school after compulsory school attendance for students who have not applied or been admitted to one of the 16 national programmes. The programme obliges the school "to provide an individually designed programme, adapted to each student's conditions and wishes, with the goal of eventually creating an interest in one of the nationally established programmes".

The Social Act defines the responsibility of the municipality to co-operate with the home in providing protection and support for children and youth showing signs of unfavourable development. The law regulates efforts for youth with substance abuse problems. The Custody of Youth Act defines the obligations of the municipality for youth under 18 and provides that those at risk of having their development and health endangered by abuse, neglect or other home conditions shall be cared for. Those endangering themselves due to substance abuse, criminal activities or other socially destructive behaviours will also be cared for.

Clearly, recent years have seen the role of the municipalities expanded as regards meeting the special needs of children and youth at risk. The move towards decentralisation and merging to create larger municipalities with flexible funding packages has enabled municipalities to assess local needs, set priorities, and address the needs of their local populations.

TURKEY

Recent efforts for children in Turkey have focused on the expansion of special education services for the estimated three million children between the ages of 4 and 18 who require such services. Those included in this group are defined as "children who could not benefit or partially benefit from the general public education because of the unnatural differences they have with respect to their physical, mental, emotional, and social characteristics", thus including children and youth at risk. With an estimated 2.5 per cent of the population of children who need special education benefiting from the special education services appropriate to their characteristics, 1993 was designated by the Ministry of National Education, "The Year of Special Education", with increased efforts to improve public awareness and build public support of initiatives.

Recent legislation in special education includes Act 3797, approved on 30 April, 1992, replacing the former General Directorate of Special Education with a more integrative body, the General Directorate of Special Education, Guidance, and Counselling Services, "to carry out the activities more effectively and extensively". In an effort to improve services and create positive public opinion, co-operation protocols between the ministries and the universities have been set up and studies have been undertaken involving the collaboration of ministries, universities, and voluntary institutions. Other activities have included examination of the various public, private, and voluntary institutions concerned with the studies of special education and guidance and the publication by the Directorate of a guidebook for those interested in special education. Radio and television programming is being used to introduce special education to the general public, and meetings have been organised in the various provinces with the co-operation of university and voluntary organisations to bring the topic of special education to the fore.

Under Act 2916, the Children Who Need Special Education Act, a number of studies related to special education are being conducted. "The purpose of this act is to provide an appropriate education for children who need special education by taking the general principles of [the] Turkish National Education System as a base, and to integrate these children to the society by helping them to have an occupation and vocation according to their education." Basic principles entail recognising that each child in need of services would benefit from services, and providing special education as early as possible. Additional principles include planning services according to the children's special needs, and maintaining vocational education and rehabilitation services consistently for children in need of special education. Additional tenets include recognising special education as "an inseparable part of the general public education", and educating special education students with their normal peers in the general public schools or institutions whenever possible. Current studies in this regard include 88 schools at the pre-school, elementary and secondary levels in 12 provinces. The schools were selected as the pilot sites in a study of integrated education in the general public schools involving all of the students including special education students, the families, and the teachers. Other studies involve the pairing of special education and general public schools with shared activities including visits to each other's schools, trips, lectures, and shared celebrations.

The Ministry of National Education is responsible for planning special education services including pre-school, elementary, secondary, vocational and diffused education services. The institutions responsible for implementing services encompassing diagnosis, vocational rehabilitation, care, education and training include guidance and research centres, units related to the school guidance services, public and private elementary and secondary schools, boarding special education schools, home-boarding special education schools and classes, and vocational schools and vocational education centres. A variety of individuals and institutions including families and relatives, municipal and police officers, health and social services administrators, census officers, school personnel, and religious personnel are responsible for providing information to the nearest civil administrative division regarding children in need of special education services. Guidance and research centres, located in the provinces, conduct examinations and make recommendations to the Board of Education in the province, which is responsible for placing the child in the appropriate programme. The guidance and research centres monitor the placements in co-operation with the schools.

The period between April 1992 and April 1993 saw the establishment of 8 Education and Practice Schools, 6 Vocational Schools and 2 Vocational Education Centres for children with learning difficulties, 2 schools for children who are hard of hearing, 4 schools for children with hearing impairment, and 8 guidance and research centres. It is reported, therefore, that "the schooling rate in special education (...) has increased approximately 100 per cent compared to previous years", thus representing significant success in the efforts towards increasing services to children with special needs including those children considered at risk.

12

UNITED KINGDOM

ENGLAND AND WALES

In England and Wales, recent legislation regarding children and youth at risk and their families has resulted in a number of reforms geared towards the integration of services. The government is funding measures fostering regeneration and encouraging economic development in socially and economically depressed areas. With regard to services integration, "the government recognises that, in order to achieve lasting change, the regeneration efforts of central and local government and the private and voluntary sectors need to be co-ordinated". In support of this goal, to be used to complement the government's main programmes including education, housing, training, employment, and social security, in April 1994, the Single Regeneration Budget combined the funds from twenty separate programmes sponsored by five government departments to create greater flexibility in addressing local needs. A Ministerial Committee on competitiveness co-ordinates overall planning. New, integrated regional offices, uniting previously separate departments will plan and set regeneration priorities for the region and bid for Single Regeneration Budget funds.

Currently, in some of the most deprived areas, the government is funding 31 City Challenge Partnerships which include in their five-year Action Plans for regeneration, improved services and facilities for children and families. Originally part of Grants for Education Support and Training (GEST), but coming under the Single Regeneration Budget in 1994-95, the government is funding a number of projects related to raising standards in inner city schools and focusing on improving literacy. Another major component of GEST, which directly benefits children and youth at risk, is funding directed at tackling the problems of truancy and disaffection. Expenditure of over 55 million pounds has been supported over the four years 1993-97 (Wales has operated a similar scheme from 1994-95). The programme seeks to keep students in regular school attendance to tackle the problems of disaffection in schools and to prevent young people becoming involved in anti-social and criminal behaviour.

Another programme for youth at risk is the Youth Action Scheme, which, with the government allocating over 4 million pounds in 1993-94, seeks to provide challenging and stimulating activities to divert young people from anti-social and criminal behaviour. The programme involves co-operation of a number of agencies including the Youth Service, the police, social services, and health authorities. The Youth Service is managed by local authorities and voluntary bodies and provides for the social education of those aged 11-25. The National Youth Agency is largely delegated the responsibility from the Department for Education and Employment to oversee the Youth Service. "The Agency is intended to assist in promoting partnership between the voluntary and statutory sectors of the youth service, securing a national focus for the support of youth work, a more effective means of implementing government policy, and a more efficient response to increasing international initiatives in this area." The Agency has broad responsibilities and is permitted to seek funding from a variety of government departments and the private sector for a wide range of activity including innovative and original work.

Education for children under 5 in England and Wales has not been mandatory, but the government is extending the opportunities for all 4-year-olds to have access to it. Along with local education authorities, the voluntary private sectors play a substantial part in the provision of pre-school care and education, and are encouraged to co-ordinate efforts at the local level. Recent reforms affecting pre-school and school age children have included passage of the Children Act 1989, which combines legislation regarding the care and upbringing of children in private law (for example, those involved in a domestic dispute such as a divorce) and public law (for example, children in care of a local authority). The law has been characterised as "the most important reform of the law concerning children this century [which] promotes partnership between local authorities and parents, and between the various local authority departments, over care for children in need".

Other legislation directly benefiting children is the Education Reform Act 1988 which requires all publicly funded state schools to provide the National Curriculum. Of particular benefit for children and youth at risk is the provision for periodic assessment with additional help provided when needed, up to the age of 16. "Through the Education Reform Act 1988 and the Education Act 1993 the government has given expression to the themes of quality and diversity of educational provision, parental choice of school, and school autonomy and accountability." Another tenet of this act is provision of funding specifically for additional education services for travellers and displaced persons. Local authorities also receive grants under section 11 of the Local Government Act 1966, the urban component of which was incorporated in the Single Regeneration Budget in 1994-95, to benefit ethnic minority children and their families, enabling communities to employ additional staff and finance supplementary projects including English as a second language, strategies for improving educational achievement, and home-school liaison.

"Guidance on educational provision for 'pupils with problems' was issued jointly by the then Department for Education and the Department for Education and the Department of Health in 1994. This sought to expand collaboration across the providers of services plans for children 'in need'. A statutory Order under the Children Act has since made the production of services plans mandatory, and required that they be the subject of cross-service consultation, and be published."

The Education Reform Act 1988 also requires schools to provide students with guidance and careers education in preparation for their transition into adulthood and the world of work. In an effort to improve the quality and availability of vocational training, as detailed in the 1991 White Paper, "Education and Training for the 21st Century", the government has introduced new General National Vocational Qualifications (GNVQs) primarily for 16-19 year olds as well as additional National Vocational Qualifications (NVQs).

In England and Wales, emphasis is placed on career planning, and beginning in 1994, additional funding was offered to include early career guidance for years 9 and 10 when students are approximately 14-15 years old. In most schools, students at the age of 15 are offered opportunities for practical work experience and schools are encouraged to integrate their programmes with those of the local Careers Service. The Compact programme, with 50 inner city compacts and extension later to other areas, includes partnership agreements between employers and schools. Under this programme, students who meet certain academic and attendance standards are offered a variety of further education and training opportunities. The programme contains "provision for monitoring the progress of individual students and for identifying and supporting students at risk". For those considered most at risk in Compact and other schools, the earlier Department for Employment sponsored "Compact Plus" to target increased support to these students and to help them to successfully transition from school into work, training or further education. National Targets for Education and Training were released in 1991 with government support by the Confederation of British Industry. These targets seek to involve business, education and training organisations, as well as government in an effort to achieve "improved levels of participation and attainment in high quality education and training". Education, employer and trade union representatives comprise the advisory board which reports to the government on progress towards the objectives. In 1992, the government passed the Further and Higher Education Act which "established a new further education sector in England and Wales funded by new national Funding Councils, so bringing greater coherence to post-16 further education". Co-operation between this further education sector and various other organisations including the Careers Service, the Training and Enterprise Councils, and the Department of Employment is promoted by a Charter for Further Education.

Since April 1991, another programme, the Youth Credits programme, offers credits carrying a financial value to aid students trying to make career decisions at the age of 16 or 17. Students may present the credits to an employer or training provider in exchange for approved training. In addition, for all 16- and 17-year-olds who are not in full-time education, who are unemployed, and are seeking training, the government guarantees a training experience, with Training and Enterprise Councils co-ordinating with Careers Services to ensure achievement of this goal.

For families, the earlier Department for Education and the Welsh Office funded a new initiative on family literacy. In an endeavour to improve both children's and parents' literacy, this programme builds partnerships and integrates efforts among national organisations as well as those of various local organisations including schools, further education colleges, local education authorities and voluntary organisations. Another integrative programme aimed at children and youth at risk and their families is the Drugs Prevention Initiative. By 1994, the experimental programme, begun in 1990, funded 20 local teams in urban areas to develop drugs prevention programmes and to encourage co-ordination of all drugs prevention activities in the community.

Legislation and programmes in England and Wales are being developed with increasing attention to services integration of programmes affecting children and youth at risk. This is a general trend in programme reforms with a large number of measures focusing particularly on youth as they seek to make the transition from school and training to the world of work.

NORTHERN IRELAND

While public services in Northern Ireland operate under a similar policy context to that in England and Wales, a number of differences exist in administration, service delivery, and the legislative framework affecting children and youth at risk and their families. For example, the present law in Northern Ireland related to the care and protection of children and the provision of social services dates back to the 1968 Children and Young Persons Act. A proposal for a draft Children (Northern Ireland) Order currently exists which would consolidate the public and private law much like that accomplished in England and Wales under the Children Act 1989. Education reform in Northern Ireland, as in England and Wales, has shifted greater responsibility to the boards of governors of schools and colleges, and currently, alternative models for future administrative structures are being considered. The Education Reform (Northern Ireland) Order 1989 contains similar reforms to those promulgated by the 1988 Education Reform Act in England and Wales including a statutory Northern Ireland Curriculum. Compulsory education in Northern Ireland, however, begins at age 4, with pre-school provision left largely to the discretion of the Education and Library Boards. New policy on day care and early education was to be released in 1994. Regional Health and Social Services Boards and the Health and Social Services Management Executive provide an integrated management structure for service delivery. Proposed legislation would allow the provision of child care services to be delegated to Community Trusts. The development of day care services in the voluntary sector has been supported by the Department of Health and Social Services.

Targeting Social Need (TSN) is a major government policy priority which "aims to meet greatest need, reduce unfair social and economic differentials and promote equality and equity by focusing resources more precisely on Northern Ireland's most disadvantaged areas and people, Protestant and Catholic". Urban regeneration programmes such as Making Belfast Work, like those in England and Wales, seek to address the complex economic, educational, social, health, and environmental problems associated with inner city poverty, and to co-ordinate community, private sector, voluntary sector and government efforts. A similar initiative is targeted to Londonderry. The Belfast Action Teams, under the Department of the Environment, provide guidance and funding to community organisations for anti-poverty projects including those targeted to young people at risk. Governmental grant support, for projects promoting cross-community contact and mutual under-standing as well as respect of cultural diversity, is available as a result of the Community Relations (Amendment) (Northern Ireland) Order 1975 and the Transfer of Functions (Northern Ireland) Order 1989. The Grants for Education Support and Training Scheme (GEST) in England and Wales does not extend to Northern Ireland, but it is believed that much the same outcome is achieved through support for in-service teacher training (INSET) in high poverty areas.

The Northern Ireland Committee on Drug Misuse, established in 1984, under the Department of Health and Social Services, is responsible for monitoring and prevention of drug use as well as promoting co-operation between the various agencies and professions. Since drug abuse is a relatively small problem in Northern Ireland, the Drugs Prevention Initiative in force in England and Wales, does not include Northern Ireland. In the absence of a severe problem, low-profile community based activity has been supported as opposed to highly visible national campaigns which it is feared could actually inadvertently encourage experimentation. Similarly, truancy is not as severe a problem in Northern Ireland as elsewhere in England and Wales, but support is available through the Education and Library Boards where necessary. For example, three of the boards have provided additional traveller liaison teachers to help ensure the integration and regular school attendance of traveller children. The new initiative in "family literacy" adopted in England and Wales does not extend to Northern Ireland.

Northern Ireland boasts a Careers Service similar to that in effect in England and Wales. The service functions under the direction of the Training and Employment Agency which also endorses the National Education and Training Targets.

Training and Enterprise Councils do not exist in the region, and the Training and Employment Agency is charged with the responsibility of ensuring a skilled workforce. Careers education is a compulsory element in the secondary school curriculum with non-statutory guidance issued by the Northern Ireland Curriculum Council. Youth aged 14-16 may, as in England and Wales, choose vocational or academic options outside the statutory curriculum. Training credits may be earned to secure National Vocational Qualifications as part of the Training and Employment Agency's new pilot "Jobskills" programme. A Compact Scheme, involving partnerships between employers and schools through which students may receive opportunities for jobs with training or training leading to jobs, exists in Belfast.

Similar to England and Wales, Northern Ireland does have an established Youth Service with statutory provisions included in the Education and Libraries (Northern Ireland) Order 1986 and the Youth Service (Northern Ireland) Order 1989. The service is comprised of both a statutory sector including some 180 youth clubs and 20 residential centres under the Education and Library Boards, and a voluntary sector with some 2 000 voluntary groups which receive grant aid from the Education and Library Boards. The Boards have developed Specialist Intervention Schemes for young people identified as being at risk and not achieving up to their potential. The Youth Council for Northern Ireland, established under the Youth Service Order 1989, seeks to address the problem of marginalised, unattached youth and has among its functions "to encourage and assist the co-ordination and efficient use of the resources of the youth service".

Several important pieces of legislation were pending in 1994 in Northern Ireland that would encourage greater integration of services to children and youth at risk and their families. Nevertheless, recent policy changes have also encouraged such a trend.

SCOTLAND

Recent government proposals for reform in Scotland have reflected a commitment to increasing the level of partnership between the public and private sectors. The Scottish Office, in its 1992 publication, *The Structure of Local Government in Scotland*, maintains that "[local authorities] have to act much more in partnership with the private sector, and with the powerful public sector agencies". Interdisciplinary teamwork is also a construct which the government supports as a means to provide for the care, education and health needs of children and youth.

Corresponding to government efforts in England and Wales, the Scottish government is promoting regeneration programmes in Scotland's urban areas. The emphasis in these programmes is to improve social, economic and physical conditions, while working in partnership with the private sector, and involving local people in the process of assuming greater responsibility. Some partnership initiatives are led by the Scottish Office, with others led by Scottish Homes and other agencies. Local participation is encouraged and in those led by the Scottish Office, the Office contributes 75 per cent of the funding with the remainder contributed by local authorities. "The programme encourages local authorities to place the management of projects in the hands of local community groups and voluntary organisations."

In Scotland, as in England and Wales, the Children Act 1989 requires that all pre-school and care programmes for children under 8 be reviewed by the social work department in conjunction with the education department. Goals include involving voluntary organisations, health boards, the private sector, employers and parents in a co-ordinated effort to provide comprehensive services for young children. However, many communities "are still at an early stage in their plans to promote, support or develop any childcare provision in their local areas". To assist rural communities in developing childcare services, Highlands and Islands Enterprise is supporting three-year development programmes in rural Scotland and is encouraging partnerships among communities. While education for under fives is not mandatory, local authorities are obliged to carry out an assessment if it appears that a child may have special educational needs.

In recent guidance, the government has called for interagency collaboration. At the national level, an AIDS Prevention Co-ordinating Group for Scotland, comprised of health boards, local authority representatives, national representatives from the voluntary sector, the Health Education Board for Scotland, and the Police and Prisons' services, unites key groups in an endeavour to foster planning and co-ordination and promote services integration. At the local level, AIDS co-ordinators, appointed by the health boards, are charged with co-ordinating cross-sectoral activities involving local authorities and voluntary organisations.

Another integrative programme in Scotland is the Scottish children's hearing system to which children under 16 may be referred for a variety of reasons including: offending, truancy, child abuse, or because they are in need of care or protection. The system, legislated by the Social Work (Scotland) Act 1968, operates under the auspices of the Secretary of State jointly with local authorities, to protect the best interests of children. The system requires collaboration of reporters, hearings, and service providers. In addition, in an effort to combat abuse, co-operation has been encouraged among various professionals and services including social work, education, police, and health. To combat youth homelessness, the government in 1994 planned to introduce demonstration projects "bringing together all the relevant agencies – social work, housing, employment and social security – to tackle the problems in concert".

Similar to that in England and Wales, the Careers Service in Scotland is charged with providing information, guidance and assistance to young people seeking education, training and employment. In this endeavour, careers services co-ordinate with education authorities, local enterprise companies, schools, colleges, employers and training providers. The Trade Union Reform and Employment Rights Act 1993 requires that career guidance and placement services be provided to those attending or leaving state and independent schools and colleges.

Education providers and employers are increasingly being called upon to collaborate in developing and assessing training programmes. Training programmes include Youth Training, sponsored by Scottish Enterprise, which provides two years of training for 16 and 17 year olds, and Skill-seekers which "gives young people the support and spending power to determine their own career training needs". Education Business Partnerships are being encouraged to develop co-ordinated links between education providers and the business community. Contributing to the effort to boost the economy and create jobs are the Scottish Enterprise Network and the Highland and Islands Enterprise which, through representation of local enterprise companies, involve private business in co-ordinating efforts with the public sector. Both of these enterprise organisations support efforts to assist communities in developing childcare services. Both also contributed to the establishment of the Scottish Quality Management System, in 1993, which developed quality criteria for vocational education and training.

The at risk status of children may well be compounded by the needs of family members requiring special services including elderly people, people with a mental or physical disability or with a mental illness. In Scotland, under the Community Care programme, local authorities are obliged to provide services and prepare action plans in conjunction with other community services including health boards, housing authorities, voluntary agencies, and the private sector. Another measure benefiting children and youth at risk and their families is the 1992 Out of School Childcare Grant whereby the government authorised 45 million pounds sterling over a three-year period to support childcare, thus enabling some parents of school-age children to further their education, training and employment opportunities.

A variety of integrative approaches are being tried in Scotland to better serve children and youth at risk. Clear guidance recognises the need for interdisciplinary teamwork and a close partnership with the private sector in providing a wide range of care, education, and health programmes.

13

UNITED STATES OF AMERICA

A growing interest in services integration for children and youth at risk and their families in the United States has emerged as a result of several important factors including: *i)* a demographic picture which shows that in 1993, approximately 33 million persons or 13.3 per cent of the United States population lived at or below the poverty line, with 20.4 per cent of children living in poverty; *ii)* the realisation that fiscal constraints require doing more with less, thus leading to efforts to find more cost-efficient ways to meet people's needs; *iii)* a recognition that social problems are growing more complex and more severe; and *iv)* an awareness that the current service delivery system is a complicated and often cumbersome one, making it difficult for those in need to negotiate the system and gain access to necessary services.

While the federal government funds many services and programmes benefiting the population at risk, and can therefore, influence policy and programmes by attaching legal requirements to these funds, the system of service delivery in the United States is such that historically and constitutionally, many responsibilities are reserved to the States. Additionally, many county and local governments administer and contribute to the costs of social, health and welfare services, with education traditionally held as a local function with local school boards responsible for determining policy. While traditionally, government has funded many support services, the debate continues as to the extent to which government, and especially the federal government, should intervene. Many non-governmental entities including private, not-for-profit organisations, private businesses, and foundations provide funds and programmes as well. In a historical context, the concept of services integration in the United States is not a new one, and indeed, as part of the 1960s "War on Poverty", the federal government created local "community action agencies" to deliver a host of services to families living in poverty, it is also true, however, that over the years, a large array of programmes have emerged, many of them "categorical" in nature and designed to respond to a specific problem as opposed to addressing the wide range of issues generally faced by children and their families. "Overlapping purposes and sometimes contradictory or inconsistent implementation policies, such as varying eligibility requirements, pervade the services delivery system." Policy makers seeking to effectively meet needs in a cost-efficient manner are moving towards services integration in the context of several other strategies, including "(...) creating outcomes-based systems, fostering new community governance, combining funds and using other resources innovatively, and designing new approaches to leadership and professional development (...)".

At the national level, one recent example of the growing emphasis on outcomes and the move towards services integration, is the adoption in March 1994 of a law which codifies eight "National Education Goals" and offers States additional funding for the purpose of achieving these goals. Embodied in the goals are objectives to provide all disadvantaged and disabled children with a quality pre-school program, to increase parental involvement in their children's education, and to provide nutrition and health care necessary for children to be effective learners at school. To achieve the goals, the United States Department of Education has asked parents, schools and service agencies to "(...) link community resources, (...) strengthen family support programmes, [and] promote interagency collaboration".

In the area of child care and child development, as early as the 1960s, the Head Start programme provided a comprehensive programme with a broad spectrum of services for children at risk and their families including social, nutritional, health, and education services. Head Start currently serves 36 per cent of eligible children and the current administration is hoping to expand services so that by 1998, all eligible children and their families will receive services. Recent legislation regarding child care policy has sought to foster integration and focus on planning and prevention. In 1991, the Child Care Development Block Grant and grants to support "At-Risk Child Care" required co-ordinated planning for all child care services within States and required state agencies to co-ordinate new services with other, federal, state and local child care and child development programmes. Another programme provides child care for mothers receiving welfare benefits through the Aid to Families with Dependent Children programme and participating in work or training under the Family Support Act JOBS programme, designed to help mothers to move into the workforce. In addition, the Transitional Child Care Programme offers one year of child care to women after they discontinue receiving welfare payments.

For school age children, the federal government's largest education programme, the Chapter One programme of the Elementary and Secondary Education Act, granted nearly $7 billion in funding to assist schools to provide services targeted to the needs of children at risk. The re-authorisation proposal for the law includes the stipulations that schools co-ordinate Chapter One services with other education, health and social services programmes, that they increase parent involvement, and in schools with high concentrations of poverty, that they provide health programmes for early identification of health and/or nutritional problems.

For families and children, recent legislation has sought to move from a focus on crisis intervention to an effort towards prevention and strengthening families. Legislation creating the Family Preservation and Support Services Programme was passed in August, 1993. "Family preservation programmes are for families in crisis, including those at risk of having their children placed in foster care (...). Family support programmes (...) aim to keep families healthy and intact by providing or linking them to a wide range of voluntary preventive and supportive services such as parent education, prenatal classes, and early intervention for young children whose development is delayed."

For youth in transition to work, the federal Job Training Partnership Act (JTPA) allocates $2 billion per year to "assist youth in making successful transitions from school to work, apprenticeship training, the military or post-secondary education and training", but the law does not stipulate a requirement for co-ordination with other health or social services. In 1994, the School-to-Work Opportunities Act, to be jointly administered by the Departments of Education and Labour, will serve as a catalyst for partnerships of employers, educators and others to build a high quality school-to-work transition system to prepare young people for careers in high-skill, high-wage jobs. At the local level, employers, educators, labour leaders, and other community leaders are responsible for collaborating in planning and administering the programme to meet local needs. Funding will include federal grants to States, waivers, direct grants to local partnerships, and grants to areas with high poverty rates. The legislation also supports co-ordination of state, local and other federal resources and requires that after initial demonstration periods, States and localities find other sources of funding.

Another programme requiring the co-operation of departments is the Empowerment Zone and Enterprise Community programme. Under this programme, rural areas designated by the Department of Agriculture and urban areas designated by the Department of Housing and Urban Development will receive funds and tax incentives, and waivers to address local needs such as the following: "1) drug and alcohol prevention and treatment; 2) training and employment of adults; 3) support to promote home ownership; and 4) non-school services for children and families provided by community-based organisations". These communities will also have priority for other federal programme funds. "This approach represents a major innovation in co-ordinating and focusing federal resources from many different agencies on high-risk communities, and requires an unprecedented degree of state and local level collaboration as well. The Enterprise Board to oversee implementation of this initiative includes the Secretaries of all domestic Cabinet agencies."

A strong trend exists in the United States to encourage services integration for children and youth at risk and their families. The United States recognition of the problems caused by current demographic and social trends, limited resource availability, and the need to improve service delivery and effectiveness, has encouraged the integration of services. The debate continues, however, as to the degree to which government should intervene.

Annex I

STUDY ON SERVICES INTEGRATION FOR CHILDREN AND YOUTH AT RISK AND THEIR FAMILIES

COUNTRY REPORT QUESTIONNAIRE: LEGISLATION AND POLICIES

In the first part of the report please would you provide a description of the legislation and policies existing in your country which are relevant to the integration of services for children and youth at risk and their families. Preferably, this should involve consultation with government officials from all of the relevant ministries (*e.g.* Education, Social Welfare/Social Services, Health, Labour, Agriculture) since they will have different perspectives.

In countries with both federal and state governments, particularly where the state governments are numerous, an outline of federal legislation and policies along with the main differences between states' legislation and policies will be ample.

Legislation and policies need to be considered, in turn, in relation to services for pre-school children, school children, youth in the transition to work, and the families of children and youth at risk. Any one piece of legislation or policy may apply to more than one of these groups. However, as far as practicable, the laws and policies relevant to services for each of these four different client groups should be described separately.

Please address the following questions:

- *Philosophy*: What is your government's philosophy or outlook concerning the integration of services? Is the government interested in integrating services and, if so, why?
  - For pre-school children:
  - For school children:
  - For youth in the transition to work period:
  - For families of children and youth at risk:

- *Laws and policies/promoting*: Describe fully the laws and policies in your country which promote services integration.
  - For pre-school children:
  - For school children:
  - For youth in the transition to work period:
  - For families of children and youth at risk:

- *Laws and policies/inhibiting*: Do any laws or policies in your country act to inhibit integration and, if so, which and how? Are there any other obstacles to integration?
  - For pre-school children:
  - For school children:
  - For youth in the transition to work period:
  - For families of children and youth at risk:

- *Laws and policies/change*: Is the government planning to change any laws or policies relevant for services integration and, if so, what is planned?
  - For pre-school children:
  - For school children:
  - For youth in the transition to work period:
  - For families of children and youth at risk:

- *Legislation/importance*: Assess the relative importance of legislation for services integration. To what extent is integration the result of government legislation and policies, and to what extent is it the result of local or community initiatives?
  - For pre-school children:
  - For school children:
  - For youth in the transition to work period:
  - For families of children and youth at risk:

- *Benefits/policies*: Describe the present policies and aims of your government with respect to the provision of social security benefits for children and youth at risk and their families (*e.g.* low income families, the unemployed, one parent families, the homeless, immigrants, refugees, aborigines, gypsies and travellers). Please give special attention to the homeless, immigrants, refugees, aborigines, gypsies and travellers, if relevant.
  - For pre-school children:
  - For school children:

- For youth in the transition to work period:
- For families of children and youth at risk:

- *Benefits/change*: Is the government planning to change any of the benefit policies mentioned above and, if so, how?
  - For pre-school children:
  - For school children:
  - For youth in the transition to work period:
  - For families of children and youth at risk:

- *Benefits/descriptions*: Describe in the tables attached the social security benefits which are available in your country for children and youth at risk and their families (*e.g.* low income families, the unemployed, one parent families, the homeless, immigrants, refugees, aborigines, gypsies and travellers). Please photocopy the tables if necessary.
  - For pre-school children:
  - For school children:
  - For youth in the transition to work period:
  - For families of children and youth at risk:

- *Benefits/special groups*: Are there any social security benefits to which children and youth at risk and their families (*e.g.* low income families, the unemployed, one parent families, the homeless, immigrants, refugees, aborigines, gypsies and travellers) are NOT entitled? If so, what are these? Is the country of origin of immigrant a factor in determining whether or not they are entitled to certain benefits (*e.g.* European Community versus non-European Community immigrants)?
  - For pre-school children:
  - For school children:
  - For youth in the transition to work period:
  - For families of children and youth at risk:

- *Funding*: How is the utilisation of funding for integrated services evaluated? Is funding being used by services in the way the government intended?
  - For pre-school children:
  - For school children:
  - For youth in the transition to work period:
  - For families of children and youth at risk:

- *Decentralisation*: If your government has a policy of decentralisation of services for children at risk (otherwise no response necessary): What are the implications of decentralisation for the control of services development?
  - For pre-school children:
  - For school children:
  - For youth in the transition to work period:
  - For families of children and youth at risk:

- *Communication/ministries*: Describe the interfaces between different government ministries or departments responsible for integrated services. What is the nature and quality of the communication between them?
  - For pre-school children:
  - For school children:
  - For youth in the transition to work period:
  - For families of children and youth at risk:

- *Communication/services*: How, and how effectively is government legislation and policy on integration communicated to the relevant services?
  - For pre-school children:
  - For school children:
  - For youth in the transition to work period:
  - For families of children and youth at risk:

- *Authority*: Who, according to government laws and policies, is given the responsibility for implementing integrative measures?
  - For pre-school children:
  - For school children:
  - For youth in the transition to work period:
  - For families of children and youth at risk:

- *Implementation of legislation/policies*: How are legislation and policies on integration implemented, and by what means is implementation monitored? To what extent are legislation and policies put into practice?
  - For pre-school children:
  - For school children:
  - For youth in the transition to work period:
  - For families of children and youth at risk:

- *Service quality*: How is the quality of integrated services monitored, evaluated and promoted?
  - For pre-school children:
  - For school children:
  - For youth in the transition to work period:
  - For families of children and youth at risk:

- *Preventive services*: To what extent, as reflected in legislation, policies and funding, does the government promote preventive as opposed to remedial services?
  - For pre-school children:
  - For school children:
  - For youth in the transition to work period:
  - For families of children and youth at risk:

- *Voluntary services*: What view, as reflected in legislation, policies and funding, does the government take on voluntary sector services? How, and to what extent does it support them?
  - For pre-school children:
  - For school children:
  - For youth in the transition to work period:
  - For families of children and youth at risk:

- *Parental participation*: With reference to legislation and policies, what view does the government take on parental participation in legal processes, decision-making, and service provision? In these three different areas, are there laws or policies which require or encourage it?
  - For pre-school children:
  - For school children:
  - For youth in the transition to work period:
  - For families of children and youth at risk:

- *Client rights*: What are clients' (including parents) legal rights regarding complaints? Are they able to take complaints to a ministerial level?
  - For pre-school children:
  - For school children:
  - For youth in the transition to work period:
  - For families of children and youth at risk:

– *Client choice*: What view, as reflected in legislation and policies, does the government take on client (including parental) choice? Do they have the right to decide which services they (or their children) benefit from?

- For pre-school children:

- For school children:

- For youth in the transition to work period:

- For families of children and youth at risk:

INTEGRATED SERVICES

In the second part of the report please would you describe the national and community level integrated services available for children and youth at risk and their families in your country. In most Member countries, service provision varies extensively, and the task of providing a fully comprehensive picture would not be practicable. It is suggested therefore that you provide examples of the main TYPES of integrated services available in your country. These examples should cover the four different client groups (pre-school children, school children, youth in the transition to work, and families), the major at risk categories, preventive and remedial services, and government and voluntary programmes. Foundations and independent experts may be useful points of contact in addressing voluntary provision. The examples should NOT be confined to sites of best practice; at this stage we are interested in gaining a picture of the range of integrated services in your country.

As for legislation and policies, integrated services should be described under four separate headings: pre-school, school, transition to work, and families of children and youth at risk. This should be the broad structure, although it is understood that some programmes may span over more than one of these groups. Process, outcomes, attitudes and working practices will be considered at a later date, in case studies of selected services, and therefore do NOT need to be included in your descriptions.

Please address the following questions:

– *Population at risk*: What proportion of your country's child and youth population is defined as at risk? (If you participated in the Children and Youth at Risk Study, you do not need to answer this question unless there have been any notable changes.)

- For pre-school children:

- For school children:

- For youth in the transition to work period:

- For families of children and youth at risk:

– *Services/provision*: For approximately what proportion of children and youth at risk does the government plan to provide relevant services each year? What proportion of the at risk group actually benefits from services (*i.e.* take-up)?

  – For pre-school children:

  – For school children:

  – For youth in the transition to work period:

  – For families of children and youth at risk:

– *Services provision/change*: Is the government satisfied with the present extent of services provision for children and youth at risk? Are there any plans for change in coverage and, if so, what are they?

  – For pre-school children:

  – For school children:

  – For youth in the transition to work period:

  – For families of children and youth at risk:

– *Services/examples*: Describe examples of the main types of integrated services which are available to the major at risk client groups in your country (statutory/non-statutory, mainstream/specialised, preventive/remedial, large scale/small scale, community-based/other-wise). Please consider the following questions in this respect:

  – For pre-school children:

    – What is the name of the programme? If possible, please also provide an appropriate contact name, address, telephone number and fax number. Where many programmes bear the same name, one typical example is sufficient.

    – Is it a statutory or non-statutory programme?

    – What is the scale of delivery (*e.g.* local, regional, state, national)?

    – What proportion of its target population does the programme serve?

    – Which services and professionals are involved in it?

    – Who are the clients?

    – What is the location of services delivery (*e.g.* school, social centre)?

    – What are the aims of the programme?

    – How is it organised?

    – How is it funded? What conditions are attached to the funding available, and do these conditions encourage or inhibit services integration?

- What aspects of the programme are integrated?
- For how long has the programme been practising an integrated approach?
- Why did the programme adopt an integrated approach? Was it the result of national legislation or of a local initiative?
- Does any one agency take the lead in collaboration? If so, which and how?
- How is integration promoted? What role does training play in its promotion, and what form does this training take?
- Are there any obstacles to integration? If so, what are they, and how do they inhibit it?
- For school children:
  - As above.
- For youth in transition to the work period:
  - As above.
- For families of children and youth at risk:
  - As above.

Thank you very much for completing this questionnaire.

Four separate tables were supplied for pre-school children, school children, youth in the transition to work and families of children and youth at risk in the form exemplified below for pre-school children.

Services integration for children and youth at risk and their families benefits table

Pre-school children

Name of benefit	Type of benefit[1]	Administrative organisation[2]	NT or T[3]	Eligibility[4]

1. e.g. child, family, unemployment.
2. Who administers the provision of the benefit?
3. For non-targeted or universal benefits enter NT, and for targeted or means-tested benefits enter T.
4. Who can apply? What are the qualifying conditions?

CASE STUDY FRAMEWORK: PART 1

STRATEGIC LEVEL INTERVIEW SCHEDULE (FOR SENIOR MANAGERS)

Introduction

The research is concerned with services integration for children and youth at risk and their families and is being carried out as part of a study by the Organisation for Economic Co-operation and Development (OECD). The OECD is an international, intergovernmental organisation whose aim is to promote social and economic welfare in its 24 Member countries.

The study is looking at good practice in integrated services provision (*i.e.* the way in which services are co-ordinating their work to meet the needs of children and youth at risk and their families), and your programme has been chosen as an example.

We want to find out what has made this programme successful, and also the problems which have been experienced in adopting an integrated approach.

Interview details
- Name of person interviewed:
- Job title:
- Main professional responsibilities:
- Name of agency/institution/programme:
- Contact address/tel. no./fax no.:
- Date:

Context

Description of area

1. Can you tell us a little about the nature of the area you serve?
    - PROBE
    - Demographic characteristics
    - Socio-economic characteristics
    - Social/educational problems

Services provided

2. What services do you offer for children and youth at risk and their families?

Services integration

3a. Do these services work together or separately? Assuming answer is "together":

3b. For how long have these services been working together?

3c. How were they organised before they started working together?

3d. Who are the key partners?

3e. Does any one service take a leading role in the partnership?

3f. What led these services to cooperate?
   - PROBE
   - Legislation
   - Policies
   - Initiative by managers or professionals
   - Grass roots movement
   - Anything else?

3g. What were the objectives of adopting an integrated approach?

Input

Support for integration

4a. Was there any (political) support for an integrated approach to services provision? If "yes":

4b. Who provided this support?
   - PROBE
   - Politicians
   - Managers/administrators
   - Professionals
   - Community (including business)
   - Clients

4c. What kind of support did they provide?

Initial planning for integrated services

5. Who was involved in the initial planning of integrated services provision?
   - PROBE
   - Politicians

- Managers/administrators
- Professionals
- Community (including business)
- Clients

Resources to implement integration

6. Were any extra resources made available to implement an integrated approach?
   - PROBE
   - Funding
   - Training
   - Personnel
   - Buildings
   - Office equipment
   - Information systems
   - Anything else?

Evaluation of integrated approach

7. Were any pilot projects initiated or evaluation reports utilised to assess the benefits of an integrated approach?

Process

Actors in decision-making and planning

8a. Who is currently involved in the decision-making and planning for integrated services?
   - PROBE
   - Politicians
   - Managers/administrators
   - Professionals
   - Community (including business)
   - Clients

8b. Are there any individuals or groups who you feel should be involved in decision-making and planning who are not at present?

Strategies for implementation of an integrated approach

9a. What strategies have been used to implement an integrated approach?

      – PROBE

- Funding
- Training
- Committees
- Shared service location
- Any others?

9*b*. Has the approach to implementation been reviewed and changed in any way?

9*c*. What strategies and practices have been most effective in implementing an integrated approach?

9*d*. What have been the obstacles to adopting an integrated approach?

Product

Benefits of integration:

10*a*. What have been the benefits of services integration so far?

      – PROBE

- Increased efficiency
- Financial gains
- Better services
- Improved social/economic/educational outcomes
- Improved service relations
- More comprehensive databases
- Shared knowledge
- For you personally
- Anything else?

10*b*. What are the expected future benefits of services integration?

      – PROBE

- Increased efficiency
- Financial gains
- Better services
- Improved social/economic/educational outcomes
- Improved service relations
- More comprehensive databases
- Shared knowledge
- For you personally
- Anything else?

Problems with integration

11. What have been the negative or unanticipated consequences of services integration?
    - PROBE
    - Reduced efficiency
    - Financial disadvantages
    - Poorer services
    - Worse social/economic/educational outcomes
    - Strained service relations
    - Confidentiality problems
    - Communication difficulties
    - For you personally
    - Anything else?

Client information

12a. What kind of client information do you keep?
    - PROBE (IMPORTANT)
    - Information on client outcomes

12b. How is this information recorded and stored?

12c. Is this data shared with other services?

12d. Is confidentiality an issue for information sharing?

Client outcomes

13. How would you describe client outcomes?
    - PROBE
    - Personal perceptions of outcomes
    - Recent data on outcomes

CASE STUDY FRAMEWORK: PART 2

OPERATIONAL LEVEL INTERVIEW SCHEDULE (FOR MIDDLE MANAGERS)

Introduction

The research is concerned with services integration for children and youth at risk and their families and is being carried out as part of a study by the Organisation for Economic Co-operation and Development (OECD). The OECD is an international, intergovernmental organisation whose aim is to promote social and economic welfare in its 24 Member countries.

The study is looking at good practice in integrated services provision (*i.e.* the way in which services are co-ordinating their work to meet the needs of children and youth at risk and their families), and your programme has been chosen as an example.

We want to find out what has made this programme successful, and also the problems which have been experienced in adopting an integrated approach.

Interview details
- Name of person interviewed:
- Job title:
- Main professional responsibilities:
- Name of agency/institution/programme:
- Contact address/tel. no./fax no.:
- Date:

Context

Description of area

1. Can you tell us a little about the nature of the area you serve?
   - PROBE
   - Demographic characteristics
   - Socio-economic characteristics
   - Social/educational problems

Description of clients

    2. Can you tell us about the clients you serve?

       – PROBE

       • Demographic characteristics

       • Socio-economic characteristics

       • Social/educational problems

Services provided

    3. What services do you offer for children and youth at risk and their families?

Description of services

    4a. Are they statutory or non-statutory?

    4b. What is the scale of service delivery of these services?

    4c. What proportion of your target group do you serve?

    4d. What are the aims of the services?

    4e. Where are the services located?

Services integration

    5a. Do these services work together or separately? Assuming the answer is "together":

    5b. For how long have these services been working together?

    5c. How were they organised before they started working together?

    5d. Who are the key partners?

    5e. Does any one service take a leading role in the partnership?

    5f. What led these services to co-operate?

       – PROBE

       • Legislation

       • Policies

       • Initiative by managers or professionals

       • Grass roots movement

       • Anything else?

    5g. What were the objectives of adopting an integrated approach?

Input

Support for integration

6a. Was there any (political) support for an integrated approach to services provision? If "yes":

6b. Who provided this support?

- PROBE
- Politicians
- Managers/administrators
- Professionals
- Community (including business)
- Clients

6c. What kind of support did they provide?

Initial planning for integrated services

7. Who was involved in the initial planning of integrated services provision?

- PROBE
- Politicians
- Managers/administrators
- Professionals
- Community (including business)
- Clients

Resources to implement integration

8a. Were any extra resources made available to implement an integrated approach?

- PROBE
- Funding
- Training
- Personnel
- Buildings
- Office equipment
- Information systems
- Anything else?

8b. Were any inputs lacking?

Evaluation of an integrated approach

9. Were any pilot projects initiated or evaluation reports utilised to assess the benefits of an integrated approach?

Process

Actors in decision-making and planning

10a. Who is currently involved in the decision-making and planning for integrated services?
  - PROBE
  - Politicians
  - Managers/administrators
  - Professionals
  - Community (including business)
  - Clients

10b. Are there any individuals or groups who you feel should be involved in decision-making and planning who are not at present?

Strategies for implementation of an integrated approach

11a. What strategies have been used to implement an integrated approach?
  - PROBE
  - Funding
  - Training
  - Committees
  - Shared service location
  - Any others?

11b. Has the approach to implementation been reviewed and changed in any way?

11c. What strategies and practices have been most effective in implementing an integrated approach?

11d. What have been the obstacles to adopting an integrated approach?

Organisation of integrated services

12. How do you manage, organise and deliver integrated services?
    - PROBE FULLY FOR EACH OF THE FOLLOWING
    - Joint planning (committee meetings?)
    - Sharing of personnel
    - Joint training
    - Joint funding
    - Information sharing
    - Sharing of buildings and office equipment
    - Multi-professional approach to client
    - Holistic family approach
    - Involvement of community/clients

Product

Benefits of integration

13a. What have been the benefits of services integration so far?
    - PROBE
    - Increased efficiency
    - Financial gains
    - Better services
    - Improved social/economic/educational outcomes
    - Improved service relations
    - More comprehensive databases
    - Shared knowledge
    - For you personally
    - Anything else?

13b. What are the expected future benefits of services integration?
    - PROBE
    - Increased efficiency
    - Financial gains
    - Better services
    - Improved social/economic/educational outcomes
    - Improved service relations

- More comprehensive databases
- Shared knowledge
- For you personally
- Anything else?

Problems with integration

14. What have been the negative or unanticipated consequences of services integration?
    − PROBE
    - Reduced efficiency
    - Financial disadvantages
    - Poorer services
    - Worse social/economic/educational outcomes
    - Strained service relations
    - Confidentiality problems
    - Communication difficulties
    - For you personally
    - Anything else?

Client information

15a. What kind of client information do you keep?
    − PROBE (IMPORTANT)
    - Information on client outcomes
15b. How is this information recorded and stored?
15c. Is this data shared with other services?
15d. Is confidentiality an issue for information sharing?

Client outcomes

16. How would you describe client outcomes?
    − PROBE
    - Personal perceptions of outcomes
    - Recent data on outcomes

CASE STUDY FRAMEWORK: PART 3

FIELD LEVEL INTERVIEW SCHEDULE (FOR PROFESSIONALS)

Introduction

The research is concerned with services integration for children and youth at risk and their families and is being carried out as part of a study by the Organisation for Economic Co-operation and Development (OECD). The OECD is an international, intergovernmental organisation whose aim is to promote social and economic welfare in its 24 Member countries.

The study is looking at good practice in integrated services provision (*i.e.* the way in which services are co-ordinating their work to meet the needs of children and youth at risk and their families), and your programme has been chosen as an example.

We want to find out what has made this programme successful, and also the problems which have been experienced in adopting an integrated approach.

Interview details
- Name of person interviewed:
- Job title:
- Main professional responsibilities:
- Name of agency/institution/programme:
- Contact address/tel no./fax no.:
- Date:

Context

Description of area

1. Can you tell us a little about the nature of the area you serve?
    - PROBE
    - Demographic characteristics
    - Socio-economic characteristics
    - Social/educational problems

Description of clients

2. Can you tell us about the clients you serve?
    - PROBE
    - Demographic characteristics
    - Socio-economic characteristics
    - Social/educational problems

Service provided

3. What kind of service do you offer for children and youth at risk and their families?

Description of service

4. Where is the service located?

Services integration

5a. Do you work together with other services or separately? Assuming the answer is "together":

5b. For how long have you been working together?

5c. How were things organised before you started working together?

5d. Who are the key partners?

5e. Does any one service take a leading role in the partnership?

5f. What led these services to cooperate?
    - PROBE
    - Legislation
    - Policies
    - Initiative by managers or professionals
    - Grass roots movement
    - Anything else?

5g. What were the objectives of adopting an integrated approach?

Input

Support for integration

6a. Was there any (political) support for an integrated approach to services provision? If "yes":

6b. Who provided this support?

- – PROBE
- Politicians
- Managers/administrators
- Professionals
- Community (including business)
- Clients

6c. What kind of support did they provide?

Initial planning for integrated services

7. Who was involved in the initial planning of integrated services provision?

- – PROBE
- Politicians
- Managers/administrators
- Professionals
- Community (including business)
- Clients

Resources to implement integration

8a. Were any extra resources made available to implement an integrated approach?

- – PROBE
- Funding
- Training
- Personnel
- Buildings
- Office equipment
- Information systems
- Anything else?

8b. Were any inputs lacking?

Process

Actors in decision-making and planning

9a. Who is currently involved in the decision-making and planning for integrated services?
   − PROBE
   • Politicians
   • Managers/administrators
   • Professionals
   • Community (including business)
   • Clients

9b. Are there any individuals or groups who you feel should be involved in decision-making and planning who are not at present?

Strategies for implementation of an integrated approach

10a. What strategies have been used to implement an integrated approach?
   − PROBE
   • Funding
   • Training
   • Committees
   • Shared service location
   • Any others?

10b. Has the approach to implementation been reviewed and changed in any way?

10c. What strategies and practices have been most effective in implementing an integrated approach?

10d. What have been the obstacles to adopting an integrated approach?

Nature of partnership

11. What form does your partnership with other professionals take?

Approach to clients

12. How do you approach and meet the needs of your clients?

Involvement of clients

13. Are your clients involved in decision-making regarding their treatment?

Involvement of community

14. To what extent is the community involved in service provision?

Product

Benefits of integration

15a. What have been the benefits of services integration so far?
  - PROBE
  - Increased efficiency
  - Better services
  - Improved social/economic/educational outcomes
  - Improved communication/relations between professionals
  - More comprehensive databases
  - Shared knowledge
  - For you personally
  - Anything else?

15b. What are the expected future benefits of services integration?
  - PROBE
  - Increased efficiency
  - Better services
  - Improved social/economic/educational outcomes
  - Improved communication/relations between professionals
  - More comprehensive databases
  - Shared knowledge
  - For you personally
  - Anything else?

Problems with integration

16. What have been the negative or unanticipated consequences of services integration?

  - PROBE

- Reduced efficiency
- Financial problems
- Poorer services
- Worse social/economic/educational outcomes
- Strained relations between professionals
- Confidentiality problems
- Communication difficulties
- For you personally
- Anything else?

Client information

17a. What kind of client information do you keep?
  - PROBE (IMPORTANT)
  - Information on client outcomes

17b. How is this information recorded and stored?

17c. Is this data shared with other services?

17d. Is confidentiality an issue for information sharing?

Client outcomes

18. How would you describe client outcomes?
  - PROBE
  - Personal perceptions of outcomes
  - Recent data on outcomes

CASE STUDY FRAMEWORK: PART 4

FIELD LEVEL INTERVIEW SCHEDULE (FOR CLIENTS)

Introduction

The research is concerned with services integration for children and youth at risk and their families and is being carried out as part of a study by the Organisation for Economic Co-operation and Development (OECD). The OECD is an international, intergovernmental organisation whose aim is to promote social and economic welfare in its 24 Member countries.

The study wishes to look at how useful services in your area are: what kind of support they offer and the problems experienced in using them. Your views are particularly important because the goal of these services is to meet the needs of people in the local community.

Interview details
- Name of person interviewed (or pseudonym):
- Name of agency/institution/programme used:
- Date:

Context

Socio-economic characteristics

Can I start by asking a few questions about yourself?

1a. First of all, how old are you?

1b. What do you do for a living? If still at school, please give details.

1c. (Adults) If you have a spouse or partner, what does he/she do for a living?
or
(Children) What do your parents do for a living?

1d. In which country were you born?

1e. Do you see yourself as belonging to a particular cultural group? If yes, which one?

1f. Sex: M F

Services used

2. Which of the social, health and educational services provided in this area do you use?

FROM NOW ON FOCUS ON THE SERVICE WHICH RECOMMENDED THE CLIENT FOR AN INTERVIEW.

Client needs/problems

3. What were the needs that led you to choose to use this service?

Services integration

4a. Does this service work alone or together with other services? If "together":

4b. Which services work together?

4c. How was the service organised before it started working with other services? If response other than "don't know" given:

4d. What have been the main changes?

Description of service

5. Where is the service located?

Input

Support for integration

6. Did you actively support or encourage the service to work in partnership with other services?

Process

Involvement in planning

7. Have you been consulted about or involved in the planning of the service and have your views been taken into account?

Service use and character

8a. How often do you use the service?

8b. Which professionals do you see?

8c. What form do your meetings with them take?

    – PROBE

- Family involvement

8*d*. Are they understanding, sympathetic and helpful?

8*e*. Are you involved in decision-making regarding the help you receive?

Product

9*a*. How have you and your family benefited, if at all, from using this service?

9*b*. What problems have you experienced in using the service?

9*c*. How could it be improved?

CASE STUDY FRAMEWORK: PART 5

SELF-COMPLETION QUESTIONNAIRE (STRATEGIC AND OPERATIONAL LEVELS, AND PROFESSIONALS)

- We would be grateful if you could complete this questionnaire and return it to:
- Name:
- Job title:
- Main professional responsibilities:
- Name of agency/institution/programme:
- Contact address/tel. no./fax no.:
- Date:

(please turn over)

QUESTIONS

Please could you respond to these questions on a separate piece of paper with your answers clearly numbered.

1. Please describe the socio-economic nature of the area served by your agency/institution/programme. (Please note that from now on the term "agency" will be used as shorthand for "agency/institution/programme".)
2. What type of agency is it? (*i.e.* statutory/non-statutory, mainstream/specialised, preventive/remedial, large scale/small scale, community-based/otherwise).
3. What kind of services do you provide?
4. What is your annual budget?
5. Does you agency consult with other agencies in the course of preparation of service plans? If yes, please give details.
6. Does your agency have staff members who are co-located with staff members from another agency? If yes, please give details.
7. Does your agency plan and conduct professional development and training sessions with other agencies? If yes, please give details.

8. Does your agency contribute data to a (community-level) interagency information database? If yes, please give details.

9. Does your agency's board have joint meetings with the board(s) of other agencies? If yes, please give details.

10. Does your agency have a shared intake form with other agencies? If yes, please give details.

11. Does your agency meet regularly with other agencies on an interagency children's services and planning council? If yes, please give details.

12. Is there a single or co-ordinated access point for multiple services provided by your agency and other agencies in your community? If yes, please give details.

13. Do you have any formalised interagency agreements regarding the provision of programmes/services? If yes, please give details.

14. Is there an umbrella organisation in your community, responsible for overall provision of children's services? If yes, please give details.

15. Is there an agreement in your community for there to be one primary case manager for each child and family? If yes, please give details.

16. Is your agency involved with the delivery of programmes that are the joint responsibility of two or more agencies? If yes, please give details.

17. Does your agency hold case planning and follow-up conferences with other agencies? If yes, please give details.

18. Does your agency run any group programmes which include clients of other agencies? If yes, please give details.

19. Do you share any transportation resources with another agency? If yes, please give details.

20. Do you share any other administrative resources (*e.g.* office supplies, support staff) with another agency? If yes, please give details.

21. Do you share professional resources (*e.g.* psychological, psychiatric) with another agency? If yes, please give details.

22. Has your agency jointly hired staff (*e.g.* programme, support staff) with another agency? If yes, please give details.

23. Does your agency have any agreements regarding preferential access to your services for other agency clients? If yes, please give details.

24. Are you engaging in discussions with other agencies regarding the potential benefits (and costs) of consolidation (amalgamation)? If yes, please give details.

THANK YOU VERY MUCH FOR COMPLETING THIS QUESTIONNAIRE

Annex 2

THE CIPP MODEL AND THE CASE STUDY APPROACH

by

R. Volpe

The challenge before the OECD Children and Youth At Risk Study is the creation of case study reports that describe and evaluate some of the world's best efforts to integrate services. In some situations these services have been integrated by design. Often, however, the integration of services for children and youth involves necessary blending and uniting in the face of changed government priorities. This has meant that sectorial rivalries have had to be put aside because interprofessional collaboration involves shared goals and objectives.

Implied in this observation is the recognition that children's services are usually something less than a system involving interplay and co-operation between providers and families. Rather, we have a collection of often competing, independent and increasingly specialised agencies. This mixture is difficult to understand and manage. Moreover, it is inefficient, politicised and plastic. The promise of effectively integrated services is better and more cost-effective service provision. The measurable expected outcomes of services integration would be the reduction in inequities due to accessibility, the elimination of gaps, the lessening of insufficiencies in information for planning and the lowering of the number of services operating with inadequate resources.

Services integration should be manifest on two levels: the first refers to multidisciplinary co-ordination directed to the decisions concerning individual children and their families; and the second involves interagency co-ordination that focuses on decisions concerning entire programmes. Both forms of co-ordination require considerable co-operation and communication. The concept of co-ordination is complex and requires an evaluation model that incorporates the following dimensions:

- *Organisational climate*: The atmosphere that surrounds the administration and provision of services reflects the priority given to co-operative and collaborative undertaking between agencies.

- *Allocation of resources*: The allocation of suitable resources to interagency work seen in the way that money, personnel and space are allocated.

- *Principle of practice*: The governing rules and policies affecting practice will reflect the priority given to services integration. The existence and generation of protocols, regulations, guidelines and agreements need attention.

- *Personnel*: The kind of people involved in co-ordinated efforts to a large extent determines their success or failure. The level, qualification and commitment of all involved personnel need to be known.

- *Programme implementation and operation*: The actual behaviour of service providers in communicating, meeting together and sharing decision-making can be determined to be either supportive or destructive to collaborative efforts.

- *Organisational structure*: The way decision-making and the allocation of resources are structured will determine the extent to which agencies can maintain the flexibility and adaptability to work together and be influenced by the real needs of all community participants.

The case study is a particular type of narrative approach to social science research that is well suited to the multi-level, cross-cultural examination of services integration in terms of these dimensions. The organisation of the diverse data yielded by this method, however, requires a complex evaluation model. The CIPP Model is such a model. It provides a means of organising complex information collected via a number of methods. This organisation can form the case record on which a multi-level case study or multiple case studies can be derived.

The CIPP Model was originally conceived as a way of moving evaluation research away from a narrow focus on whether programmes achieved their stated objectives to a more constructive emphasis on the general information needed for decision-making. The fundamental premise on which the model is based is that the purpose of programme evaluation is not to prove but to improve. Evaluation is, therefore, a means to make programmes work better for those they intend to serve. The rendering of the model provided here is the outcome of numerous applications in the evaluation of children's services.

The four areas referred to in this model are context, input, process and product. The first major heading, *Context,* includes the background of programme objectives, and the environment and events surrounding the development and implementation of a programme or service system. Included under this heading are previous research and evaluation studies, socio-political occurrences and community reactions. *Input* evaluation deals with the nature and kind of resources developed for, and allocated to the sites. *Process* evaluation refers to the on-going management, feedback and priority setting. Finally, *Product* includes the observable impact and outcome effectiveness of service co-ordination attempts. Furthermore, this phase provides summative analysis, interpretation, conclusions and recommendations derived from the obtained data. Information to facilitate decision-making is, therefore, possible throughout the evaluation process. The decision areas for *context* informs planning, *input* serves structuring efforts, *process* deals with implementation, and *product* focuses on recycling or extending the programme to other jurisdictions.

For application in the OECD case studies the CIPP Model needs to be elaborated. With this aim in mind it is noteworthy that the CIPP Model parallels the Van Leer Evaluation Model. The components of the Van Leer Model involve programmes being described in terms of their philosophy, activities, effects and results. To some extent these features are similar to context, input, process and product. In both of these models the nature of services needs to be portrayed, significant others or partners delineated, the process of integration captured in terms of salient facilitators/obstacles and consequent outcomes of the programme noted. The emphasis of these evaluation models is on describing means/ends and intended/actual dimensions of service delivery. *Context*, or that which is of relevance surrounding a programme, includes the apparent need for services, the legal mandates that exist in a given community, the preparation and practice traditions of associated professionals and the existence of special funding opportunities. The primary orientation here is to describe the history and background of a service programme. For the case study it is important to note how the programme has been and is currently perceived by clients, associated professionals and sponsors. The intended ends of the programme are determined in association with the needs, issues and opportunities available to the programme designers. These decisions are usually articulated as goals and objectives. *Input* to the programme involves the choice of strategies employed in the delivery of services. In this dimension it is useful to note what are the alternative implementation and service delivery strategies that are actually available. Important here is making clear the procedural design of service delivery activities and special protocols for interagency collaboration. The intended means by which articulated aims are to be achieved involves outlining procedures to be followed by providers via a series of structuring decisions. *Process* refers to the way implementation is guided on the operational level. What sort of checks on implementation have been made? What evidence exists as to the relation between what was intended in a programme design and what actually exists? The monitoring of programmes gives feedback and enables adjustments between what is intended and what actually happens on the ground. *Product* examines the actual practices of both professionals and clients. This component asks, how do practitioners, participants, and observers judge the attainments of the programme? Included here are the actual outcomes of service delivery. Both long and short-term outcomes are of interest. Legitimate vantage points for measurement, interpretation and judgement can be achieved by obtaining information from both individuals and aggregates of stakeholders. Also important is the need to examine the relation of intended ends and unanticipated positive and negative outcomes.

The field researcher gathering information for a case study record needs to encounter decision-makers on a face to face basis and identify what information is needed for the study. The actual collection of information should be derived from a variety of resources and employ multiple methods. The application of this material should be a thorough, coherent depiction of a programme or service delivery system in terms of its aims, structure, process and product. The CIPP Model makes organised information available for comparison, contrast and decision-making.

REFERENCES

AALTO, V-L. (1991), *Aikakauskirja, 32*, on organising pre-school education.

BALLAUF, H. (1994), *Europaischer Verband fur Erwachsenenbildung (Hg), Rolle und Funktionen der Erwachsenenbildung in Europa – Arbeitstitel*, Scheitern in Beruf und Lehre verhindern. Wie Jugendlichen am bergang Schule – Arbeitswelt zu helfen ist. Ein Projekt der Munchner Volkshochschule. Unveroffentlichtes Manuskript, Munchen, Germany.

BENDIGO SENIOR SECONDARY COLLEGE (1994), *Annual Report*, Bendigo.

BRAUN, F., LEX, T., SCHAFER, H. and ZINK, G. (1993), *Jugend Beruf Gesellachaft, 44, 182-187*, Offentliche Jugendhilfe und Jugendberufshilfe - Ergebnisse aus der wissenschaftlichen Begleitung des Bundesjugendplan-Modellprogramms, Arbeitsweltbezogene Jugendsozialarbeit.

BRINKMAN, G. and WALRAVEN, G. (1996), "Services integration for children and youth at risk in the Netherlands," a case study report for the Organisation for Economic Co-operation and Development concerning good practice in the pre-school and school years, Sardes, Utrecht.

BRUNER, C. (1991), *Thinking Collaboratively*, Education and Human Services Consortium, Washington, DC.

BURDEKIN REPORT (1989), *Our Homeless Children*, Report of the National Inquiry into Homeless Children, Canberra, Australia.

CALIFORNIA LEGISLATURE (1989), SB 997, Chapter 1303, Statutes of 1989.

CALIFORNIA LEGISLATURE (1991a), SB 786, Chapter 994, Statutes of 1991.

CALIFORNIA LEGISLATURE (1991b), AB 2184, Chapter 1205, Statutes of 1991.

CALIFORNIA LEGISLATURE (1992), AB 3491, Chapter 316, Statutes of 1992.

CALIFORNIA LEGISLATURE (1993a), AB 1741, Chapter 951, Statutes of 1993.

CALIFORNIA LEGISLATURE (1993b), SB 931, Chapter 985, Statutes of 1993.

CARDOSO, A. (1994), *A Outra Face da Cidade – Pobreza em Bairros Degradados de Lisboa*, Camara Municipal de Lisboa, Lisboa.

CHALLIS, L., FULLER, S., HENWOOD, M., KLEIN, R., PLOWDEN, W., WEBB, A., WHITTINGHAM, P. and WISTOW, G. (1988), *Joint Approaches to Social Policy*, Cambridge University Press, Cambridge.

CHANG, H.N., GARDNER, S.L., WATAHARA, A., BROWN, C.G. and ROBLES, R. (1991), *Fighting Fragmentation: Collaborative Efforts to Serve Children and Families in California's Counties*, California Tomorrow and the Children and Youth Policy Project, San Francisco.

CHASKIN, R.J. and RICHMAN, H.A. (1992), "Concerns about school-linked services: Institution based versus community-based models", *The Future of Children*, Vol. 2, pp 107-117.

CHILDREN ACT (1989), HMSO, London.

CHILDREN AND YOUTH SERVICES ACT (1990), Bonn, Germany.

CHILD CARE AND DEVELOPMENT BLOCK GRANT (1991), Washington, DC.

CHILD AND FAMILY SERVICES ACT (1984), Toronto, Ontario, Canada.

CHILDREN FIRST (1990), *Report of the Advisory Committee on Children's Services*, Queen's Printer, Toronto, Ontario.

CHYNOWETH, J. (1994), *Personal Communication*, California Policy Academy, in California Case Study, Mimeo, OECD, Paris.

COMMONWEALTH OF AUSTRALIA (1994), *National Review of Education for Aboriginal and Torres Strait Islander Peoples*, Australian Government Publishing Service, Canberra.

CONSENT TO TREATMENT ACT (1994), Ontario Ministry of Health, Toronto, Ontario.

COOPERS AND LYBRAND CONSULTANTS AND ASHENDEN MILLIGAN (1992), *Students At Risk Program: Case Studies*, Australian Government Publishing Service, Canberra.

DAUDEY, K. and OOSTERBEEK, H. (1995), "The feasibility of cost-effectiveness analysis of programmes for students at risk", OECD, Paris.

DELAPP, L.R. (1994), California Legislature Assembly, Office of Research (27 September, telephone interview; 24 October, personal communication).

DEPARTMENT FOR EDUCATION AND CHILDREN'S SERVICES (1990), *The Interagency Referral Process: A Service for Students with Social and Behavioural Difficulties*, South Australia.

DEPARTMENT OF EMPLOYMENT, EDUCATION AND TRAINING (1992), *Students At Risk Programme: Case Studies,* Australian Government Publishing Service, Canberra.

DEPARTMENT OF EMPLOYMENT, EDUCATION AND TRAINING (1994), *National Survey of Client Satisfaction with Youth Access Centres (YACs) December 1993 - March 1994,* Evaluation and Monitoring Branch EMB Report 12/94, Canberra.

DEPARTMENT OF EMPLOYMENT EDUCATION AND TRAINING (1995a), *Student Information Guide*, Canberra.

DEPARTMENT OF EMPLOYMENT EDUCATION AND TRAINING (1995b), *Austudy' 95*, Canberra.

EDUCATION ACT (1989), Ministry of the Attorney-General, Queen's Printer, Toronto, Ontario.

EVANS, J., EVERARD, B., FRIEND, J., GLASER, A., NORWICH, B. and WELTON, J. (1989), *Decision-making for Special Needs. An Inter-service Resource Pack*, Institute of Education, London.

FAMILY PRESERVATION AND FAMILY SUPPORT PROGRAM (1993), Washington, DC.

FODOR'S (1994), FODOR'S (1995), *Australia and New Zealand,* Fodor's Travel Publications, Inc., New York.

GEELEN, H., VAN UNEN, A. and WALRAVEN, G. with BUIS, C. (1994), Services Integration for Children and Youth at Risk in the Netherlands, Sardes, The Hague.

GOALS 2000: EDUCATE AMERICA ACT (1994), *Goals 2000: Educate America Act Summary of the Act*, Council of Chief State School Officers, Washington, DC.

HABERKORN, R., HAGEMANN, U. and SEEHAUSEN, H. (1988), Kindergarten und soziale Dienste, Freiburg im Breisgau.

HABERMAS, J. (1981), Theorie des Kommunikativen Handelns, 2 Bande, Frankfurt, Germany.

HAGEN, U. and TIBBITTS, F. (1994), "The Norwegian case: child-centered policy in action", in L. Adler and S. Gardner (eds.), *The Politics of Linking Schools and Social Services*, The Falmer Press, London.

HARRIS, R.G. (1992), *Exchange Rates and International Competitiveness of the Canadian Economy*, Economic Council of Canada, Ottawa.

HAWKE, R.J.L. and HOWE, B. (1992), *Towards a Fairer Australia: Social Justice Strategy 1991-92*, Australia Government Publishing Service, Canberra.

HAWKINS-STAFFORD ELEMENTARY AND SECONDARY SCHOOL IMPROVEMENT AMENDMENTS (PL 100-297) (1988), Washington, DC.

JAUHIAINEN, A. (1993), "School, student welfare and the welfare state. The formation of the student welfare system in the Finnish compulsory education system and its network of experts from the late 1800s to 1990s", University of Turku C 98, Turku, Finland.

JOHNSON, W. (1991), "The development of a co-ordinating mechanism: A new approach to the provision of health, education and welfare services to the school-aged population of South Australia with social and behaviour difficulties", Thesis for Masters in Education Administration, Flinders University, Adelaide, South Australia.

KAGAN, S.L. with NEVILLE, P. (1993), *Integrating Services for Children and Families*, Yale University Press, London.

KAHN, A.J. and KAMERMAN, S.B. (1992), *Integrating Services Integration: An Overview of Initiatives, and Possibilities*, National Center for Children in Poverty, Columbia University, New York, NY.

KUSSEROW, R.P. (1991), *Services Integration for Families and Children in Crisis*, Department of Health and Human Services, Washington, DC.

LAW 142/90 ON LOCAL AUTONOMY (1990), Rome, Italy.

MAHWHINNEY, H.B. (1994), "Discovering, shared values: ecological models to support interagency collaboration, in L. Adler and S. Gardner (eds.), *The Politics of Linking Schools and Social Services*, The Falmer Press, London.

MALONEY, C. (1990), *Children First*, COMSOC, Toronto.

MCDONALD, P. (1993), *Confronting the Chaos. A Report of the SANS Project*, Salvation Army, Melbourne.

MCEETYA (1993), *National Report on Schooling in Australia*, Curriculum Corporation, Carlton, Victoria, Australia.

MCEETYA (1994), *National Strategy for Equity in Schooling*, Curriculum Corporation, Carlton, Victoria, Australia.

MELAVILLE, A.I. and BLANK, M.I. (1993), *Together We Can*, US Government Printing Office, Washington, DC.

MINISTERIAL COUNCIL OF OVERSEAS SKILLS RECOGNITION (1991), *Australia*, Australian Government Publishing Service, Canberra.

MINISTRY OF EDUCATION AND SCIENCE (1989), *Richness of the Incomplete*, Zoetermeer, the Netherlands.

MINISTRY OF WELFARE, HEALTH AND CULTURAL AFFAIRS (1993), *Youth Deserves the Future*, Memorandum intersectoral youth policy, The Hague.

MINISTRY OF WELFARE, HEALTH AND CUTURAL AFFAIRS (1994), *Directing Youth Care Services, Government Viewpoint*, The Hague.

MIRAND RESEARCH ASSOCIATES INC. (1993), *Project Highroad: Programmatic and Policy Evaluation. Interim Report on Implementation Progress*, Mirand Research Associates, Inc. New York, United States.

MULFORD, C.L. and ROGERS, D.L. (1982), "Interorganizational coordination: Theory, research, and implementation", in D.L. Rogers and D.A. Whetten (eds.), *Definitions and Models*, Ames, Iowas State University Press, Iowa.

MUNICIPAL EDUCATIONAL ADMINISTRATION ACT (1992), Helsinki, Finland.

NATIONAL CENTER FOR CHILDREN IN POVERTY (1993), "The effects of the 1990-1991 recession on children under six living in poverty", *News and Issues Newsletter Fall 1993*, Columbia University School of Public Health, New York, NY.

NEW BEGINNINGS (1990), *A Feasibility Study of Integrated Services for Children and Families*, Final Report, New Beginnings, San Diego.

OECD (1993), "Services integration for children and youth at risk and their families", Conclusions of the Paris Meeting, March 15th -16th, 1993 and questionnaire for completion by Member countries, mimeo, Paris.

OECD (1994), "Services integration for children and youth at risk and their Families", Conclusions of the Duisburg meeting, 29th October 1993, including four interview schedules and a self-completion questionnaire, mimeo, Paris.

OECD (1995*a*), *Our Children at Risk*, Paris.

OECD (1995*b*), *OECD in Figures*, Paris.

OFFORD, D. (1994), *Yours, Mine and Ours*, Premier's Council on Health, Well-being and Social Justice, Toronto.

OFFORD, D. and BOYLE, M. (1987), *Ontario Child Health Survey*, Ontario Ministry of Community and Social Services, Toronto.

OJALA, M. (1989), "Early childhood training, care and education in Finland", in P.P. Olmsted and D.P. Weikart (eds.), *How Nations Serve Young Children: Profiles of Child Care and Education in 14 Countries*, The High Scope Press, Ypsilanti, Michigan, United States.

ONTARIO MINISTRY OF COMMUNITY AND SOCIAL SERVICES (1988), *Investing in Children*, Queen's Printer for Ontario, Toronto.

ONTARIO MINISTRY OF EDUCATION AND TRAINING (1991), *Better Beginnings, Better Futures Project*, Toronto, Canada.

ONTARIO MINISTRY OF SKILLS DEVELOPMENT (1992), *Yearly Report*, Queen's Printer, Toronto.

PILLING, D. (1990), *Escape from Disadvantage*, The Falmer Press, London.

PLANNING AND STATE SUBSIDIES WELFARE ACT (1992), Helsinki, Finland.

RAAB, E. (1994), *Jugend Beruf Gesellschaft, 44, 5,* Schulsozialarbeit – Perspektiven fur die 90er Jahre.

RAMIREZ, M.E. (1992), *Emprego, Igualdade e Acolhimento de Criancas,* Em direçao a descentralizacao e a parceria, in Relatorio Anual.

RAUWENHOFF COMMITTEE (1990), *Education-Labour Market: Towards an Effective Pathway*, Alphen aan den Rijn.

ROYAL COMMISSION ON LEARNING (1994), *For the Love of Learning*, Government of Ontario, Toronto.

SASKATCHEWAN MINISTRY OF EDUCATION (1992), *Integrated School-Based Services for Children and Families*, Regina, Saskatchewan.

SCHAFERS, B. (1981), Sozialstruktur und Wandel der Bundesrepublik Deutschland, Stuttgart, Germany.

SCHMIDT, G.B. (1992), Schulerhilfe Weinheim. Schulbezogene und ausserschulische Sozialarbeit als Hilffe fur sozial benachteiligte Jugendliche, Weinheim, Germany.

SCHOOL TO WORK OPPORTUNITIES ACT (1994), Washington, DC.

SCOTTISH OFFICE (1992), *The Structure of Local Government in Scotland: Shaping the New Councils*, The Scottish Office, Social Work Services Group, Edinburgh.

SEEBOHM REPORT (1968), Committee on Local Authority and Allied Personal Social Services, HMSO, London.

SINGLE REGENERATION ACT (1994), HMSO, London.

STALLINGS, J.A. (1995), "Ensuring teaching and learning in the 21st century", *Educational Researcher*, Vol. 24, pp 4-8.

STRATMANN, P. (1988), *Interagency Responses to School Children with Social and Behavioural Problems*, Department of Premier and Cabinet, Adelaide, Australia.

STUFFLEBEAM, D.L. (1971), "The relevance of the CIPP evaluation model for educational accountability", *Journal of Research and Development in Education*, Fall, pp 492-501.

TAKALA, M. (1992), *"School Allergy" – A Problem of the Individual and the Society,* Acta Universitatis Tamperensis ser A vol 335, Tampereen yliopisto, Tampere, Finland.

TOBIN, M. (1994), *Students at Risk Program Sunshine Deanery, Interim Report August 1993-December 1994. An Evaluation and Overview of the Star Program*, Sunshine Deanery, Melbourne.

VALDE, E. (1993), *The Role of Student Counselling in Senior Secondary School in Orientation Towards Working Life and in Vocational Choice*, University of Turku, Turku, Finland.

VASCONCELOS, L. (1993), *Pobreza em Portugal – Variaçao e Decomposiçao de Medidas de Probeza a Partir de Orçamentos Familiares de 1980/81 e 1989/90*, Documentos de Trabalho, CISEP, No. 2.

VEENMAN, J., DIJKSTRA, A. and GOEZINNE, B. (1995), *Best Practices: Transitions from School to Work for Youth at Risk in the Netherlands*, Erasmus University, ISEO, Rotterdam.

WAGNER, M., GOLAN, S., SHAVER, D., NEWMAN, L., WECHSLER, M. and KELLEY, F. (1994), A *Healthy Start for California's Children and Families: Early Findings from a Statewide Evaluation of School-linked Services*, SRI International, Menlo Park, California, United States.

WALLER, V. (1992), *Review of the Interim Coordination Role of Youth Access Centres (YACs)*, DEETYA, Evaluation and Monitoring Branch, Canberra, Australia.

WEBB, A.L. and WISTOW, G. (1982), *Whither State Welfare? Policy Implementation in the Personal Social Services, 1979-80*, Royal Institute of Public Administration, London.

WEBB, S. and WEBB, B. (1963), *English Poor Law Policy*, Frank Cass, London.

WILSON, W. (1990), "Race-neutral programs and the democratic coalition", in *American Prospect*, pp. 74-81.

YOUNG OFFENDER'S ACT (1984), Federal Government of Canada, Ottawa.

ZIGLER, E. (1989), *Schools of the 21st Century*, presentation to the Nexus conference, Child, Youth and Family Policy Research Center, Toronto, Canada.

ZIGLER, E. and MUENCHOW, S. (1992), *Head Start: The Inside Story of America's Most Successful Educational Experiment*, Basic Books, New York.

The following documents have not been published, but are available at the OECD:

1. *Services Integration in the United States: An Emerging Agenda*, Blank, M.J., Hoffman, E., research and technical support by Goldblatt, L.A. and Marshall, M.E, prepared for U.S. Department of Education, Office of the Undersecretary, Planning and Evaluation Service and U.S. Department of Health and Human Services, Office of Assistant Secretary for Planning and Evaluation, 1994.

2. *Integrated Services for Children and Youth at Risk*, Dahl, M., Sweden, 1994.

3. *Services Integration for Children and Youth at Risk in the Netherlands*, Geelen, H., van Hunen, A. and Walraven, G., Country Report, The Hague, 1994.

4. *Report Research into Children and Youth Risk Groups by Slovenia*, Lebaric, N. Justin, J., Kobal D., Zerovnik, A. and Klopcic, V., 1994.

5. *The Integration of Health and Social Services for Children and Young People Attending Schools in Quebec*, Rodrigue, Y., Canada, 1994.

6. *Enfants et Jeunes en Situation de Risque/Intégration de Services: Portugal*, 1994.

7. *France: Questionnaire for Country Reports*, France, 1994.

8. *Integrated Services for Children and Youth at Risk and Their Families: German National Report*, Germany, 1994.

9. *Integration of Children and Youth at Risk and Development and Present State of Special Education in Turkey*, Turkey, 1993.

10. Reply to Questionnaire, Italy.

11. *OECD/CERI Questionnaire on Services Integration for Children and Youth at Risk*, Ontario.

12. *Responses to the OECD Study on Services Integration for Children and Youth at Risk and Their Families*, Saskatchewan, Canada.

13. *Services Integration for Children and Youth at Risk and Their Families, The Case of Finland*, Country Report, Finland, 1994.

14. *Services Integration for Children and Youth at Risk and Their Families: Report of the Flemish Community*, Brussels, 1994.

15. *Services Integration for Children and Youth at Risk and Their Families, Student Support Grants Program*, Manitoba, Canada.

16. *Services Integration for Children and Youth at Risk and Their Families: Country Report*, Alberta, Canada.

17. *Services Integration for Children and Youth at Risk and Their Families: Country Report Questionnaire*, Scotland.

18. *Services Integration for Children and Youth at Risk and Their Families: Response for England and Wales to Country Report Questionnaire*, England and Wales.

MAIN SALES OUTLETS OF OECD PUBLICATIONS
PRINCIPAUX POINTS DE VENTE DES PUBLICATIONS DE L'OCDE

AUSTRALIA – AUSTRALIE
D.A. Information Services
648 Whitehorse Road, P.O.B 163
Mitcham, Victoria 3132   Tel. (03) 9210.7777
Fax: (03) 9210.7788

AUSTRIA – AUTRICHE
Gerold & Co.
Graben 31
Wien I   Tel. (0222) 533.50.14
Fax: (0222) 512.47.31.29

BELGIUM – BELGIQUE
Jean De Lannoy
Avenue du Roi, Koningslaan 202
B-1060 Bruxelles   Tel. (02)
538.51.69/538.08.41
Fax: (02) 538.08.41

CANADA
Renouf Publishing Company Ltd.
1294 Algoma Road
Ottawa, ON K1B 3W8   Tel. (613) 741.4333
Fax: (613) 741.5439
Stores:
61 Sparks Street
Ottawa, ON K1P 5R1   Tel. (613) 238.8985
12 Adelaide Street West
Toronto, ON M5H 1L6   Tel. (416) 363.3171
Fax: (416)363.59.63

Les Éditions La Liberté Inc.
3020 Chemin Sainte-Foy
Sainte-Foy, PQ G1X 3V6 Tel. (418) 658.3763
Fax: (418) 658.3763

Federal Publications Inc.
165 University Avenue, Suite 701
Toronto, ON M5H 3B8   Tel. (416) 860.1611
Fax: (416) 860.1608

Les Publications Fédérales
1185 Université
Montréal, QC H3B 3A7 Tel. (514) 954.1633
Fax: (514) 954.1635

CHINA – CHINE
China National Publications Import
Export Corporation (CNPIEC)
16 Gongti E. Road, Chaoyang District
P.O. Box 88 or 50
Beijing 100704 PR   Tel. (01) 506.6688
Fax: (01) 506.3101

CHINESE TAIPEI – TAIPEI CHINOIS
Good Faith Worldwide Int'l. Co. Ltd.
9th Floor, No. 118, Sec. 2
Chung Hsiao E. Road
Taipei   Tel. (02) 391.7396/391.7397
Fax: (02) 394.9176

DENMARK – DANEMARK
Munksgaard Book and Subscription Service
35, Nørre Søgade, P.O. Box 2148
DK-1016 København K   Tel. (33) 12.85.70
Fax: (33) 12.93.87

J. H. Schultz Information A/S,
Herstedvang 12,
DK – 2620 Albertslung   Tel. 43 63 23 00
Fax: 43 63 19 69
Internet: s-info@inet.uni-c.dk

EGYPT – ÉGYPTE
Middle East Observer
41 Sherif Street
Cairo   Tel. 392.6919
Fax: 360-6804

FINLAND – FINLANDE
Akateeminen Kirjakauppa
Keskuskatu 1, P.O. Box 128
00100 Helsinki
Subscription Services/Agence d'abonne-
ments :
P.O. Box 23
00371 Helsinki   Tel. (358 0) 121 4416
Fax: (358 0) 121.4450

FRANCE
OECD/OCDE
Mail Orders/Commandes par correspondance
:
2, rue André-Pascal
75775 Paris Cedex 16 Tel. (33-1) 45.24.82.00
Fax: (33-1) 49.10.42.76
Telex: 640048 OCDE
Internet: Compte.PUBSINQ@oecd.org
Orders via Minitel, France only/
Commandes par Minitel, France exclusive-
ment :
36 15 OCDE
OECD Bookshop/Librairie de l'OCDE :
33, rue Octave-Feuillet
75016 Paris   Tél. (33-1) 45.24.81.81
(33-1) 45.24.81.67
Dawson
B.P. 40
91121 Palaiseau Cedex   Tel. 69.10.47.00
Fax: 64.54.83.26

Documentation Française
29, quai Voltaire
75007 Paris   Tel. 40.15.70.00

Economica
49, rue Héricart
75015 Paris   Tel. 45.75.05.67
Fax: 40.58.15.70

Gibert Jeune (Droit-Économie)
6, place Saint-Michel
75006 Paris   Tel. 43.25.91.19

Librairie du Commerce International
10, avenue d'Iéna
75016 Paris   Tel. 40.73.34.60

Librairie Dunod
Université Paris-Dauphine
Place du Maréchal-de-Lattre-de-Tassigny
75016 Paris   Tel. 44.05.40.13

Librairie Lavoisier
11, rue Lavoisier
75008 Paris   Tel. 42.65.39.95

Librairie des Sciences Politiques
30, rue Saint-Guillaume
75007 Paris   Tel. 45.48.36.02

P.U.F.
49, boulevard Saint-Michel
75005 Paris   Tel. 43.25.83.40

Librairie de l'Université
12a, rue Nazareth
13100 Aix-en-Provence Tel. (16) 42.26.18.08

Documentation Française
165, rue Garibaldi
69003 Lyon   Tel. (16) 78.63.32.23

Librairie Decitre
29, place Bellecour
69002 Lyon   Tel. (16) 72.40.54.54

Librairie Sauramps
Le Triangle
34967 Montpellier Cedex 2 Tel. (16) 67.58.85.15
Fax: (16) 67.58.27.36

A la Sorbonne Actual
23, rue de l'Hôtel-des-Postes

06000 Nice   Tel. (16) 93.13.77.75
Fax: (16) 93.80.75.69

GERMANY – ALLEMAGNE
OECD Bonn Centre
August-Bebel-Allee 6
D-53175 Bonn   Tel. (0228) 959.120
Fax: (0228) 959.12.17

GREECE – GRÈCE
Librairie Kauffmann
Stadiou 28
10564 Athens   Tel. (01) 32.55.321
Fax: (01) 32.30.320

HONG-KONG
Swindon Book Co. Ltd.
Astoria Bldg. 3F
34 Ashley Road, Tsimshatsui
Kowloon, Hong Kong   Tel. 2376.2062
Fax: 2376.0685

HUNGARY – HONGRIE
Euro Info Service
Margitsziget, Európa Ház
1138 Budapest   Tel. (1) 111.62.16
Fax: (1) 111.60.61

ICELAND – ISLANDE
Mál Mog Menning
Laugavegi 18, Pósthólf 392
121 Reykjavik   Tel. (1) 552.4240
Fax: (1) 562.3523

INDIA – INDE
Oxford Book and Stationery Co.
Scindia House
New Delhi 110001   Tel. (11) 331.5896/5308
Fax: (11) 332.5993

17 Park Street
Calcutta 700016   Tel. 240832

INDONESIA – INDONÉSIE
Pdii-Lipi
P.O. Box 4298
Jakarta 12042   Tel. (21) 573.34.67
Fax: (21) 573.34.67

IRELAND – IRLANDE
Government Supplies Agency
Publications Section
4/5 Harcourt Road
Dublin 2   Tel. 661.31.11
Fax: 475.27.60

ISRAEL – ISRAËL
Praedicta
5 Shatner Street
P.O. Box 34030
Jerusalem 91430   Tel. (2) 52.84.90/1/2
Fax: (2) 52.84.93

R.O.Y. International
P.O. Box 13056
Tel Aviv 61130   Tel. (3) 546 1423
Fax: (3) 546 1442

Palestinian Authority/Middle East:
INDEX Information Services
P.O.B. 19502
Jerusalem   Tel. (2) 27.12.19
Fax: (2) 27.16.34

ITALY – ITALIE
Libreria Commissionaria Sansoni
Via Duca di Calabria 1/1
50125 Firenze   Tel. (055) 64.54.15
Fax: (055) 64.12.57

Via Bartolini 29
20155 Milano   Tel. (02) 36.50.83

Editrice e Libreria Herder
Piazza Montecitorio 120
00186 Roma   Tel. 679.46.28
Fax: 678.47.51

Libreria Hoepli
Via Hoepli 5
20121 Milano   Tel. (02) 86.54.46
                      Fax: (02) 805.28.86
Libreria Scientifica
Dott. Lucio de Biasio 'Aeiou'
Via Coronelli, 6
20146 Milano   Tel. (02) 48.95.45.52
                      Fax: (02) 48.95.45.48

JAPAN – JAPON
OECD Tokyo Centre
Landic Akasaka Building
2-3-4 Akasaka, Minato-ku
Tokyo 107   Tel. (81.3) 3586.2016
                      Fax: (81.3) 3584.7929

KOREA – CORÉE
Kyobo Book Centre Co. Ltd.
P.O. Box 1658, Kwang Hwa Moon
Seoul   Tel. 730.78.91
                      Fax: 735.00.30

MALAYSIA – MALAISIE
University of Malaya Bookshop
University of Malaya
P.O. Box 1127, Jalan Pantai Baru
59700 Kuala Lumpur
Malaysia   Tel. 756.5000/756.5425
                      Fax: 756.3246

MEXICO – MEXIQUE
OECD Mexico Centre
Edificio INFOTEC
Av. San Fernando no. 37
Col. Toriello Guerra
Tlalpan C.P. 14050
Mexico D.F.   Tel. (525) 665 47 99
                      Fax: (525) 606 13 07

Revistas y Periodicos Internacionales S.A. de
C.V.
Florencia 57 - 1004
Mexico, D.F. 06600   Tel. 207.81.00
                      Fax: 208.39.79

NETHERLANDS – PAYS-BAS
SDU Uitgeverij Plantijnstraat
Externe Fondsen
Postbus 20014
2500 EA's-Gravenhage Tel. (070) 37.89.880
Voor bestellingen: Fax: (070) 34.75.778

**NEW ZEALAND –
NOUVELLE-ZÉLANDE**
GPLegislation Services
P.O. Box 12418
Thorndon, Wellington Tel. (04) 496.5655
                      Fax: (04) 496.5698

NORWAY – NORVÈGE
NIC INFO A/S
Bertrand Narvesens vei 2
P.O. Box 6512 Etterstad
0606 Oslo 6   Tel. (022) 57.33.00
                      Fax: (022) 68.19.01

PAKISTAN
Mirza Book Agency
65 Shahrah Quaid-E-Azam
Lahore 54000   Tel. (42) 735.36.01
                      Fax: (42) 576.37.14

PHILIPPINE – PHILIPPINES
International Booksource Center Inc.
Rm 179/920 Cityland 10 Condo Tower 2
HV dela Costa Ext cor Valero St.
Makati Metro Manila   Tel. (632) 817 9676
                      Fax: (632) 817 1741

POLAND – POLOGNE
Ars Polona
00-950 Warszawa
Krakowskie Przedmieácie 7 Tel. (22) 264760
                      Fax: (22) 268673

PORTUGAL
Livraria Portugal
Rua do Carmo 70-74
Apart. 2681
1200 Lisboa   Tel. (01) 347.49.82/5
                      Fax: (01) 347.02.64

SINGAPORE – SINGAPOUR
Gower Asia Pacific Pte Ltd.
Golden Wheel Building
41, Kallang Pudding Road, No. 04-03
Singapore 1334   Tel. 741.5166
                      Fax: 742.9356

SPAIN – ESPAGNE
Mundi-Prensa Libros S.A.
Castelló 37, Apartado 1223
Madrid 28001   Tel. (91) 431.33.99
                      Fax: (91) 575.39.98

Mundi-Prensa Barcelona
Consell de Cent No. 391
08009 – Barcelona   Tel. (93) 488.34.92
                      Fax: (93) 487.76.59

Llibreria de la Generalitat
Palau Moja
Rambla dels Estudis, 118
08002 – Barcelona
      (Subscripcions) Tel. (93) 318.80.12
      (Publicacions) Tel. (93) 302.67.23
                      Fax: (93) 412.18.54

SRI LANKA
Centre for Policy Research
c/o Colombo Agencies Ltd.
No. 300-304, Galle Road
Colombo 3   Tel. (1) 574240, 573551-2
                      Fax: (1) 575394, 510711

SWEDEN – SUÈDE
CE Fritzes AB
S–106 47 Stockholm   Tel. (08) 690.90.90
                      Fax: (08) 20.50.21

Subscription Agency/Agence d'abonnements :
Wennergren-Williams Info AB
P.O. Box 1305
171 25 Solna   Tel. (08) 705.97.50
                      Fax: (08) 27.00.71

SWITZERLAND – SUISSE
Maditec S.A. (Books and Periodicals - Livres
et périodiques)
Chemin des Palettes 4
Case postale 266
1020 Renens VD 1   Tel. (021) 635.08.65
                      Fax: (021) 635.07.80

Librairie Payot S.A.
4, place Pépinet
CP 3212
1002 Lausanne   Tel. (021) 320.25.11
                      Fax: (021) 320.25.14

Librairie Unilivres
6, rue de Candolle
1205 Genève   Tel. (022) 320.26.23
                      Fax: (022) 329.73.18

Subscription Agency/Agence d'abonnements :
Dynapresse Marketing S.A.
38, avenue Vibert
1227 Carouge   Tel. (022) 308.07.89
                      Fax: (022) 308.07.99

See also – Voir aussi :
OECD Bonn Centre
August-Bebel-Allee 6
D-53175 Bonn (Germany) Tel. (0228)
                      959.120
                      Fax: (0228) 959.12.17

THAILAND – THAÏLANDE
Suksit Siam Co. Ltd.
113, 115 Fuang Nakhon Rd.
Opp. Wat Rajbopith
Bangkok 10200   Tel. (662) 225.9531/2
                      Fax: (662) 222.5188

TRINIDAD & TOBAGO
SSL Systematics Studies Limited
9 Watts Street
Curepe
Trinidad & Tobago, W.I. Tel. (1809)
                      645.3475
                      Fax: (1809) 662.5654

TUNISIA – TUNISIE
Grande Librairie Spécialisée
Fendri Ali
Avenue Haffouz Imm El-Intilaka
Bloc B 1 Sfax 3000   Tel. (216-4) 296 855
                      Fax: (216-4) 298.270

TURKEY – TURQUIE
Kültür Yayinlari Is-Türk Ltd. Sti.
Atatürk Bulvari No. 191/Kat 13
Kavaklidere/Ankara
                      Tel. (312) 428.11.40 Ext. 2458
                      Fax: (312) 417 24 90
Dolmabahce Cad. No. 29
Besiktas/Istanbul   Tel. (212) 260 7188

UNITED KINGDOM – ROYAUME-UNI
HMSO
Gen. enquiries   Tel. (0171) 873 0011
Postal orders only:
P.O. Box 276, London SW8 5DT
Personal Callers HMSO Bookshop
49 High Holborn, London WC1V 6HB
                      Fax: (0171) 873 8463
Branches at: Belfast, Birmingham, Bristol,
Edinburgh, Manchester

UNITED STATES – ÉTATS-UNIS
OECD Washington Center
2001 L Street N.W., Suite 650
Washington, D.C. 20036-4922 Tel. (202)
                      785.6323
                      Fax: (202) 785.0350
Internet: washcont@oecd.org

Subscriptions to OECD periodicals may also
be placed through main subscription agencies.

Les abonnements aux publications périodiques
de l'OCDE peuvent être souscrits auprès des
principales agences d'abonnement.

Orders and inquiries from countries where Dis-
tributors have not yet been appointed should be
sent to: OECD Publications, 2, rue André-Pascal, 75775 Paris Cedex 16, France.

Les commandes provenant de pays où l'OCDE
n'a pas encore désigné de distributeur peuvent
être adressées aux Éditions de l'OCDE, 2, rue
André-Pascal, 75775 Paris Cedex 16, France.

5-1996

OECD PUBLICATIONS, 2, rue André-Pascal, 75775 PARIS CEDEX 16
PRINTED IN FRANCE
(96 96 05 1) ISBN 92-64-15305-5 – No. 48951 1996